RADICAL-LOCAL TEACHING

AND LEARNING

D1614242

RADICAL-LOCAL TEACHING AND LEARNING

A Cultural-Historical Approach

Mariane Hedegaard and Seth Chaiklin

AARHUS UNIVERSITY PRESS

© The authors and Aarhus University Press 2005
© Cover photographs: Jose B. Rivera, East Harlem
Cover design: Jørgen Sparre
Graphic design: Narayana Press, Gylling
Printed in Denmark at Narayana Press, Gylling

ISBN 87 7288 829 6

Published with financial support from
The Danish Research Council for the Humanities

AARHUS UNIVERSITY PRESS

Langelandsgade 177
DK-8200 Aarhus N
Fax (+ 45) 8942 5380
www.unipress.dk

73 Lime Walk
Headington, Oxford OX3 7AD
United Kingdom
Fax (+ 44) 1865 750 079

Box 511
Oakville, CT 06779
USA
Fax (+ 1) 860 945 9468

Preface

Over the past 20 years we have been developing a perspective about subject-matter teaching and learning in relation to individual development. Although pedagogical trends and fashions come and go, some basic issues are always present as part of the defining features of pedagogical practice. Two of these problems, which are addressed in this book, are (a) how to conceptualize and organize the subject-matter content to be used in pedagogical interactions, and (b) how to develop desired psychological capabilities through pedagogical interactions with subject-matter content. While these problems can be addressed in general terms, it is also necessary to relate the general perspectives to the local historical conditions within which pedagogical interactions are conducted. From this point of view, general theoretical perspectives become interesting when they serve to guide efforts to realise a practice in a specific historical context, while practical efforts should be evaluated in relation to a general theoretical perspective. In turn, practical work challenges the further development and clarification of our theoretical understanding of how to relate subject-matter teaching to the particular conditions under which children are learning.

The practical research work in this book was conducted in an afterschool program for children in a New York City neighborhood where many of the families have a historical relation to Puerto Rico. The intention is to present an example of the dynamic interaction between theory and practice in a way that will encourage persons with a more practical interest to consider the theoretical arguments, while the more theoretically oriented reader will also consider the practical example. The hope is that the reader will reflect about the ways in which theoretical and practical aspects of pedagogical work can be integrated, to the benefit of both aspects.

At the time that we conducted the project, Mariane Hedegaard was a visiting scholar at Teachers College, Columbia University, while Seth Chaiklin was a Project Director at the Institute for Learning Technologies at Teachers College, Columbia University. The afterschool project was conducted in collaboration with Pedro Pedraza as a project at the Center for Puerto Rican Studies, City University of New York, with support from the Exxon Foundation. This collaboration was essential for the development of the project. We thank Pedro

Pedraza, the leader of the project, Jorge Ayala, a research assistant in the project, Karen Diaz Navarro, the teacher in the project, who worked with engagement and enthusiasm, and the parent helpers, Carmen and Belén, who assisted the children in the classroom.

Seth Chaiklin and Mariane Hedegaard
Copenhagen, February 2005

Contents

CHAPTER 1

Radical-Local Teaching and Learning for Education and Human Development

This book presents an approach to teaching and learning that we have designated *radical local*. To realize both general societal interests and worthwhile personal development, the content of educational programmes for children must be grounded in and draw explicitly from the local societal conditions within which the children live. Through working with this content, children should appropriate an understanding of general theoretical-dialectical concepts from subject-matter disciplines, which they can use as tools for understanding the content they have studied, and more generally for analyzing their own life conditions and future possibilities. These are distinctive features of a successful radical-local teaching and learning approach. The central concern of radical-local teaching and learning is how to relate educational practices to children's specific historical and cultural conditions – both the objective conditions in which the children live and their comprehension of and relation to those conditions.

The specific event that provided the opportunity for formulating our theoretical ideas about radical-local teaching and learning was the possibility to conduct an experimental teaching programme for a group of elementary school children in the context of an existing experimental afterschool programme in East Harlem.[1] An afterschool programme can be an ideal place to experiment

---

1   The afterschool programme was started originally by Pedro Pedraza, a researcher at the Center for Puerto Rican Studies at Hunter College, City University of New York City, with a focus on developing literacy and mathematics competences for children (Pedraza, 1989). This afterschool programme was part of the El Barrio Popular Education Program (K. Rivera, 1999; Torruellas, 1989; Torruellas, Benmayor, Goris & Juarbe, 1991), which was started by researchers at the Center for Puerto Rican Studies, in part, because of a dissatisfaction with producing research studies that contributed primarily to the professional advancement of the report writers, without affecting noticeably the conditions and possibilities for the people in the community being described.

with radical-local concerns such as bridging family and community traditions with subject-matter knowledge, because the content of afterschool activities are not usually formalized by laws, regulations and curriculum plans.

The first part of the book presents a framework for conceptualizing and designing radical-local educational interventions for schoolchildren. We start by considering the goals of education and the relation of educational practice to personal development, and then consider some of the problems faced by cultural minorities, especially Latinos in completing school. The idea of radical-local teaching and learning is introduced, along with some key principles from the cultural-historical research tradition about knowledge, psychological development, and teaching and learning. Some of the cultural-historical principles are elaborated further in relation to problems of (a) selecting subject-matter content that takes account of schoolchildren's cultural-historical background and life situation, and (b) using that selection in a way that is relevant both to their present life in their local community and their coming societal life.

The second part of the book presents a qualitative analysis of the teaching experiment. The intention of the educational programme was to develop the children's subject-matter knowledge about general social science concepts and principles from history and social studies through investigation of a theme that was central in their lives. The specific topics selected for investigation were motivated by our knowledge of the cultural-historical background of the children and their families. General subject-matter concepts are first formulated through specific investigations. In turn, as these concepts become explicitly formulated, it is possible for the children to use these concepts to reformulate their everyday understanding of their life and community. In other words, the programme was an attempt to realize our ideas about radical-local teaching and learning.

Our interest was to develop a positive intervention that addressed significant intellectual and cultural needs of the children, most of whom came from families with a Puerto Rican background, while drawing upon knowledge of the East Harlem community in which most of the children lived. We did not want to conduct another study documenting that Puerto Rican children were not achieving comparable levels of academic success as other social groups in New York City (e.g., Calitri, 1983; Santiago Santiago, 1978) nor show that the form and content of teaching that the children receive tends to be oriented to rote learning, repetitive drill, and other kinds of tasks that do not require nor encourage analytic, creative, theoretical thinking (e.g., Anyon, 1981; Orum, 1988). These points have been well-documented, and they continue to be well documented, not only for Puerto Rican children in New York City, but for other Hispanic groups in the United States (e.g., Arias, 1986; Brown, Rosen, Hill, & Olivas, 1981; De La Rosa & Maw, 1990; Goldenberg, 1990; National Commission on Secondary Education for Hispanics, 1984; Nieto, 1998, 2000).

Although it is important to document the existence of these problems, these analyses do not usually contain insights into what positive steps should be taken for intervention. Especially in the more descriptive studies, one cannot tell what a symptom of inadequate educational programmes is and what a cause is. Our interest in this book is to present a theoretically motivated approach to subject-matter teaching, which in the present case was directed toward the needs of Puerto Rican children in East Harlem.

Formal Education and Child Development

A major goal of formal education, at least as formulated in official documents, is to help children gain insight into and a capability for using subject-matter traditions to understand the social and natural world. However, the content and purpose of formal schooling are not limited only to the goals of subject-matter learning and subsequent intellectual development. There are usually expectations that formal education should prepare and motivate children to participate in a society's existing economic, political, and cultural practices, where subject-matter learning is seen as part of realizing that goal.

Radical-local teaching and learning is concerned to realize these widely-held goals for formal education, but focuses additionally on how education can contribute to the personal development of children in relation to their historical and cultural conditions. The assumption is that the relationship between schoolchildren's cultural background and the historical conditions within which they live can and should have consequences for the content of teaching if these goals are to be realized. Schooling is normally organized around specific subject-matter content such as specific content and procedures for reading, writing, calculating, analyzing physical and historical phenomena. How are these specific practices to be related to these general goals? And how should one consider them in relation to the variations found within contemporary societies such as between city and country, rich and poor families, religious and cultural differences, to name only a few of the more important dichotomies that are commonly considered.

The idea of radical-local teaching and learning presented here is an attempt to make an integrated conceptual model for educational practice that addresses this tension between valued general goals of education and the individual and diverse variations found in its concrete practice. We focus specifically on the dynamic between how general subject-matter content and specific historical conditions can contribute to children's development. The focus is on how education, through subject-matter teaching can contribute to the development of motives and competencies that are relevant for the child's societal life.

The cultural-historical research tradition provides a useful set of theoretical resources for articulating and clarifying the ideal of radical-local teaching and learning, which in turn reveals some limitations in the current theoretical development of the cultural-historical tradition.

CULTURAL-HISTORICAL THEORY OF EDUCATION

In 1931, Lev Vygotsky prepared a book-length manuscript on his cultural-historical theory of human development. This theoretical perspective provided the framework for subsequent investigations into schoolchildren's conceptual development. In several of his texts from the period 1932-1934, Vygotsky discussed this relation, considering different models. The model Vygotsky promoted was that instruction and learning should be the source of further development, where instruction should prepare and motivate the child to participate in a society's existing cultural practice as well as develop psychological functions of thinking and concept formation that were not yet fully acquired. This model contrasted with a behaviorist model which equated learning and development, or a Piagetian model in which instruction must wait for a certain level of development to be achieved (see also Vygotsky, 1926/1998b, Chap. 4 and 6).

In Vygotsky's analysis, thinking with real concepts was the major psychological function that characterized school age children, and instruction should be directed toward such development (e.g., Vygotsky, 1934/1987, Chap. 6). As part of his analysis of the development of schoolchildren's conceptual thinking, Vygotsky considered the relation between what he called spontaneous or everyday concepts and academic or scientific concepts. The former are typically learned as a result of everyday practice and tend to be strongly situated. The latter, which are usually learned as a result of formal instruction, often by verbal definition, tend to be abstract and reflect historically-developed systematic analysis of societal and natural phenomena. The acquisition of scientific concepts depends on the child's everyday concepts, and a consequence of this acquisition is that a child's everyday concepts are modified and their content further developed. This dialectic of the child's everyday knowledge and its potential transformation from theoretical knowledge acquisition provides an important conceptual model for addressing a main concern of radical-local teaching and learning, namely to use the general concepts of disciplinary knowledge as a way to develop and refine personal, local knowledge.

Vygotsky's perspective about the relation between learning and development for school age children and the theory of activity provided a conceptual framework for Vygotsky's former research assistant Daniil El'konin, who in collaboration with Vasili Davydov, started in the late 1950s to develop an approach to educational practices that aimed, in part, to support psychological development.[2] In the late 1970s this tradition started to receive attention and interest from other cultural-historical researchers outside of Moscow, especially in Northern Europe (e.g., Hedegaard, 1990, 2002; Hedegaard, Engeström, & Hakkarainen, 1984; Hedegaard & Lompscher 1999; Lompscher, 1985; van Oers, 1999), and this tradition continues to be developed today especially within Russia, Ukraine, and Latvia (Davydov, 1998; Experiment Centre, http://www.experiment.lv; International Association 'Developmental Education', http://www.maro.newmail.ru).

Developmental teaching-learning research has focused primarily on problems of subject-matter teaching (Davydov, 1988b; 1988c; Lompscher, 1985, 1999), providing an important theoretical and practical perspective for developing educational interventions aimed at promoting children's learning of theoretical-dialectical concepts. The developmental teaching-learning approach developed by El'konin and Davydov did not conceptualize sufficiently the children's cultural background and local historical conditions, even if these aspects are generally recognized within the theoretical tradition as significant.

We believe this theoretical tradition, given its grounding in the cultural-historical tradition, can be elaborated to integrate these aspects, so that cultural and social conditions and motive development can be addressed explicitly in the planning process and in the content of the teaching. The elaborated theoretical perspective provides a coherent general perspective for conceptualizing processes of learning and teaching and the role of knowledge in children's development.

SOCIAL STUDIES TEACHING WITH CULTURAL CONTENT IN A RADICAL-LOCAL PERSPECTIVE

Rather than view cultural sensitivity and disciplinary standards as necessarily standing in opposition to each other, we assume that by giving a solid disciplinary foundation through the investigation of topics that are related to their life, children will be able to better appreciate the relation between academic or disciplinary studies and their own life situations. That is, in a radical-local teaching approach, schoolchildren should develop academic knowledge and

---

2   After El'konin's death in 1984, Davydov and his colleagues continued to develop this tradition, which came to be called *developmental teaching-learning* (e.g., Davydov, 1988a). More precisely, Davydov called his approach *Oubchenie Razvitsia*. The polysemous Russian word *oubchenie* means simultaneously *teaching* and *learning*. There is not a corresponding English word that has this double meaning, so we will use the somewhat awkward 'teaching-learning' to preserve the intended meaning.

skills that correspond to those normally expected in a school curriculum, but developed through subject-matter content that is relevant to the children's life situation, and which can develop the children's capabilities for analyzing and interpreting their situation. Our goal in this book is to show how one can conduct subject-matter teaching that simultaneously draws from the participants' historical situation while contributing to their own development in relation to that historical situation.

We believe that helping children explore the historical and cultural conditions of the community in which they live can be relevant for this purpose. It is possible to select social studies subject-matter content that is relevant to children's life situation, and to investigate this content in a way that concurrently develops academic knowledge and skills typically associated with disciplinary traditions. 'Relevant' means that the content of social studies teaching should provide children with useful academic concepts and methods for analyzing existential issues that confront them in their lives. These issues include both immediate and visible issues (e.g., housing conditions, family life, and adequate resources in their neighbourhood) as well as longer-term identity issues in which one forms an attitude or position in relation to one's life situation.

A focus on relevant topics does not necessarily result in a dilemma or contradiction in which the teacher must choose between academic relevance and personal relevance. It is necessary, however, to help children integrate their experience and information into a theoretical model or perspective for understanding the significance of events and conditions, and not simply to draw on experience or provide children with specific historical facts that are culturally relevant. Ideally, such a model or perspective functions as a foundation from which children can continue to analyze and interpret their life situation. By bringing the methods of investigation of a subject-matter discipline into the classroom as a working approach, the teacher, in collaboration with the children, can develop specific substantive results which can be related to the children's concrete situation. More generally, through this process, one aims to help children acquire knowledge and skills for understanding and developing better relationships to their life conditions.

In the case of our experimental teaching programme, we assumed that it would be possible to give the children academically challenging activities that reflected disciplinary standards, despite a common tendency to assume that such goals are too demanding or inappropriate for inner-city minorities in the United States.[3] By incorporating the history and culture of the immediate community

---

3   Though there are some exceptions (e.g., Levin, 1995; Slavin, Madden, Dolan, & Wasik, 1996).

in educational activities, we aimed to help the children in the project extend their knowledge about central characteristics of the Puerto Rican community in general and in East Harlem in particular. Through this investigation, and planned instructional activities, we expected the children to acquire research methods and concepts from social science. We hoped to engage the children in these instructional activities by letting them become active in researching their community and its origins. That is, through acquiring concrete knowledge about their local community, we would at the same time develop appropriate theoretical-dialectical concepts that could be used as a tool for analyzing their own life conditions and future possibilities. Thereby we hoped that they would develop motivation for school subjects and self-respect as competent pupils.

CHILDREN'S MOTIVE DEVELOPMENT

We do not assume that children will necessarily learn about their local community simply because we introduce this subject-matter content as part of teaching. Even though experience with their local community is part of their everyday life, it is often necessary to develop a motivation for wanting to investigate this experience in a more systematic way. One task in a teaching-learning programme is to create activities that are interesting for the children so that they develop interest for the kind of knowledge presented in the programme and hopefully thereby a general motive for learning.

Vygotsky's colleagues El'konin (1999) and Leontiev (1978) both extended Vygotsky's theory by introducing development of motives as a central aspect of human development. Motives are seen as culturally created through the child's participating in institutional activities. El'konin describes how cultural-historical practice in institutions influences children's development and how new motives that become dominant result in qualitative changes in the child's relations to the world and therefore can be seen as markers of new periods in development.

Plan of the Book

The first part of this book describes the theoretical background that was the foundation for formulating the teaching intervention described in the second part. Chapter 2 contextualizes the intervention by discussing the goals of education, the nature of problems experienced by children from minority families, and reviewing research about school completion. Chapter 3 introduces the concept of radical-local teaching and discusses some of the research and intervention projects that have considered the use of local community knowledge in relation to teaching.

Chapters 4, 5, and 6 present the main theoretical ideas that were used to plan, conduct, and analyze the teaching intervention. Chapter 4 contains an analysis of different forms of knowledge and how they are related to school teaching and what this implies in relation to children's personal knowledge. This combination is seen as the primary process by which persons can relate their theoretical knowledge to their daily life. In the case of cultural minority children, this would mean acquiring a theoretical-dialectical understanding of their local community so that it could be used to interpret their daily situation. Chapter 5 presents a theory of child development. Development is described as a societal and cultural process, in which the interaction between motivation and knowledge acquisition are the main developmental processes, and the development of motives is the central aspect of personality development. Chapter 6 describes a theory of radical-local teaching characterized as a double move between the goals of teaching and the conditions and interests of the child. There is a special interest in clarifying the relation between subject-matter knowledge and the cultural procedures and understanding from everyday life. Chapter 7 gives a historical overview of the history of the community of East Harlem. Chapter 8 describes some of the educational conditions in East Harlem along with the specific problems that motivated the teaching experiment. Chapter 9 gives a brief overview of the content and organization of the teaching experiment conducted in an afterschool setting in East Harlem, along with methods of data collection and analysis. Chapters 10 through 13 give a narrative report and some analysis of the teaching experiment, while Chapter 14 discusses the competencies the children achieved through participating in the experiment. The book concludes with Chapter 15 which discusses the implications of radical-local teaching and learning for planning teaching of cultural minorities and majorities.

CHAPTER 2

Education in a Societal Perspective

Education is viewed today as a basic human right. Any self-respecting nation-state has, as a minimum, a primary educational system; international treaties and conventions on civil and political rights recognize the right to education; and the value and importance of education is praised worldwide. Within this historical condition, educational researchers should have an integrated perspective on teaching and learning that engages the main aspects of a satisfying educational practice in relation to societal interests.

The function and purpose of education in contemporary society is difficult to explicate, especially if one wants to separate what might be realistic to achieve from what is idealistically expected by interested persons such as politicians, government officials, educators, and parents. A systematic historical investigation and analysis of the purposes of and expectations for education are beyond the scope of this book, which is focused on a theoretically-grounded approach for planning educational practices (radical-local teaching and learning) that aims to contribute to the improvement of children's life situation, especially for cultural minority children. It is important, however, in formulating a perspective about a satisfying educational practice, to consider the relations between general visions and expectations about the goals of education and how these practices might relate to the broader goals and interests found in societal life. It is not enough to assume the sufficiency of intentions to make improvements; we need to have an analysis that clarifies the relations among educational practice, educational goals and our expectations of what can be achieved by education in relation to societal interests. Such an analysis is likely to reveal the need to refine goal formulations and expectations of education relative to predominant conceptions, as well as identify issues that need to be addressed more directly in specific research and intervention efforts.

In the previous chapter, we mentioned some of the most typically expressed purposes of education, namely to help prepare and motivate children to participate in a society's existing economic, political and cultural practices as active, productive citizens (e.g., Burstyn, 1996; White, 1990). These interests, when formulated in general terms, appear transnationally. Examples of official documents with these kinds of formulations can be found from a variety of countries with diverse political and economic systems such as the United States, the Soviet Union, Denmark, and Great Britain. They can also be found in formulations from cultural minorities (e.g., Royal Commission on Aboriginal Peoples, 1996, Chap. 5; Fisher with Pérez, González, Njus, & Kamasaki, 1998, pp. 87-89).

Formal documents often focus only on the global qualities that should be developed among children in relation to these general goals for participation in societal life. For example, subject-matter teaching, aimed at the development of children's motives and competences, should be a central and essential goal in education. This kind of goal is reflected in curriculum standards formulated by the National Council for the Social Studies (1994), which argues that a consequence of social studies education should be that children acquire knowledge, skills, and attitudes that are directed toward the common good.

At the same time, we presume there is also a societal belief, at least implicitly, that these global qualities provide relevant resources for each individual to have a fuller, richer life, preferably a 'good life'.[4] The relations between education and a good life are complicated because of the tension between a desirable societal goal ('a good life'), the insufficiency of education alone to realize that goal, and the strong likelihood (if not actual necessity) that some forms of education can contribute in significant ways to helping persons develop knowledge and skills that would be relevant and useful to the development of a good life.

Additional complications arise between the psychological or experiential dimension that characterizes a 'good life' and the material conditions within which one lives, and the relation between individual and collective conditions. It is possible to have a positive orientation or attitude to one's life, even if living in difficult material conditions. On the other hand, there is no reason why one should have to continue to live in those conditions, as a matter of moral view or economic necessity. That is, the question of a good life cannot be reduced solely to the psychological state of the individual, but must also consider the concrete, societal conditions within which life is lived.

---

4   A philosophical analysis of the concept of 'good life' is complicated. Persons living in difficult and relatively impoverished material conditions can still experience their lives in positive terms. Others, with considerable material wealth can experience their life in miserable terms. For example, consider the extent of drug and alcohol abuse, and stories of psychological misery among movie and rock music stars. It is likely to be impossible to specify which material conditions are elements of a 'good life'. However, to start, we think it is valuable to create some minimal social conditions (e.g., in terms of health care, freedom from physical violence, access to qualifying education, and employment opportunities).

Moreover, realizing a good life is not always a matter of individual development. It will probably depend critically on the conditions for and state of collective societal relations. In other words, education alone will not be sufficient for helping a person to realize a good life, yet a satisfying educational practice should help individuals to develop knowledge and skills that would be relevant to living in relation to their current living conditions, which includes developing a critical understanding both of what should be protected and what might be worthy of further improvement. In a radical-local perspective (see Chapter 3), we want to consider how the development of motives and competences through specific subject-matter learning is necessary or useful for leading a richer, fuller life. At the same time, we need to recognize that the question of a good life must take into account the diverse background of persons who are being educated.

This tension between societal and personal goals for education raises the possibility that these two aspects are not necessarily satisfied simultaneously in every case. This tension is recognized, at least implicitly, in the previously-mentioned curriculum standards, and the pro-offered resolution is a suggested need for personal, academic, pluralist, and global perspectives. However, the standards do not confront the possible or even likely conflicts between individual needs and interests in contrast to dominant societal interests.

In addition to a focus on individual development, education is also often viewed as having an important contribution to the resolution of problems of social justice that arise from inequalities in material resources and access to economic opportunities. A popular belief in the United States (and many other countries) is the idea of education as a social equalizer, providing an opportunity for advancement and improvement.[5] Assuming this belief is true, then it would appear that one could address (or at least reduce) the societal problems faced by children from cultural minorities by ensuring that their educational achievements and qualifications correspond to those of the majority.

We do not expect to find a simple causal relation between education and the quality of an educated child's societal life. Moreover, there are many reasons to doubt, that education alone can resolve the unacceptable societal conditions under which many minority children must live, especially when they come

---

5   As a substitute for full justification of this assertion, we will only point to the numerous examples from everyday experience in the United States in which sports and music stars exhort children to stay in school, public advertising campaigns, popular slogans, 'a mind is a terrible thing to waste', and so forth. As we discuss later, there are also some empirical grounds for holding this belief (e.g., clear statistical evidence for the economic advantages of having a high school diploma).

from poor families. It is necessary to consider the variety of societal conditions involved in a life situation.

There is a tension between (a) wanting educational practices to address societal problems in a comprehensive way, (b) likely limitations for educational practices alone to realize those goals, yet (c) possibilities to make significant improvements in relation to existing practices that contribute in a meaningful way to addressing societal problems, without mistaking these improvements as necessarily being sufficient to all the issues of societal life that must be addressed.

As a simple way to elaborate this tension between educational practice and more general societal goals, especially in relation to a good life, let us consider the following example.[6] Many of the general societal goals formulated by cultural minority groups, especially societally and economically disadvantaged groups, are not fundamentally different from the goals of dominant groups, though some of the particular goals of ethnic groups may conflict with the dominant groups. Consider, for example, the kinds of goals formulated by the National Council of La Raza (NCLR) in their report *State of Hispanic America 1991.*[7]

The primary goal is formulated in the Foreword as 'equality'.[8] The specific issues presented in the report's Executive Summary include a focus on socio-economic issues in relation to major population groups, where the general goal is to reduce 'the economic disparity and gaps in opportunity between Hispanics and the rest of the U.S. society'. For example, the Executive Summary notes that Hispanics have 'the lowest levels of educational attainment of any major population group, but are underrepresented in pre-school programmes and other education programmes designed to help at-risk students', and that Hispanics are more likely to be members of the working poor, more likely to contract certain diseases while being less likely to have access to health care, to suffer from substantial levels of discrimination in education, employment and

---

6   Given that the teaching intervention described in this book is concerned with the education of children from Puerto Rican families in East Harlem, the rest of this chapter will draw primarily from examples that are either oriented to Latinos in general in the United States, and to Puerto Ricans in New York City.

7   According to the statement on the back of the report's cover page, 'The National Council of La Raza (NCLR), the largest constituency-based national Hispanic organization exists to improve life opportunities for the more than 22 million Americans of Hispanic descent' (National Council of La Raza, 1992).

8   '[I]t is in everyone's interest to join in our struggle for Hispanic American equality' (Yzaguirre, 1992).

housing, yet receive minimal attention from federal civil rights enforcement agencies.

It is interesting to note that although these issues are formulated in terms of rights, equal opportunities and access, the NCLR suggests that it 'is not simply a moral preference, it is a social and economic imperative' (p. 33). Their argument seems to be directed to the idea that regardless of one's sense of human rights and dignity, the material conditions of the future well-being of the United States will depend on the socioeconomic conditions of Hispanics. What is important to recognize here is that there is not a call for changing the general or typical practices and goals of the American social, political, or economic traditions, but rather a call for programmes, policies, and interventions that will enable Hispanic persons to participate with comparable conditions as other Americans. One might wonder, as we do, whether there are any special characteristics or conflicts between the needs and traditions of Hispanic persons that might interact with these general socioeconomic demands. The Executive Summary gives a small indication of this possibility when it states that current programmes 'do not necessarily take into account the special characteristics and needs of Hispanics or serve them equitably.' Without developing the analysis further, we can say that these characteristics partly refer to cultural traditions (e.g., emphasis on the family), but may also refer to material conditions that are not particular to Hispanics alone.

One would expect that NCLR and other organizations would not advocate material equality if the price to be paid would be existential misery. Education can have an important function in this connection, because of its possibilities and potentials for addressing the experiential and existential aspects of life, even if material conditions are difficult. Furthermore, this education does not have to adopt a pacifying or institutional justifying function as illustrated, for example, by the work of Paolo Freire (1968/1970) with adult literacy in Brazil, Oskar Negt (1971) with industrial workers in Germany, or examples from American high schools described in Delpit (1988).

Several important points arise when one starts to analyze the goals formulated in this example as an indication of what characterizes a 'good life'. First, there are likely to be multiple visionary goals (related to health, education, work, living conditions, and so forth). Second, many of these goals may need to be addressed simultaneously if a general effect is to be realized. Third, the concrete actions that are taken or needed to realize these multiple goals may sometimes contradict or affect each other.

Let us suppose, for the sake of analysis, that it was unproblematic to change the existing schooling conditions and practices for the children referred to in NCLR's report; that it was possible to offer educational programmes that would qualify these young people for participation in economic life. Even with this problem of education wished away, there are still many other problems, involving additional interactions with the family and their problems in maintaining basic living conditions (housing, food, health, physical safety), that can overwhelm the effects or possibilities of schooling. A similar point was illustrated in the context of prenatal healthcare programmes that were successful with middle-class women, but were not successful with impoverished women, because so many other problems hindered or overwhelmed the success of the programme (Schorr, 1988).

Often the practical problems that children in East Harlem face and the solutions that they sometimes find (e.g., drug-dealing) are perceived as more practical and relevant (Bourgois, 1989) than a friendly chat about the value of getting a good education (Inclán & Herron, 1989). It is important to note that these children's capabilities may be comparable to other children in the United States, but when one looks at the actual conditions within which cultural minority children, such as those living in East Harlem, must grow up (described further in Chapters 7 and 8), then one can better understand why their life conditions can often overwhelm their possibilities for developing and using their capabilities, and why educational programmes alone can be overwhelmed or undermined by the other problems and conditions that these children face.

From a societal perspective, it is clear that educational programmes often have (or are given) goals and interests that extend beyond a well-functioning classroom. The brief analysis given here is meant to remind us that it is unlikely that significant changes in the societal conditions for large groups of people will be addressed or affected solely by individual educational programmes. We should not expect that educational interventions will necessarily be sufficient to eradicate social problems for these children, nor always succeed, if one does not also address other problems of health, child care, nutrition, physical safety, and so forth.

Realistic expectations for societal improvement may require more systematic and comprehensive analyses and interventions in community development and social services to help families and individuals achieve conditions of living that correspond to the demands and resources of New York City and the United States (e.g., Schorr, 1988). Programmes that provide comprehensive, integrated social support are probably needed if one wants to have significant numbers of impoverished minority children achieve the kinds of success considered typical or acceptable for middle-class children. Research about basic problems – such as sustaining school attendance and promoting sufficient educational activity to get, as a minimum, the certification needed for many societal opportunities (e.g., high school diploma) – that aims to move from describing these conditions and exploring possible effective interventions, toward developing intervention for ongoing practices, may have to take these additional aspects directly into account in their implementation,[9] or in coord-ination with complementary programmes (see Swanson, Mehan, & Hubbard, 1995, for one example).

At the same time, it should be obvious that addressing these issues about life conditions does not solve the specific educational problems, such as what should be taught – and how. We should not undersell the possibilities of education for contributing to societal improvement, if there is some conscious effort to take account of and integrate societal conditions into specific teaching programmes for the cultural-historical conditions of the children.

Attention to the broader societal issues gives a better opportunity to try to formulate educational interventions that can coordinate conceptually with other societal conditions, rather than hoping that one's educational contribution will in some unspecified way contribute to a qualitative change. As we become more knowledgeable about the concrete, specific societal conditions and challenges within which the children are growing up, it becomes possible to think more explicitly about the content of the educational programmes in relation to those conditions and experiences, and our possibilities for formulating relevant and realistic educational interventions are likely to increase.

To get some sense of the complexity involved in understanding schooling practice in a societal perspective, we look at the issue of school completion, with a focus on cultural minorities and particularly, when possible, for Latino students in the United States and Puerto Rican children in New York.

School Completion

In Western, wage-based economies, formal state-approved schooling is not usually an end in itself. The institutionally-defined, objective status 'gradu-

---

9 Schorr (1988) describes Eugene Lang's 'I have a dream' project, which started originally from a generous impulse in which the wealthy industrialist promised in a speech to the graduating sixth-grade class of his old elementary school that he would pay their col-lege tuition if they came into college. Having made this promise, he subsequently hired a full-time worker to support the children. Lang originally thought that this person could organize enrichment activities such as trips to museums, concerts, and libraries. It quickly became apparent that this was unrealistic, when this person was using much of the time for such things as making sure that some of the children were simply getting out of bed in the morning to go to school. Incidentally, Lang's initial promise was made in an elementary school in the same area where our teaching project was conducted.

ated' is important, both in societal interactions and in educational research and intervention. In societal interactions, school completion is usually taken as a necessary requirement for acceptance into employment, military service, training, further education, and other activities usually related to one's economic activities and standard of living,[10] so one function of schooling is to provide this certification. In the United States, the acquisition of a *high school diploma* (or an equivalent examination, GED) is the primary educational pathway that persons are expected to complete.[11]

Much research and political advocacy in the United States has focused on questions of high school retention and graduation, because a high school diploma will usually give access to more and higher-paying jobs (Fashola & Slavin, 1997). In the United States, there is a strong correlation between level of education and lifetime earnings (e.g., Bowles, Gintis, & Osborne, 2002; Sewell & Hauser, 1975; U.S. Census Bureau, 2002). For example, among Puerto Ricans who have had 0-11 years of schooling (i.e., no high school diploma), 30%-39% have an annual income below the poverty line, while only 16% of Puerto Ricans who graduated from high school are living below the poverty line (De La Rosa & Maw, 1990). Many cultural minority groups tend to have lower rates of high school completion than societally dominant groups. For example, in 1983, 80% of the Puerto Ricans who entered the New York City schools did not graduate from high school (Calitri, 1983). In 1991, 51.3% of Hispanics over the age of 25 had completed four years of high school compared with 80.5% of non-Hispanics (National Council of La Raza, 1992). In 1999, 38% of all Hispanic youth between the ages of 16-24 had dropped out of school, compared with 13% non-

---

10 There are, of course, some persons who are economically successful despite not completing school, or who are given access to societal institutions that usually require that one has formally completed school. While these exceptional cases are relatively few, they are also consistent with the analysis to be presented here. If persons are capable of achieving a good life (including a societally-accepted economic self-sufficiency, self-satisfaction), then there may be less concern about completion of schooling. School typically has an enabling function that focuses on the qualification that one has completed the institution. It is neutral about whether a person has acquired specific knowledge and skills that can be used. It is seen as a typical, maybe sufficient, and often, but not always necessary accomplishment to achieving a good life.

11 Other countries sometimes have additional pathways through apprenticeship systems, and other kinds of technical and practical educations. Examples include Great Britain (Kerckhoff, 1990), Denmark (Vibe-Hastrup & Mørkøv Ullerup, 1988), and Germany (Hamilton, 1990).

Hispanic Black and 7% White youth in the same age range (Kaufman, Kwon, Klein, & Chapman, 2000, Table 3, p. 12; see Pérez, 2000, pp. 8-9, for similar statistics). Even when various mediating factors are controlled (immigration status, socioeconomic status, language status), the pattern remains that youth with a Hispanic background are relatively less likely to complete high school (Fernández & Shu, 1988; Lockwood & Secada, 1999).

The interpretations or explanations of the relationship between achieved education level and economic condition can be complicated. For example, those with high school education may also come from economically stronger families who provided other social and cultural resources, thereby facilitating future employment. Nonetheless, the empirical relationship supports the suggestion that in terms of basic economic levels, remaining in the schooling system until one can obtain a high school diploma is a critical factor in terms of the economic outcomes for Puerto Rican students.[12] Therefore, there has been considerable interest in supporting Hispanic students, as well as students in general, to complete high school (see Fashola & Slavin, 1997, for a review of programmes that have had a significant and replicable impact on reducing the number of dropouts in a broad range of secondary schools).

The vital importance of completing high school in the United States has made this process an important focus for both educational research and intervention. Research about school completion focuses on the question of whether or not students complete a legally-prescribed or societally-acceptable quantity of schooling. There is considerable scientific and practical interest in understanding why some groups of children are less likely to complete (or even enter) high school than others, why pupils remain in school, and what interventions can be made to support the likelihood of children completing high school. Many research studies on cultural minority students comment directly or indirectly about the meaning of their investigations for school completion.

Four main research perspectives, relevant to high school completion are considered here. The first focuses on knowledge development about school completion, through analyses of possible reasons for not completing school. The other three perspectives – institution-directed interventions, student-directed interventions, community-directed interventions – correspond to interventions into ongoing practice.

---

12 However, Brown, Rosen, Hill, & Olivas (1981) found that a Puerto Rican high school dropout was more likely to be employed than a Puerto Rican high school graduate, which may reflect more about the historical employment conditions for Puerto Ricans than the qualities of the high school graduates.

ANALYSES OF FACTORS THAT AFFECT HIGH SCHOOL GRADUATION

An interest in the description and analysis of relatively lower school achievement, both quantitatively and qualitatively of cultural minority students in the
United States, arose partly in reaction to the initial theoretical explanations that
focused on genetic differences and cultural deficits. An historical account of early
explanations for these observations can be found in Jacob and Jordan (1993).

The empirical problem that motivates this research is rooted in the well-
documented and noticeable differences, on a number of indicators (e.g., percentage of high school dropouts, scores on standardized tests) that show that some
groups, especially minority groups, have higher rates of early school-leaving
and lower scores of academic achievement than societally dominant groups.
The research problem is to understand the causes or influential factors for these
differences.

Many factors have been identified and investigated (see Fashola & Slavin,
1997 for an overview), but specific causes for school dropout and poor school
performance are difficult to investigate systematically. Many general factors are
likely to contribute to dropping out of school, including problems with safety,
poor instruction, inadequate teachers, uncaring environments, poor physical
conditions (books, buildings, other resources), as well as individual problems
such as drug use, pregnancy.

The current views reject single-factor causal explanations. The empirical
realities are more complicated. For example, mismatch between communication
or interaction styles may contribute to young people dropping out of school,
but there are also many cases in which immigrants to the United States are
relatively successful in American high schools, although they would also be
subject to these differences (Gibson, 2000; Gibson & Ogbu, 1991; Ogbu, 1987;
Suarez-Orozco, 1993). Similarly, some individuals within minority groups that
historically have been relatively unsuccessful at completing school can be highly
successful, while some individuals from historically-successful majority groups
also fail.

If we ignore the rhetorical attempts to organize existing research literature on
minority school failure into opposing classes of single-factor explanations (e.g.,
Jacob & Jordan, 1993; Erickson, 1993), and focus on current viewpoints, then it
is interesting to see some common points of view among researchers purport-
edly in opposition or disagreement with each other. The current tendency is
toward dialectical models built on an interaction between objective conditions
in the schools and society, with the subjective interpretations and reactions by
the children and their families (Erickson, 1993; Foley, 1991; Ogbu, 1993).

It seems that the main issue, according to these theoretical models, is whether
students feel good about what is happening to them in school. The school does
not necessarily have to acknowledge their culture, language, communication

styles, if they do not experience these differences as threatening their culture. When these aspects are experienced as threatening to one's cultural or social identity, then forms of resistance can appear, and students develop a negative orientation to acquiring the skills needed to accomplish school-defined tasks (Hoffman, 1988; Matute-Bianchi, 1986). This theoretical view is also consistent with empirical investigations for reasons for remaining in school (C. Rodriguez, 1992), and reflects recommendations from the Hispanic Dropout Project (Secada, Chavez-Chavez, Garcia, Muñoz, Oakes, Santiago-Santiago, & Slavin, 1998).

A common aspect that runs through these various theoretical and empirical accounts is the importance of a student's interpretation of their experiences in relation to schooling. Many factors can affect how young people interpret their school experience, including effects from the peer group (Steinberg, Dornbusch, & Brown, 1992); a positive cultural self-definition (Hoffman, 1988), which may reflect more generally the ethnic community's expectations or demands (which can be reinforced with direct social demands and punishments) (Gibson, 1993); support from individual teachers or mentors (Adi-Nader, 1990); historically accumulated experience of rejection and exclusion by majority groups (Ogbu, 1993); and changing economic opportunities for an ethnic group (Foley, 1991).

The variability observed in these studies would appear to reflect the specific historical development and current societal relations that characterize various minority groups in the United States. An important implication of this variability is, however, that if one wants to move from knowledge-development studies (i.e., description and analysis of high school dropouts) toward intervention in ongoing practice, then it will be necessary to develop analyses for specific minority groups in relation to their specific historical conditions (e.g., Vélez-Ibáñez & Greenberg, 1994). Moreover, one should expect a certain amount of variability for a specific minority group, even when living in the same city (e.g., Tapia, 1998). A generic analysis, in which one describes, for example, an intervention to prevent or reduce the numbers of minority children dropping out of high school in the United States, is unlikely to be effective (Bartolomé, 1994).

INTERVENTIONS TO SUPPORT HIGH SCHOOL GRADUATION

Institutional Interventions

Some political and research work has focused on trying to improve the quality of existing institutions. In some instances, the problem was simply to get adequate resources to conduct the existing programmes. In other instances the problem was to get new programmes or extend existing programmes to serve more persons.

Santiago Santiago's (1986) account of the difficulties and persistence that has been needed to achieve even minimal action on the part of the New York City school system (e.g., to use Spanish as a language of instruction) attests to the complexity involved in achieving significant changes in New York City schooling practices for Puerto Rican students. And conditions for the continued use of bilingual education in New York City are regularly threatened (del Valle, 1998; Reyes, 2003).

Equal access to educational opportunities has been another important issue because of structural racism. The focus on legal rights and equal opportunities is important and necessary. One can see the importance and necessity of conducting the legal and political campaigns to achieve reasonable conditions for addressing the social and educational problems that characterize the community (e.g., Schneider, 1976).

Research based on attempts to identify schools that were especially effective at educating minority students (Edmonds, 1979), has inspired some attempts to make these large-scale institutional changes at the level of entire schools or a group of schools in a school district. Evidence for success in these specific interventions has been debated (Brookover, 1987; Purkey & Smith, 1983; Stedman, 1987; Stedman, 1988), and continues to be debated (e.g., Teddlie & Reynolds, 2001), but some positive examples have been identified (Stedman, 1987). A striking characteristic is that often the entire school environment (leadership, physical plant, teacher morale, community support) are present in effective programmes (T.P. Carter & Chatfield, 1986; Lucas, Henze, & Donato, 1990; Fashola & Slavin, 1997). Similar characteristics have also been observed in the same neighbourhood where our teaching experiment was conducted (Alvarez, 1992; Meier, 1995a).

This focus on transforming the entire school environment (governance structure, parental involvement, teacher-pupil relations, teacher expectations) also characterizes several long-term projects that were developed specifically with a focus on schools where children have traditionally been failing (e.g., Chasin & Levin, 1995; Comer & Joyner, 2004; Levin, 1995; Slavin, Madden, Dolan, & Wasik, 1996). These projects are not specifically directed to the issue of school completion, and are often implemented in elementary or middle schools. However some of these efforts are motivated by a research-based evidence that it may be better to help children get started in a good direction at the middle-school age, because it may be too late or more difficult to make adequate interventions at high-school age (for summaries see Ascher, 1993, Lockwood, 1995). These examples reiterate the point that systematic changes in the educational possibilities for minority students will extend far beyond the teaching methods.

Intervention for Supporting Students

In addition to working toward institutional changes for supporting school completion, there have been programmes and interventions that focus primarily on supporting children to remain in school. There are several examples in which a concerted effort has been made to support Puerto Rican (and other minority students) to remain in school through a variety of methods (extra teaching, mentoring, enrichment activities). There is often considerable financial and institutional support from public school systems, universities, private foundations and private businesses in these programmes (e.g., Adi-Nader, 1990; A. Rodríguez, 1992; Trueba, 1988).

Community-Directed Intervention

A third target of intervention has been directed at the community within which the children are going to school. One kind of intervention focuses on parents, helping them to support their children through a variety of methods (how to help with homework, joint reading activities). Another kind aims to develop better relations between the parents and the schools (e.g., communicate the goals of the school), with an assumption that this might lead to better support of the school.

There is accumulating evidence that parental involvement in schooling leads to better student achievement, school attendance and graduation rates (Flaxman & Inger, 1992). Many projects have been conducted in recent years that have attempted to involve Latino parents in the schooling, and these experiences have helped to identify practices that facilitate their participation in schools (Delgado-Gaitan, 1991, 1994; Nicolau & Ramos, 1990; Orum, 1991). Similarly, studies of school effectiveness have noted that parental or community involvement is one characteristic of schools that have been more successful in educating Latino minority children (e.g., Alvarez, 1992; T.P. Carter & Chatfield, 1986; Lucas et al., 1990).

Summary Remarks

The problems of and interest in school completion and the research that aims to address these problems and interests arise from a set of societal conditions that extend far beyond the schools themselves. We have described three kinds of efforts that have attempted to make direct interventions into existing practices in an attempt to improve the rate at which minority children will graduate from high school. Striking characteristics of these efforts have been the significant number of years needed to develop and implement these programmes. T.P.

Carter and Chatfield (1986) speculate that a minimum of three years is needed for changing school practice, and the considerable institutional resources and activities that have to be mobilized. Comer (1999) tells about the five years of concentrated efforts needed to make changes in schooling practices. In Bloom, Ham, Melton, & O'Brien's (1998) evaluation study of eight schools that were implementing the ideas of an accelerated school, they noted that it was often five years before baseline improvements in standard reading and mathematics performance scores were observed, because the first three years were often used for implementing organizational changes, with instructional changes only starting in the third year and solidifying by the fifth year (p. 58). These characteristics are understandable when one considers that these interventions tend to involve comprehensive changes in the school's practices. Given the complexity of even a single school, and the time needed to see the effects of interventions, it will be difficult to evaluate whether all these changes are needed as a package or the extent to which single aspects can be effective alone.

It is important to note that this focus on school completion often does not consider what children are learning in school, just that they have been there sufficiently long to achieve at least the minimal requirements for a high school diploma. Evaluations of the large-scale reform efforts mentioned before often focus on standardized test scores and relative performance levels. This is not to say that there is not a concern with the quality of the education, but these concerns are often formulated in generic terms like 'problem solving' or 'higher order thinking skills'. These projects have been important for showing the considerable effort that is needed to create institutional conditions that can support good teaching, but if we assume that schools should be doing more than providing the minimal skills needed to get a high school diploma, then we must also be concerned with the content of the schooling. (We also assume there are interactions between the content of schooling and the interest to complete high school.)

There are many examples from diverse projects (e.g., accelerated schools) that show that children living in difficult societal conditions, coming from cultural groups that historically have been conceptualized as intellectually inadequate by dominant groups, have capabilities and interests to engage in theoretical, analytical, reflective thinking, and their communities offer more resources than one might normally think. Therefore it should possible to make interventions where the focus becomes the intellectual content of the teaching.

In the beginning of this chapter, we mentioned a tension between wanting educational practices to address societal conditions, but being limited in relation to what one wants to realize. This tension was illustrated in considering the considerable efforts that are needed to create the support services that are often needed to help children from poor conditions be successful in school. At the same time, we believe that it is possible to use schooling to support child development in a way that goes beyond the mere acquisition of the institutional credential of a high school diploma. The remainder of this book is concerned with presenting a perspective for planning educational activities that are aimed at contributing to the development of a good life. The analysis presented in this chapter makes it clear that good educational activities alone will not be sufficient to realize that goal, but we believe that it is a necessary part that has not received adequate attention.

Line of Children ©Jose B. Rivera, East Harlem.

CHAPTER 3

An Introduction to Radical-Local Teaching and Learning

The preceding chapter examined briefly some of the goals and interests normally connected to education, and considered the issue of school completion, because of the important consequences that it has for one's future life conditions, the historically low rates of school completion recorded for Puerto Rican children, and for helping to illustrate the complex relation between educational intervention and societal conditions. Without minimizing the significance of high school graduation, we now shift the focus to issues of how education can contribute to helping children prepare to live a good life, which we assume is not achieved simply because one has completed high school, without regard to the content of that education. As noted previously, education is expected to help children develop competences and motives that are relevant for participation in societal life. The content of the education that one receives is also relevant to the quality of life that one lives afterwards. An exclusive focus on easily measurable goals (e.g., standardized test scores in reading and mathematics) may hinder the realization of life quality more than it promotes (Smith, Gilmore, Goldman, & McDermott, 1993).

The idea of radical-local teaching and learning is a theoretical perspective for how to organize educational programmes. The simultaneous goal of radical-local teaching and learning is to develop general conceptual knowledge about subject-matter areas, with content that is related specifically to the children's life situation. This does not mean that the scope of subject-matter teaching should be limited to the knowledge and experience that children bring to school. Rather the interest is to understand the dynamic relation between subject-matter knowledge, life situation, and personal development such that general subject-matter understanding is developed through and in relation to children's life situation. To realize this goal, we need to have a more explicit conceptual analysis of the relations between conceptual knowledge and life situations and the psychological processes involved in acquiring this knowledge in a form that can be used actively in relation to one's life conditions and situations.

As noted in Chapter 1, Vygotsky was interested in children's concept development. His analysis of the relation between children's everyday concepts and scientific concepts is relevant to our interest to integrate children's everyday knowledge with a theoretical understanding that is relevant to the specific local conditions in which the child is living. Ultimately Vygotsky's analysis is insufficient for our purposes, because it does not have an analysis of the relation of knowledge to children's societal lives, and his analysis of the relation between forms of practice and forms of knowledge was not sufficiently explicit. It is useful, however, to consider his analysis because it provides a way to understand how subject-matter knowledge can become 'personal' (i.e., an active part of a person's thinking), and thereby transforming everyday knowledge. At the same time, this review helps to clarify the need for a more explicit analysis of institutional practice in relation to knowledge development and use.

Vygotsky's Analysis of Everyday and Scientific Concepts

The core of Vygotsky's distinction between everyday concepts and scientific concepts is motivated by (a) different histories for the psychological developmental of the two kinds of concepts, and (b) substantive differences in their psychological form. When children come to school, they have already learned the meaning of many words, even if they have not had systematic instruction about these words. These *everyday concepts* are usually 'saturated with the child's own rich personal experience' (Vygotsky, 1934/1987, p. 178), and tend to be used spontaneously, unreflectively, and unrelated to any system of concepts.

The label, *scientific concept,* is used to refer to concepts that are part of a well-defined system of conceptual relationships. The defining features of a scientific concept are its systematic relationships to other concepts and a mastering of one's conscious awareness of concept meaning.[13]

'Scientific concept' refers broadly to all concepts that are formulated in systematic relationships, and not only to concepts within (natural) scientific disciplines. Vygotsky uses some simple examples of hierarchical relations to

---

13 '[W]e can state the core of our hypothesis … Only within a system can the concept acquire conscious awareness and a voluntary nature. Conscious awareness and the presence of a system are synonyms when we are speaking of concepts, just as spontaneity, lack of conscious awareness, and the absence of a system are three different words for designating the nature of the child's concept' (Vygotsky, 1934/1987, pp. 191-2, emphasis in the original).

illustrate the idea of systematic relationships, concepts such as *flower* and *rose* or *furniture* and *table* can come into systematic relationships when persons become consciously aware of their superordinate and subordinate relationships, which is not automatically true for children.

Vygotsky's distinction is sometimes misinterpreted as describing a hierarchical organization with concrete everyday concepts on the bottom and abstract, scientific concepts on the top, or a replacement of everyday concepts with scientific concepts. In fact, Vygotsky viewed everyday and scientific concepts are being parts of a single psychological system,[14] where the development of scientific concepts results in changes in the everyday concepts.[15]

When children enter school, there has been sufficient development of their everyday concepts so that it is possible for them to be familiar with many different aspects of the social and natural world, such that they can view films, read stories, hear news reports, while having some idea about the content being presented; throughout their schooling they also encounter many concepts that are everyday concepts for them. At the same time, the child's inability to control all the concepts involved in these practical and educational situations usually serves to create an interest for the child to engage in actions that help to achieve this control.

In analyzing conceptual development, Vygotsky emphasized the inseparability of forms of thinking from the content of thinking. This view stands in contrast to many researchers who tend to view the form and content of concepts as separate. This common view arises, according to Vygotsky, from a belief that content is culturally developed, and socially and historically determined, while thinking forms are biological processes determined by organic maturation, running parallel to the brain's organic development. In Vygotsky's view, the forms of thinking are also cultural accomplishments, developed as part of thinking with particular contents. Thus, the interdependence between form and content characterizes both the historical evolution of mankind and the development of the single person (Scribner, 1985; Vygotsky, 1930/1998a, p. 42).

---

14 'Piaget ... does not see that they [spontaneous and non-spontaneous concepts] are united in a single system that is formed in the course of the child's mental development' (Vygotsky, 1934/1987, p. 174).

15 'The emergence of higher types of concepts (e.g., scientific concepts) will inevitably influence existing spontaneous concepts. These two types of concepts are not encapsulated or isolated in the child's consciousness. ... They interact continually. This will inevitably lead to a situation where generalizations with a comparatively complex structure – such as scientific concepts – elicit changes in the structure of spontaneous concepts' (Vygotsky, 1934/1987, p. 177).

Vygotsky's analyses are helpful for clarifying some of the psychological background that motivates the kinds of pedagogical actions needed to realize radical-local teaching and learning. The analyses provide a conceptual model for understanding the relations between everyday concepts and formal subject-matter concepts, why children would be interested to learn scientific concepts, what it would mean for scientific concepts to become part of personal knowledge, and the consequences for personal development.

The orientation to be engaged in conceptual learning comes from the social situation of development (Vygotsky, 1933/1998, p. 198). This general theoretical concept focuses on the contradiction between the demands of the social relations within which a person functions and the present state of their developed psychological capabilities. These capabilities enable a person to be interested in and enter into these social relations, while at the same time being inadequate to meet all the demands and possibilities of the situation. This inadequacy is a contradiction that creates felicitous conditions for the development of new psychological functions.

The strength of scientific concepts, compared to everyday concepts, is that children learn to work consciously with the logical relations defined by the concept. The conscious use of systematic conceptual models, discussed in the next chapter, is a central aspect in the practical realization of radical-local teaching and learning, and an example of the interconnection of the form and content of thinking. But children's scientific concepts tend to be weak when it comes to 'spontaneous, situationally meaningful, concrete applications' (p. 220). The task of instruction is to develop scientific concepts so that they have the concrete specificity and ease of application of everyday concepts, while everyday concepts are drawn into a scientific system of concepts. Subject-matter knowledge thereby becomes integrated with the content of the tasks and situations in the child's life outside of school and can develop into functional conceptual tools for the child.

Children's conceptual development in Vygotsky's analysis is characterized by an increase in complexity of knowledge about the relations between concrete events and abstract aspects of a subject domain. From a radical-local point of view, the potential meeting between everyday and scientific subject-matter concepts gives the possibility for children to develop more systematic, analytic understanding of the issues, conditions and problems that are present in their living conditions. Teaching should aim at developing the ability to work with these relations. In developing this ability the child becomes able to use the learned subject-matter content as tools for analyzing and reflecting on everyday local activities. The abstract aspects help the child to relate local events with possible events. If the coherence and dialectic between the abstract and concrete aspects of a subject domain can be acquired through teaching activities, then the person has a way to combine general knowledge with personal competence and to become actualized for the person in local practice. A young person's acquisition of conceptual systems that relate to the social, societal and political aspects enables the young person to become conscious of the societal ideologies and of himself as a person in a society (i.e., his self consciousness develops) (Vygotsky, 1931/1998, p. 42). Through this process children come to acquire historically-produced societal knowledge.

Although Vygotsky's analysis of everyday and scientific concepts is useful for elaborating the idea of radical-local teaching and learning, there are still many aspects of these ideas that need to be developed further in a radical-local theoretical perspective. Vygotsky did not develop a detailed theoretical or concrete analysis of the social situation of development for schoolchildren in his published works, especially an analysis of the dynamics involved in conceptual development. The concept of motive, as part of a more general analysis of activity, introduced by Leontiev and further elaborated by El'konin, provides a useful way to elaborate and extend Vygotsky's idea of the social situation of development by providing a more explicit analysis of the dynamics of development. We will discuss this idea further in Chapter 5.

Although Vygotsky defined scientific concepts in terms of their participation in a system, he did not actually study concepts in their systematic relations. Rather he focused on the relation between single scientific concepts and their everyday forms (Vygotsky, 1934/1987, pp. 239-40). One consequence of this limitation, in our view, is that his analyses about everyday and scientific concepts did not take sufficient account of the relation between scientific concepts and the societal practices from which they were generated. We address this problem further in Chapter 4.

In some sense, the social situation of development can be understood as an implicit concept of 'practice', and Vygotsky's arguments reflect an orientation to the idea of practice as the source of psychological development, for example in his discussion of the differences between everyday concepts learned at home and academic concepts learned at school. But his focus was primarily on the personal meaning of concepts. He did not elaborate an analysis of practice, and therefore did not consider the meaning of concepts in relation to societal practice or the social situation of development.

We need therefore to introduce the notion of institutional practice, which we will use in the next two chapters, as part of our analysis of knowledge and development, and in this chapter as part of a more elaborated account of what we mean by radical-local teaching and learning.

Institutional Practice

We limit our attention to the idea of institutional practice, because pedagogical practices in our society are usually institutionalized, and because the interest in radical-local teaching and learning is focused on the idea of education as preparation for participation in institutionalized practice (including both further education and work practices).

On the one hand, a concrete institutional practice is an integral whole, realized by the actions and interactions among multiple participants. At the same time, an institutional practice always has at least three different aspects or perspectives that are present in the practice, and which contribute to the conditions for the production, reproduction and development of this practice. These perspectives are: *societal,* reflected in historically evolved traditions and interests in a society that are formalized into laws and regulations; *general,* which can be seen as guided by generalized or theoretical outlines for institutional activities; and *individual,* which characterizes the shared activities of persons in specific institutions. All three perspectives are necessary to understand an institutional practice and the variations within an institutional practice. Without one of these three aspects, then the idea of an institutionalized practice does not exist. Each aspect – societal, general, individual – are conditions for the others. Figure 3.1 presents a graphic representation of a general model of institutional practice.

The first important institution for a child is usually the family. Practice within a specific family is usually unwritten, and often unspoken, including aspects that are unique for this family. In terms of the model, this is the individual aspect. Aspects of individual family practice that are shared with other families in a community can be characterized as general family practice. The general aspect of family practice is often found in traditions that are common for several generations of family life in a specific society, which through a historical process have become traditions for how to live and act in families. Individual families are often aware, in some sense, of these general traditions (through knowledge of practices in other families, as acquired from personal acquaintance, fictional

Figure 3.1. General model of institutional practice.

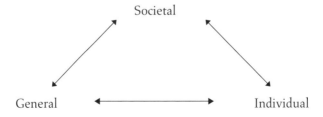

representations in movies, novels, and theatre, documentary and news reports, and so forth). In our model these traditions would be called the general perspective of family practice. Some of these traditions have become formalized into laws and bureaucratic regulations about family life through laws (e.g., inheritance, divorce, birthright, educational requirements for children). In other cases, societal requirements are imposed or inspired by specific interests – political beliefs, professional consultants, programmes implemented to respond to societal problems. These formal requirements are the societal aspect of family practice.

Schooling, as an institutional practice, can also be analyzed or characterized with this model. In each nation-state, an individual school always has its own characteristics reflecting the historical actions and decisions of the persons – administrators, teachers, consultants, and children – who have acted in that school in relation to the material resources and conditions that were available. The individual aspect of practice for each school within a given nation has typically some characteristics found in all schools, reflecting their interpretation of general practices that have developed within the school system, often developed and reinforced through teacher training institutions, further education, professional magazines, and so forth. Individual and general traditions of school practice are developed in relation to the societal aspect of school practice, which reflects national or societal interests, such as formulated in formal laws and regulations, curriculum plans, policy papers, instructional guides, specific testing goals, and other official demands on school practice. All three aspects are present in any concrete practice, though the contribution and interaction between aspects will vary for specific, individual practices.

This perspective on institutional practice gives a way to understand differences in the forms of practice that dominate at home and in school. At home the individual aspects of practices are usually dominant with mild influence from general family traditions. In most homes there is no explicit focus on societal practice (i.e., on laws and regulations) for how families should care for children except in conflict situations such as divorce, mistreatment, or death in the family. In school the societal practice dominates the activities both in content (subject-matter areas, curriculum plans, and examinations) and form (time and space characteristics such as school hours, pupil and teacher locations in the school and in the classroom).[16]

---

16 If the societal and general practices dominate more than the actual needs, then the human interactions in the home become formal and lacking positive emotional content. In contrast, if the societal and general aspects are not the basis for the school practice, then the societal value of schooling and the importance of theorizing activity are neglected. In effect, the school practice becomes 'headless' or egocentric.

This difference between home and school in dominance of individual versus societal traditions is important to take into consideration when creating radical-local teaching, because children's knowledge, grounded in individual practice traditions from home and community, is informal and often not formulated explicitly. In contrast the knowledge presented in school is dominated by the societal aspects of practice and is formulated through demands for activity in school and at examinations. The goal of radical-local teaching is to create an integration between the child's spontaneous knowledge from home and community and the subject-matter knowledge presented in school as prescribed through subject-matter areas and curriculum plans.

Radical-Local Teaching and Learning

The term *radically local* or *radical localist* has been used historically within political, religious, and academic practices. In political contexts, the term was used in the late 1700s to refer to persons in colonial America who were opposed to the formation of a federal system that became the United States of America. Radical localists wanted political decisions made at a local level by the persons who would be affected by such decisions. A similar meaning is still used today to describe persons or groups who emphasize the idea of community control and decision making that considers primarily the needs and desires of the community, without considering its relation, responsibility or obligation to larger, more common political units. A similar meaning to this concept has also been used in contemporary discussions of Christian churches, where a radically local church is one that focuses on the specific needs of an individual church and its congregation, without considering broader ecumenical issues. In academic contexts, the concept has been used to describe a research perspective in information systems design that tries to break with universal methods and guidelines and pay attention to local conditions and practices (Henriksen, 2003).

The notion of *radical-local teaching and learning* that we develop here is a dialectic transformation of the traditional radical-local concept. Our concept shares in the concern of the traditional concept by paying attention to the local, specific characteristics and needs of a specific institutional site of action. In terms of the model shown in Figure 3.1, the religious and political meanings of *radically local* have focused almost exclusively on the local aspect of a practice, without considering the institutional and societal aspects. In calling our teaching-learning approach *radical local,* we are not trying to advocate that we should restrict our attention to the local, but rather that we must enrich our understanding of the general by understanding its expression and manifestation in the local, while enriching our understanding of the local by using general subject-matter concepts. This dialectical perspective is distinctly different from the meaning of the traditional radical-local concept.

We use the term, 'radical local' to refer to a complex of related ideas. When we started the teaching experiment, the term was used to express the idea that educational research should be focused on the specific conditions and needs of a particular cultural-historical location. This formulation, inspired in part by Rene Dubos's formulation of 'Think globally, act locally', was directed to the idea that one needed to act in relation to the local conditions, even while one was thinking about the meaning of those actions in a larger perspective. This view stands in contrast to a more common, often implicit, assumption in educational research that one should seek a universal theory of education for all children in all places (or dissociated from time and place), so that educational researchers in, for example, Japan, Finland, and Brazil could meet to discuss the same analysis with each another. This universal model has been attractive in the history of sciences, but it seems like it has been adopted or accepted, perhaps too uncritically or unreflectively within educational research. Inspired by the cultural-historical perspective, it seemed worthwhile to develop a theory of educational practice that could take local conditions into consideration, in this case for Puerto Rican children in East Harlem.

The notion of *radical local* subsequently became an alternative way to think about the idea of culturally-sensitive teaching, which was another motivation for the teaching experiment reported here. We came to see that a formulation like culturally sensitive (or culturally responsive) tends to direct one's attention primarily to the cultural aspects, without providing a way to recognize the individual variations among persons within a cultural group or a way to understand or relate the specific cultural aspects to the general characteristics found within a multicultural society. The idea of radical-local is not meant to drop the idea of cultural sensitivity, but rather to see that teaching and learning for all children, regardless of their background should be related to their local conditions, where cultural aspects are one, albeit important, part of those conditions. We discuss this point further in Chapter 15.

The term *radical local* has also become a useful way to express an additional aspect about relations between the general and the individual in the formation or selection of specific examples of subject-matter content. The individual is usually understood to be a concretization of the general. Implicit in the idea of concretization is that adaptations and accommodations are made to local conditions, but it is also possible to make an individual concretization that is used universally. For example, one can take an abstract pedagogical idea (e.g., teaching arithmetic with *measure* as the initial basic relation) and make it concrete (e.g., measuring the length of wood blocks) such that it is used uniformly throughout the world. In a radical-local perspective, the concretization of subject-matter material must also take into account the relations between specific subject matter, the characteristics and conditions of the pupils, and the expected future practice in which the children will participate. The specific interpretation of this general idea emphasized in this book is the need to formulate general and societal knowledge in relation to local knowledge and conditions of children's home and community, while they learn about these local knowledge and conditions formulated through more general concepts of subject-matter traditions. When subject-matter learning is properly organized, then it has the possibility for helping to contribute to the general and societal aspects of individual knowledge development.

Finally, the model of institutional practice in Figure 3.1 gives us a way to express the differences between a radical-local approach to educational research and the historically predominant approaches to educational research. Traditionally, educational research has focused primarily on the societal and general aspects of educational practice without having an adequate way to conceptualize individual aspects in relation to the general and societal. The idea in radical-local teaching and learning is that all three aspects, the societal, the general and the individual must be integrated in subject-matter teaching and learning.

There are many reasons why we believe that a radical-local perspective is useful in pedagogical planning. For now, we will mention three. First, we expect that it will be easier to develop teaching-learning situations that are motivating to children, because of the connections to their local community, which is the source of their everyday knowledge. Second, the focus on relating subject-matter content to aspects from the children's local community makes it easier for them to use their prior knowledge in teaching-learning situations. Third, the focus on relating general academic concepts in relation to local, everyday situations gives better conditions for trying to realize the idea of making academic concepts into rich, active concepts that are used by children in their thinking and acting. The radical-local perspective is focused not simply on a better way of teaching academic concepts; rather the focus is on how to develop an understanding of academic concepts through the topics and issues of local life situations, which in turn can be used to relate in a more competent way to those situations.

Relevant Research and Practice in a Radical-Local Perspective

As far as we know, the expression *radical-local teaching and learning* has not appeared previously in educational research literature. As a way of elaborating the radical-local perspective further, we will consider some examples from the many completed or ongoing research studies, intervention projects, and innovative schools that have some aspects or features that seem consistent with or relevant to a radical-local perspective on education. We will focus particularly on examples of studies that have been oriented toward education for children with a Puerto Rican, Latino, or minority background.

Aspects of the idea of radical-local teaching and learning are emerging, often independently, in diverse projects around the world. For example, the School Development Program focuses on the conditions of development for the whole child (Comer & Joyner, 2004), and is concerned for how schooling should be providing knowledge that is relevant for one's life (Comer, 2001). Similarly, the idea that there must be more explicit attention to the choice and use of school subject-matter content in relation to the content of community life is not unique to radical-local teaching and learning. In these respects, a radical-local perspective does not necessarily provide new goals or interests for education beyond those discussed at the beginning of Chapter 2, or new ideas for existing pedagogical practice. Rather its general contributions are to provide a theoretical framework for analyzing and conceptualizing the goals of pedagogical interventions and a set of theoretical and practical tools for planning and implementing educational activities that aim to realize these goals. More specifically, it provides a more explicit analysis about the relation between subject-matter knowledge and local knowledge together with a theoretical and practical analysis of how teaching can be conducted to integrate these kinds of knowledge.

TEACHING PROJECTS THAT FOCUS ON COMMUNITY

There are a variety of projects that have either used children's immediate community as a source of material for the content of teaching, or have tried to use characteristics of the children's community and/or cultural background as an inspiration for organizing teaching. The use of community studies in educational contexts has a recorded history in the educational literature that is at least thirty-five years old. Community-oriented studies have been used in many different contexts, and even institutionalized in some instances. For example, the Foxfire project, which originated in Georgia in 1967, has been one example in which students have been motivated to engage in literacy activities through the investigation of their local Appalachian community and culture (Puckett, 1989; Wigginton, 1989). In the same vein, Cazden (1982) describes a summer-camp activity in upstate New York that was organized around children's investigation of local culture. Studies of local or regional family history have also been used as teaching material in England (Steel & Taylor, 1973; Steel, 1980), and Sweden (e.g., Sutter & Grensjo, 1988).

The main idea in these projects is usually to investigate ongoing forms of life that the children are able to observe and experience directly. This kind of information is not usually included in the typical school civics textbook that describes the formal political and institutional arrangements in a community. These kinds of projects often hope to make the content of school instruction more relevant to children's background and experience, and in some cases to help children become engaged in the conditions of their local community.

Similar examples of community-oriented studies, developed through practical experience, have also been reported for cultural minority children. Hime (1977) started to conduct science projects, often in collaboration with community organizations or institutions, with Navajo Indian students in 1966. The projects were initiated from student-formulated interests, with an explicit requirement to use community-based knowledge sources and topics rooted in Navajo traditions. Quintero (1989) describes a project that aimed to improve the quality and success of schooling for children in an unsuccessful school district in San Juan, Puerto Rico in which the children displayed an interest in their community after they were allowed to make some theatrical presentations of problems in their community. These interests were further developed into specific community studies in which the children learned more about their history and the special accomplishments of their specific community. Quintero reported that this improved the children's self-image and self-respect.

Mercado (1992) describes her attempt to introduce a research activity within the normal classroom teaching of an elementary school in the South Bronx. The children chose topics to investigate, usually focusing on questions that directly affected their community. Her work shows that children are capable of taking more responsibility for doing intellectual work, and with greater sophistication and complexity than might be typically assumed from children with their societal position. Torres-Guzmán (1992) describes an example in which students' personal experiences of, or with, racism are used as a starting point for following a traditional textbook unit on writing about racism. She also described an example in which students became engaged in investigating industrial pollution in their own neighbourhood. Diaz, Moll, and Mehan (1986) describe an example in which students, organized by their teacher, conducted a community survey about attitudes toward bilingualism as a foundation for writing a report about bilingualism. Vasquez, Pease-Alvarez, and Shannon (1994) describe *La Clase Mágica* in which elements of Spanish and Mexican culture were drawn explicitly into the context of literacy activities in an afterschool programme. Hill (1992) has collected a large number of examples of sayings, songs, and rhymes that are commonly known among Puerto Rican children, and suggested that these could be a good source of material for use in the classroom. She expects that this will have positive effects on self-esteem (pp. 95-99).

Project EXCEL, a nationally-organized effort by the National Council of La Raza, aims to support Hispanic community-based organizations to help improve the educational opportunities for Hispanic children, youth, and parents (Orum, 1991). Started in 1985, six model educational programmes have been developed, disseminated, and systematically supported through training and technical advice. These programmes include family reading, a teacher support network, and preparation for the General Equivalency Degree (a high school equivalency degree). Particularly relevant for the present discussion is the programme called *Academia del Pueblo*. Organized primarily through local community centres, this afterschool (and sometimes summer) programme is 'designed to help elementary school children build the skills which promote school success and love of learning' (p. 8). There is a required core curriculum with a thematic focus on language-development and problem-solving skills through the study of community building, and a required complementary parent education and involvement programme. These programmes typically meet twice a week for two hours a day during the school year. The core curriculum explores the issue of 'communities', including the structures and rules that govern local life and solve problems, and the jobs held by adult community members. The children have to construct a model community, during which they have to write stories and articles about their work, design a physical environment, and design a set of laws for their model community, often including policies for transportation, housing, waste disposal, zoning, and public services (p. 19). In the evaluations made to date, there are indications that children participating in these programmes make positive improvements in their math and language skills and other school-related behaviours. Like the effective schools research (see Chapter 2, pp. 26-27), these programmes have been more successful when parent participation was successfully integrated into them. The primary focus in EXCEL has been on implementation, rather than educational method development. This initial project has been elaborated, partly in response to requests from local project coordinators for new teaching materials because they were uncertain about how to continue with children who return for a second year. The project has now developed a considerable amount of detailed curriculum plans, both for elementary and junior high schoolchildren (National Council of La Raza, 1996, 1999) and adolescents (National Council of La Raza, 1998), though not all of it is community-oriented.

The diversity of settings in which these examples occurred suggest that many groups of children may be interested in investigating their communities, especially when they are given some choices about what to investigate and are supported to produce genuine, high-quality products as a result of their work (e.g., Foxfire produces magazines, records, films, television programmes; the children in Cazden's example presented their work to the local townspeople; the

Navajo children presented their results to local groups; the children in Puerto Rico started to work in a team to develop and produce a play about their community; the children in South Bronx participated in academic research conferences). Furthermore, in many of these examples, the researchers note that the children express positive affect in relation to these activities (e.g., comments about the value of the work, about their good feelings from doing the work).

Radical-Local Subject Matter

Within the radical-local perspective on education, the community study is not an end in itself, or a mediating device for creating conditions for developing basic skills in literacy and mathematical skills. It is also to take seriously that the academic content of schooling should be related to the child's local life situation. One of the most comprehensive efforts to systematically link community conditions with the content of teaching materials, in a way that also aims for the educational and personal development of the students, is described in Freire (1968/1970). The content of teaching in Freire's interventions – which focused on adult literacy development – were planned explicitly based on anthropological and sociological analyses of the life conditions of the students, which were used to choose content and topics for teaching that demanded the participants to confront, reflect, and analyze their societal relations. That is, the concern was not only to develop the literacy skills of the participants, but to do so in a way that would develop capabilities for the participants to analyze and understand their local community and life situation in a critical way that could give motivation and knowledge for acting to change those conditions.

These characteristics of Freire's project – the analysis of the societal conditions in order to identify content and themes of instruction, the systematic use of local content as part of developing subject-matter knowledge, the integration and use of subject-matter content with the participants' life situation, respect for the personal, human development of the participants (see especially Chapter 2 in Freire, 1968/1970) – are in the spirit of the radical-local teaching and learning ideal. Although Freire's project was not directed toward children, we mention it to acknowledge the inspiration that it provides for thinking about relating academic teaching to life situations, an aspect that we think should be further developed in educational research. At the same time, Freire's work should not be considered an adequate ideal for children's education, because it does not present a sufficient analysis of the historical conditions, and an analysis is needed of the societal relation between children and adults.

Another important programme of work in relation to the idea of radical-local teaching and learning is the funds of knowledge methodology (González, Moll, & Amanti, 2004). The basic idea is that there is a wide variety and depth of knowledge to be found among families that is not usually acknowledged. In the original work, there was a focus on working-class Mexican families (Moll & Greenberg, 1990; Vélez-Ibáñez & Greenberg, 1992), and efforts were made to have this knowledge brought into the classroom, not only in terms of its substance, but literally embodied by persons from the community who come to the classroom to talk with the children (Moll, Amanti, Neff, & González, 1992). Many positive benefits seem to arise from these interactions. The children can understand the relation between their schooling and future employment activities; their parents and neighbours receive a kind of official recognition and acknowledgement as having valuable capabilities. Subsequently a methodology has been developed so that teachers can learn how to make ethnographic interviews with families (González & Moll, 2002), which provides topics and themes that can be used as part of classroom teaching. Mercado and Moll (2000) describe interventions that share a radical-local focus on the importance of local knowledge, but there does not seem to be a corresponding conceptualization of how to relate this local content to the systematic development of academic concepts (e.g., Civil, 1994).

FAMILY BACKGROUND

The use of academic subject matter in relation to the local community is the main aspect of the radical-local perspective on education investigated in this book. However, there are other aspects of educational practice that should be thought through in a radical-local perspective. Given the focus on child development, it is relevant to consider the local traditions of practice at home and in the community in relation to children's subject-matter learning.

Some research approaches have investigated the dynamics of interaction between teachers and pupils who have come from cultural backgrounds whose traditions of interaction between adults and children differ from the traditional interaction forms found in traditional schooling (e.g., Philips, 1983). These projects have provided valuable information for helping to better understand how the conditions for interactions between teachers and pupils can create better conditions for learning, but again these projects do not conceptualize the relation between home practices and school subject-matter content.

The Kammehameha Early Education Project (KEEP) in Hawaii has focused primarily on developing specific interventions for the development of reading skills for Hawaiian children in the first three grades. An important part of the project was to understand interactions of teaching and learning that are common to the children's daily life outside of school. Anthropological observations helped researchers to identify interaction forms that could be adapted to classroom activities (e.g., Vogt, Jordan, & Tharp, 1993).

The experiences in KEEP have shown that explaining sources of cultural conflicts to the classroom teachers, or improving their use of motivational techniques so that the children were engaged with the instructional tasks were not sufficient for improving the acquisition of reading skills. The KEEP approach was to modify the traditional instructional practices by selecting some ways of interacting among peers and adults that children had learned at home and avoid other ways of interacting that seemed to interfere with learning activities (Jordan, 1985).

COMMUNITY-ORIENTED SCHOOLS

In recent years, there have been possibilities in the United States from various sources to create small, innovative public schools. Several of these schools, both elementary (e.g., Academia Semillas del Pueblo Charter School, Los Angeles, http://www.dignidad.org/english/history.html) and secondary (Pedro Albizu Campos High School, Chicago, Antrop-González, 2003; Ramos-Zayas, 1998; El Puente Academy for Peace and Justice, Brooklyn, NY, Rivera & Pedraza, 2000; Nueva Esperanza Academy Public Charter High School, Philadelphia, http://www.neacademy.org/) have been opened in predominantly Latino communities, and whose self-descriptions reflect goals and concerns of radical-local teaching. Examples are found in other parts of the world where there is a concern of academic instruction that is grounded in indigenous educational traditions (e.g., in New Zealand, Corson, 1993). The stated goals of these schools look very interesting from a radical-local perspective, because of the focus on using community as a source and focus of instruction. What is more difficult for us to evaluate, because we have not seen the details of the school practices, is the extent to which the community-oriented studies are used to develop general subject-matter understanding (i.e., theoretical knowledge) that can be used in relation to societal practice.

Concluding Comments

We have introduced the idea of radical-local teaching and learning as a theoretical perspective for thinking about the relationships between child development and subject-matter teaching. The general idea of radical local expresses a tension between the local and the general in an educational practice. There is a need to attend to the individual practice in a community in relation to the choice and use of general subject matter, as part of realizing societal goals for full development of children.

We have tried to show that aspects of the idea of a radical-local perspective are emerging, often independently, in diverse projects around the world. Some researchers have started to describe the idea, theoretically, of using subject-matter teaching for personal development (e.g., Cummins, 1994), or identity development, although the idea is still not found as a central theme within present-day educational research. Curriculum developers have progressed in developing specific ideas for how to incorporate relevant material (e.g., Banks, 1994; McIntyre, Rosebery, & González, 2001). However, many of the practical interventions and virtually all the research discussed in this chapter (including our own), do not have any significant interaction with or influence on each other.[17]

Moreover, we did not find examples of educational research where there was a clear focus on linking explicitly subject-matter teaching with the personal development of the students. In contrast to the practical work developed in Freire and the innovative schools, educational researchers have not often directly investigated the implications of their interventions for the personal development of the children (e.g., the relation between the content of school activities and the specific knowledge and capabilities that children develop and their life outside of school). A radical-local perspective on education provides a unified way to conceptualize the relations between subject-matter teaching, local community conditions and content, and child development, so that an integration of these aspects are seen as being necessary for, rather than in conflict or contradiction to, each other.

This focus on the necessary interrelation between subject-matter content, local community, and child development in pedagogical practice is the core of the radical-local perspective. From this point of view it is not sufficient to use familiar material from pupils' everyday lives simply because they might have a better chance to become engaged in the teaching material and have a greater chance to integrate this material into their understanding of their life situation. As a general principle, it is dubious that the mere presence of culturally-relevant materials is sufficient for children to both understand the significance of these materials in relation to the subject-matter traditions or in relation to the implications and possibilities for their own lives. In other words, it is not community-studies alone that are critical, but also their potential to develop a closer connection between the content of schooling, the interests and motives of the students, the development of their conceptual understanding, and its relation to their social development. While it is useful, maybe even important, to

---

17 But see R.T. Carter and Goodwin (1994) whose scholarly reflection moves in that direction.

use material from the children's daily social environment as a way to activate
them into engaging in intellectual and literacy activities, it is not sufficient as
an educational objective. Being activated is not the same as using this material
in a way that builds up disciplinary and critical relations between the material
and one's life situation. In the next chapter we develop our analysis further by
considering how to use subject-matter teaching in relation to personal development.

CHAPTER 4

The Relation of Knowledge to Teaching and Learning from a Radical-Local Perspective

In their research S. Scribner (1984, 1992) and Lave (1988, 1992) identified different ways that arithmetic is learned and used in community, home, school and work. These researchers argued that school has its own type of knowledge that in most cases is unrelated to the knowledge used in community, home and work life.

Different arenas of life – home, community, school, and work – have different forms of practice and knowledge which contribute differently to children's concept formation and thinking. It can therefore be a difficult task for children to relate school knowledge to their everyday knowledge from community and home life. This difference between knowledge in community, home, school and work life is not often recognized by teachers and therefore they do not provide help for bridging the gap between academic and 'local' knowledge. If teachers acknowledge these differences and succeed in establishing a connection between local and academic knowledge, then pupils get the possibility to draw upon local knowledge in learning subject matter and to use subject matter or academic knowledge in home and community settings. In Chapter 3 we characterized the principles for teaching that can create these connections as radical-local. The idea of radical-local teaching is to support children to appropriate subject-matter concepts to analyze their everyday life in home and community so that they become better to understand their community and act in relation to their future life. To design teaching practices that create conditions for forming these connections, we must have a more differentiated conceptualization of subject-matter knowledge and local knowledge.

To analyze subject-matter knowledge, we draw on Davydov's (1972/1990) theory about theoretical and empirical knowledge and Bruner's (1986) conception of narrative knowledge. To relate these knowledge forms to local knowledge, we want to introduce a differentiation between societal, general, and personal kinds of knowledge.

Societal, General and Personal Knowledge in Relation to Academic Knowledge

General knowledge is always located in relation to a specific arena of life (e.g., home, school, and work). Practice within an arena of life has problems to be handled, goals to be realized, and new possibilities to be created. General knowledge (which can be expressed in empirical, narrative, and theoretical forms) refers to that knowledge which is used commonly to address these needs.

Societal knowledge was originally a general kind of knowledge that evolved through practice in a specific arena but has now been extended to other arenas of life. In solving a problem within a specific arena, a logic of analysis or investigation is developed. When this logic can be extended or adapted to other arenas of life (which do not necessarily have the same problems or needs as the original arena), then we speak of it as *societal knowledge* (which can take empirical, narrative, theoretical forms).

We will focus on the general knowledge connected to school practice which we will call *academic* or *subject-matter knowledge*. General knowledge in home and community we will call *local knowledge*. In this chapter we analyze three forms of knowledge – empirical, narrative and theoretical – that characterize academic knowledge and discuss how they can be related to local knowledge.

As discussed in Chapter 3, Vygotsky differentiated between academic and personal knowledge.

Personal everyday knowledge refers to knowledge and skills that a person uses spontaneously in everyday activities (e.g., a three-year-old child playing with his automobile, or a physicist calculating in her laboratory) in home, community, school, work, clubs, sports arrangements and so forth. In educational practice the pupil should recognize that there is academic knowledge that transcends his personal knowledge which should motivate him towards classroom teaching and academic knowledge. The goal of radical-local teaching is that pupils appropriate academic knowledge so that it becomes personal knowledge that is used in relation to community and other everyday arenas.

Societal, general and personal knowledge are not mutually exclusive. There is no societal knowledge if there is no institutional practice that requires general knowledge and no persons to interpret the meanings of events, objects or symbols in a specific practice. Personal knowledge is always located in a historical and societal setting.

For children who are first entering school, local knowledge found in family and community practices are already transformed into personal knowledge. This personal knowledge continues to develop as the child is introduced to new practices in school as well as in home and community. How children's personal knowledge from home and community life will be related to academic knowledge in school depends on the form of academic knowledge and the teaching practice.

Forms of Knowledge Characterizing School Teaching

EMPIRICAL KNOWLEDGE AND PARADIGMATIC THINKING MODES

Empirical knowledge is reflected in abstract concepts that are attained through observation, description, classification and quantification (Bruner, Goodnow & Austin, 1956; Davydov, 1988, 1972/1990; Gagné, 1966). This form of knowledge presupposes that the world can be represented correctly, and correct representation gives possibility for accurate measurement. Empirical knowledge presupposes the use of categories for its representation. Similarities and differences are distinguished, which is the foundation for the construction of categories. Categories can be organized hierarchically into super and subcategories, and hierarchical systems and networks can be created. Paradigms of classical logic are the methods for combining knowledge categories.

Paradigmatic thinking is the thinking mode of empirical knowledge (Bruner et al., 1956; Bruner, 1974). In paradigmatic thinking, the focus is on creating consistency in information by using categories. Paradigmatic thinking transcends the observable by seeking higher forms of abstraction that combine observable categories (Bruner, 1986, p. 13).

Empirical knowledge or factual knowledge influences a great deal of everyday life for people in Western industrialized societies and characterizes the educational activity of most schools today (Davydov, Lompscher, & Markova, 1982; Davydov 1988, 1972/1990). In an empirical perspective knowledge is conceptualized as mental building blocks that can be stacked up, or as puzzle pieces that can be collected. Acquired knowledge does not change unless the information is proved wrong. Just as a building is constructed or a puzzle is assembled, one can construct a conceptual system from elements of knowledge that remain the same. This assumption is reflected in many of the school instructional materials today (e.g., in biology, national history) where the aim is to present parts from all the different areas of a subject domain, and where the presentation of the knowledge is given as facts.

When school teaching is organized around empirical knowledge, then methods of investigation and subject-matter content are not usually taught together. Subject matter can be differentiated into skill subjects (reading, writing, mathematics, foreign languages) and content subjects (history, geography, biology). The skill subjects are then usually taught as 'paradigms' without caring about the content, while the content subjects can be presented as lectures to be heard and remembered without caring about the skill aspects (Davydov & Markova,

1983; Lompscher, 1985). If instruction is based only on empirical knowledge it will orient pupils to acquiring concepts from different subject domains that are not related to each other or to their local life world.

NARRATIVE KNOWLEDGE AND DIALOGICAL THINKING MODES

Bruner is the main proponent for formulating the epistemological characteristics of narrative knowledge and thinking. The key characteristics of narrative knowledge are: (a) changeableness in intentions, (b) possible mutual perspectives and goals which interact, and (c) involvement of feelings and emotions (Bruner, 1986, pp. 16-25).

Narrative dialogical thinking modes are connected to the problem of giving meaning to personal experiences by transcending their situated character and relating them to general themes of human life. Bruner describes the method for this in three categories: *presupposition*, the creation of implicit rather than explicit meaning; *subjectification*, the depiction of reality through a personal view; and *multiple perspectives*, beholding the world not universally but simultaneously through different views which each express some part of it (Bruner, 1986 pp. 25-26). Examples of narrative knowledge are epic descriptions, novels, comedy, drama and poetry. Narrative knowledge and thinking modes can also be seen in 'folk theories' about daily life events.

Narrative knowledge and thinking characterizes the communication in children's daily life practices at home and among peers but is not usually promoted in school. Educational theories that prefer dialogue as the primary pedagogic form can be seen as promoting narrative knowledge and dialogical thinking. Ziehe's (1978) pedagogical project at the Glocksee School, based on Habermas's ideas about an ideal speech situation (e.g., free from the use of power and domination), can be seen as an example of a narrative pedagogy. This pedagogy has been very influential in the Danish school system. When narrative knowledge is the dominant form of academic knowledge in pedagogical situations, then key conceptual relations that have developed through the history of different subject-matter traditions are difficult to reveal to the students.

THEORETICAL KNOWLEDGE AND DIALECTICAL THINKING MODES

Subject-matter concepts are related to each other in systems where the concepts are complementary to each other so that if a change in a concept takes place it will be reflected in all the central relations of the system. This kind of knowledge can be conceptualized as 'mental tools' in the form of theories and models of subject matter areas that can be used to understand and explain events and situations (concrete life activities) and to organize actions.

Theoretical knowledge and dialectical methods have not been predominant in school teaching or scientific traditions. Examples of this form of knowledge are usually found in professional and scientific areas such as biology (e.g., Charles Darwin), political economy (e.g., Karl Marx), physics (e.g., Niels Bohr), psychology (e.g., Lev Vygotsky and Kurt Lewin), pedagogy (e.g., John Dewey) sociology (e.g., Pierre Bourdieu) and philosophy (e.g., G.W.F. Hegel).

A core model is a central thinking mode within the theoretical knowledge tradition. Core models contain germ-cells – the basic relations, oppositions and complementarities that appear within the diverse phenomena studied within a subject-matter area (Davydov, 1972/1990; Davydov et al., 1982). For example, in biology a germ-cell is the relation between *organism – context*. This relation can easily be recognized in all specific biological matters. Such a core relation can be extended with a new relation, which influences and changes the meaning of the initial concepts, which were defined through the initial relation. For example, in the subject domain of zoology, the general core relation organism – context can be formulated more specifically as *animal – nature*. This relation is further specified when it is applied in the investigation of specific problems such as the evolution of animals. The core relation animal – nature is elaborated into relations among the concepts of *species, population* and *ecological niche*. After this elaborated germ cell is formulated into a core model, it can be recognized and used in analyses of the conditions for a species to survive in a habitat.

Theoretical knowledge of a problem area usually emerges because of a need, or interest, to solve problems and contradictions that are central for society. This knowledge is developed through a process of experimentation, in which methods and strategies are used to introduce changes in the phenomenon being studied (Lektorsky, 1999), and relating the results to theoretical models that postulate the core relations that are involved in the appearance of the observed variations. The forms of experimentation used to introduce changes can involve real, physical changes in a phenomenon or imaginative changes. Imagined experimentation can become a tool for analyzing and reflecting about the content being investigated, which can then be used to develop theoretical dialectical knowledge.

Imaginative experimentation was used in the Danish teaching experiment in which children worked with the core model of species, population and ecological niche (Hedegaard, 1990). After having worked for some time with studying animals in the desert and in the arctic, third-grade pupils were asked to imagine what would happen to the polar bear if it was moved to the Kalahari Desert and the desert hare was moved to Greenland. The children took the ecological niches of the polar bear and the desert hare into account in this imagined experimentation, from which they concluded that each species adapts to its own special ecological niche. They generalized this conclusion to other species, thereby formulating a general conceptual relation between species and ecological niche.

By using theoretical dialectical knowledge and thinking strategies within a problem area, pupils are given the possibility to organize concrete experiences in relation to a conceptual core model that can be used for analyzing new experiences and empirical knowledge, connecting them into a coherent theoretical system. When these concrete experiences are drawn in part from personal and local knowledge, and the acquired core models in different subject-matter areas are related to local knowledge, together with methods of investigation that enable children to analyze and understand the complexity of different practices, then we start to realize the idea of radical-local teaching and learning.

FORMS OF KNOWLEDGE AND HISTORICAL TRADITIONS OF SCHOOLING PRACTICE

Subject-matter traditions in schooling practice reflect a combination of societal demands and forms of knowledge that characterize the different subject matters. In primary education, within the same subject matter, different forms of knowledge have dominated at different times. A narrative form of knowledge is predominant in literacy/mother-tongue and history teaching through the history of school reforms in Western societies. Empirical knowledge forms have been dominant in the natural science and mathematics school curriculum. To illustrate the idea of the historical change of dominant knowledge forms, we review briefly the changing views about the content and purpose of education within the Danish school system, with a special focus on literacy and history teaching.

When obligatory, universal school education was introduced in Denmark in the early 19th century, the main objectives were to teach children to read (particularly the Bible), to become good Christians, and to obey the state laws. The Lutheran Protestant church was (and still is) the state religion. Bishops supervised the schools. Theological knowledge dominated the curriculum. Lutheran catechism was used both as a subject matter and as a reading book. After a school reform in the early 20th century the curriculum changed because other objectives also became important, but the formation of the 'good Christian person' still remained central. With a second large school reform in the late 1950s other objectives, such as skills in reading, writing, mathematics, and knowledge of the physical and biological world, became important as a foundation for further education. Preparation for work and participation in a democratic society became explicit goals for school education. Protestant religious teaching remains part of subject-matter teaching, but it does not dominate reading and writing instruction and there is no longer a state-regulated examination connected to this subject. Reading and writing are now taught in the elementary grades on an empirical basis, where the main objective in the Danish lessons is to teach the child to decode written text (Johansen & Kreiner, 1992). The content of the texts or literary forms in the Danish primary school are still not conceptualized as important.

History was introduced as a subject in Danish schools in the early 20th century. The narrative form of knowledge characterized history teaching up until the 1950s, and formation of national identity was the aim of history teaching when first introduced This aim changed (after the Second World War) in the 1950s, when a massive societal change from an agricultural to an industrialized welfare society took place in Denmark. This change was reflected in the 1950s school reform, when the subject of history changed from a narrative to an empirical (fact-oriented) curriculum (*Historiedidaktik i Norden 2*, 1985; Sødring-Jensen, 1978; Hedegaard, 1998). Today the value of the narrative form of teaching history is again promoted by several researchers in history didactics (Depew, 1985; *Historiedidaktik i Norden 3*, 1988; Sødring-Jensen, 1990) who argue, as the educators did in the 1800s, that this form of knowledge is important for the formation of the children's personality and identity.

Forms of Knowledge in Everyday Activities

One aim of all educational practices, radical-local or otherwise, is to develop academic knowledge that can be used spontaneously in individual activities in home, community, school, work, clubs, sports, and so forth. The particular ways in which academic knowledge can be used depends on its form. Empirical and narrative academic knowledge are not particularly effective for changing children's everyday activity, while theoretical academic knowledge is not usually found in everyday use.

The materials and tasks in typical school instruction are dominated by *empirical knowledge*, usually in the form of facts or text knowledge. As such it rarely becomes useful for the pupil's life outside the school context. Many schoolbooks are composed primarily of empirical knowledge, presenting facts about many different things within a subject domain in a disintegrated way, without an easy-to-understand organizing principle that connects the different parts and surpasses the specific domain. Pupils taught in this way do not acquire a method for enquiring about how specific facts within a subject domain are related to specific conditions. They do not learn to use their appropriated abstract school knowledge to relate to and enquire into their local and lived world.

In typical teaching practices today, empirical subject-matter knowledge is often combined with local knowledge by using this knowledge for illustrations (e.g., mathematics examples use familiar situations, biology teaching draws on local mammals and plants). However, the empirical form of knowledge has little possibility for supporting children to use their subject-matter knowledge in contributing to everyday practice. Paradigmatic thinking can function as paradigms for grammatical rules or mathematical calculation, but there is no inner logic between these activities and everyday activities outside school.

Subject-matter knowledge in narrative form can be combined easily with local everyday narratives through examples from the children's own experience. Narrative knowledge can also be created as shared experiences among students through different kinds of project work within a subject-matter area. The use of dialogue, a main characteristic of narrative knowledge, is a central method for developing social competencies and an important method for developing democratic institutions in society. However if one does not have a framework for anchoring the dialogue, then one must accept a relativism in which the most fluent or persuasive speaker determines which knowledge is valuable. If different persons select different narratives, then the procedures that characterize the production of narrative knowledge do not provide a way to resolve the conflict of what knowledge to rely on.

It is difficult to find examples of school knowledge that have become local theoretical knowledge so that this knowledge can function as the student's tool for reflection and skillful actions. We believe this reflects more about the existing traditions of school teaching than any fundamental limitation in schoolchildren's ability to think theoretically. Young children in preschool and early school age often have developed a connected system of understanding through play and participating in activities with older children and adults and through their own reflection about phenomena that are important to them. They ponder about relations that they cannot experience directly such as the relation between life and death, the size of the world and where it ends, and many more of these philosophical questions about 'world and life'. These forms of thinking are precursors for thinking dialectically with theoretical knowledge. The goal of radical-local teaching and learning is to create conditions so that it becomes possible for children to acquire theoretical knowledge that can be integrated into everyday use.

The Significance of Theoretical Knowledge for Integrating Academic, Local and Personal Knowledge

In this chapter we have outlined different forms of knowledge to extend Vygotsky's idea (see Chapter 3) that the development of subject-matter knowledge and children's everyday local knowledge can enrich each other. Everyday knowledge can be a precondition for a child to learn subject-matter knowledge, but a child's development of everyday knowledge does not stop being important. Conversely, subject-matter knowledge can be integrated into everyday knowledge through the child's learning activity. The kind of learning activity that promotes this integration is guided by theoretical knowledge where core models guide children's exploration and experimentation.

The educational task in school should be to teach subject-matter concepts to children by relating to local and personal knowledge. Taking an instructional approach that emphasizes theoretical knowledge and dialectical methods within a subject-matter area, gives the child a possibility to relate appropriated local knowledge in a methodological way to subject-matter concepts and s/he can enquire into and perhaps analyze the conditions for specific local matters. Children's everyday concepts can thereby be extended by subject-matter concepts. By using subject-matter concepts, integrated into core models to analyze everyday local activity, teaching provides children with new skills and possibilities for action.

We believe that a focus on local matters in the process of developing theoretical subject-matter knowledge will be important for the development of children's personal knowledge. Similarly, a focus on local matters in relation to children's background regardless of whether the classroom is culturally diverse or homogenous provides a way to engage the children's interests and draw upon their everyday knowledge in developing subject-matter knowledge.

Long Parade ©Jose B. Rivera, East Harlem.

CHAPTER 5

Child Development and Learning

How can learning be developmental? That is, with regard to schoolchildren, how can subject-matter learning contribute to their psychological development?

We conceptualize child development as a cultural process in which a child appropriates motives and knowledge through participation in institutional practices. In Chapter 3, we introduced a general model of institutional practice that specified three aspects of practice that are conditions for each other. One aspect refers to the societal traditions for educational practice, another refers to general traditions, and a third refers to local practice and individual activity. The main educational institutions for schoolchildren are family, school, and afterschool institutions. Traditions for practice in these institutions are the conditions for, and source of, children's development of motives and competencies. The question is how to relate children's motives and the competencies appropriated through family and community life with subject-matter teaching in school. We will present our conceptualization of the relation between children's development and learning, focusing on motive development, and drawing upon our ideas about institutional practice and cultural-historical theories of child development.

Periods in Child Development

Children appropriate motives and competencies through upbringing and education, where they both contribute to and learn from participation in these institutionalized activities. Appropriation of motives and competencies are necessary to actively and fully participate in family and school life, work and community life.

Development can be initiated by qualitative changes in the practices in which a child participates. Change in practice can appear in several ways, the most obvious is when a child is introduced to a new institution such as a kindergarten, school, or afterschool institution and thereby is introduced to new activities. Additionally, change or introduction of new activities in the institutions in which the child already participates can also contribute to development. Whether a change in practice or new activities will influence a child's development of motives, knowledge and skills, depends on the child's possibility to realize his intentions and create his own goals in these new activities.

Daniel B. El'konin (1999) has described children's personality development as proceeding through three main periods (early childhood, childhood, adolescence), where each period reflects the most important traditions for practice in the characteristic institutions of industrialized societies: family/day-care, school/afterschool, and work place. Transcendence from one period to the next is dependent on qualitative shifts in the child's social situation (Vygotsky, 1998, Chapter 6) that often reflects change of institutional practices.

In D.B. El'konin's theory each period contains two stages that are characterized according to the relative dominance of motive and competence. The first stage is characterized primarily by motive development, while the second stage is characterized primarily by knowledge/skill appropriation that is needed to realize the motives formed in the first stage. The appropriated knowledge and skill gives the possibility to participate in new practices, which opens the way for the acquisition of new motives and a new period of development in which the further development of these motives are the focus of this period's first stage.

In the early childhood period, the social situation of development is one in which the child is dependent on the adult to meet all its needs. The first stage of this period is therefore dominated by orientation to direct emotional contact to other people, which in turn motivates a stage of acquiring knowledge about the manipulation of objects that are part of those interactions. In learning to manipulate objects, children have the possibility of entering a new period of development, childhood, in which they can use their ability to manipulate objects to enter into interactions oriented towards the development of roles in relation to other people (i.e., the first stage of this new period). Through these interactions, usually in the form of role play, children have the possibility to acquire knowledge about the tasks and activities conducted by adults (i.e., the second stage of the childhood period). This knowledge supports the development of children's motives to acquire the knowledge needed to participate in these activities, which in turn supports a stage of formal learning that is normally associated with the schoolchild. The adolescence period starts with a stage of close personal relations, followed by occupation/work.[18]

Children participate in creating the specific and local forms of the activities that characterize family life and school life[19] and thereby also influence the conditions for their own development. The interrelation between a child's knowledge and motive development and his/her surroundings starts from birth, because the newborn child introduces a new dynamic into a family. Parents both create and adapt to the child's demands and the child's demands adapt and create new ways of interaction between parent and child, between parents themselves, and between parents and other persons. Similarly, the school class and afterschool institutions are influenced by the children who attend these institutions – it is not a one-way process.

Our conceptualization of child development can be summarized by the following points:

1. Children's psychological development takes place through a creative reproduction of cultural practices through interaction and communication with other people in these activities.
2. Through these practices they appropriate cultural needs, motives, skills and knowledge.
3. These appropriations take place through interaction and communication, primarily in institutional practices which become contexts for the child's personal activities, (i.e., the family, the school, the afterschool).
4. Institutional practice can initiate change in a child's personal activity. This change can be imposed by interactions, opposition, conflicts between the significant adults' demands and the child's motivations for joining an activity, or his self-initiated activities.

----

18 Today with the societal change into a postindustrial society, another period is needed to understand child development connected to the long period between finishing primary school, getting an occupation and setting up a family. The main institutions in this period are high school, college or other forms of preparation for work life. The activities in this period are oriented more toward youth culture and professional qualification, than towards work life and planning a family. Therefore new types of dominant motive characterize young people today, which are motives for being part of the youth culture and for professional qualification.

19 Examples of how children contribute to the activities in which they participate in school and thereby to their own development are described in McDermott (1993) and Willis (1977).

Cultural Practice and Personal Motive Development

We conceptualize motivation and motives as the dynamic relation between person and practice. Motives are conceptualized as culturally created through practice and therefore have a structuring influence on practice (Leontiev, 1975/1978). A person acquires motives through participating in institutional practice. A person's motives develop through change in the dynamic of a person's social situation by participation in practice. A person's motives can develop from biological needs, where the cultural way of satisfying these needs becomes more important than the needs: For example, the craving for specific motive objects associated with needs such as hunger, which transforms into wants for special kinds of food; and sex, which transforms into wishes to be with the person one loves. Motives can also be developed independently of needs through acquisition of cultural values of institutionalized practices, such as a motive for intellectual discourse, a motive for musical experience, a motive for being believed and trusted by friends.

Personally appropriated motives become a more permanent aspect of a person's life, giving direction to activity across different situations. An activity or a task can be motivating if it relates to a person's motives. Motivation deals with the dynamic of the local practice a person is engaged in and describes the dynamic aspects of actions in concrete everyday situations.

A person's motives are related to each other. The relation between the different motives can take the form of a hierarchy, but for children this hierarchy is not very stable. What is most important at one point can change when the child is introduced to new activities. If play is the dominant motive for a child starting school, other motives will be subordinate to this. For example, a child, for whom play is the dominating activity, can perform a task much longer if it is embedded in a role play, than if it is given alone (D.B. El'konin, 1988). Conversely, a school child who has acquired a learning motive will engage for a longer time if he thinks the activity is serious and not a play activity. This child will, for example, participate in sport activities for getting points or winning but he will lose interest if the sport activity is only performed as a play. This does not imply that a child's earlier dominant motive disappears; only that it gets another position in the child's motive hierarchy.

Both Vygotsky and D.B. El'konin build on the presupposition that social relations between children and adults give content and form to children's development of motives and cognition. However, social relations alone are not developmental. Rather, development is understood as a result of the demands created in the social situation of development, which arises from the interaction between the children's motives and the adult demands associated with the practice in which they are engaged. In developing this issue further, Boris

D. El'konin (1993) takes D.B. El'konin's idea of *archetype of adulthood* as the ideal form upon which children can imagine their future. These ideal forms are made manifest through events, the real actions of persons who mediate these forms. Adults have an important role as teachers or mediators in presenting these forms, both in the everyday events of home and community life and in school.

These ideal forms must have the possibility to be combined with real life through 'events' in which the image of adulthood is exemplified as a key category that posits the integrity of childhood. The child's life and the adult's model of life have to be eventful.

The task of the teacher who is going to create conditions for learning, so that the learning will be developmental, is to help the child move from the perspective of local events and capacities of everyday life to the perspective of possible events and capacities.

In D.B. El'konin's model of development, learning is depicted as the dominant motive in early school age. This does not mean that the child is not learning in other periods. But learning in the different periods differs qualitatively. Preschool children in their play-activity are oriented towards the adult world. Through their play activities, children explore adult relations and thereby formulate their visions and questions about adult activities. At the transition to school age, children start to acknowledge the insufficiency of the knowledge and skills used to 'perform' in their play-activities. 'As if' is not sufficient anymore for the children who are at the early school age. They want to be able acquire the skilled activities of adult life (e.g., to be able to read, calculate and handle tools like adults). Play as a dominant motive starts to become subordinated to the motive of learning which begins to dominate the child's world in the early school age. The learning motive is initiated much earlier, but this motive first becomes dominant when the learning activities in school are introduced. It is important to note that this change in a child's motives is connected both to changes in his social relation, to the introduction of new activities in school, and to changes in his cognitive capacities. Through his play activities the child has developed cognitive capacities for imagination and using symbols and thereby gets ready for the literate demands of school practice. For the teacher it is important to focus on this change in dominating motives, supporting the learning motive if it is there, and helping the child to acquire this motive if it is not developed. If the learning motive does not yet dominate a young schoolchild's activities, then it will be possible to take departure in play to motivate the child for classroom activities. But to develop learning motive the activities should be created so that they are directed forward, toward learning activities.

Motivation can be created through offering eventful play activities and these activities should also have a learning motive.

An activity is always multiple motivated (Leontiev, 1975/1978). Students can develop new motives by engaging in a local activity, and through being in the activity appropriate new motives. Educators can create motivation in a teaching situation by taking students' motives into consideration when creating learning tasks. A child can enter the activities in his local class initially to please the teacher (e.g., go to a museum to find out how the Vikings lived in earlier times). The shared local activity between the teacher and the class can engage individual children in a learning activity, which can become motivating for them. They can then appropriate a new motive through their involvement in the new aspects of the activity. In the example of the class going to a historical museum, a child can become engaged in researching how people lived in earlier times if the museum activity catches his/her interest and is supported by other activities. In this way the child has developed another motive in addition to the one he/she had upon entering the activity (i.e., to please the teacher). In researching how people lived in earlier times the child has become multiple motivated, because he/she will now contribute to the class activity both to please the teacher and to engage in researching about people from earlier historical periods.

SCHOOL PRACTICE AND MOTIVATION

The motives the child has acquired through family and community life can be used to engage in class activities in school. Schoolchildren are aware to some extent that there is academic knowledge that transcends local knowledge and their personal knowledge, which gives them a motive for participating in classroom teaching and the expectation for learning subject matters. In school the child starts to become able to distinguish between traditions for practice in different contexts (distinguish between their own life world and the life worlds of other persons). Because the child can distinguish between differences in practice traditions they become able to relate intentionally to the activities in school. This implies that the child is ready both to initiate his own learning as well as leave the instructional activity (either physically or mentally) if the school activity does not acquire sense for the child in relation to his other life activities (Berger & Luckmann, 1966).

The concepts of subject-matter teaching can be combined with the child's personal knowledge from his family and community life through the child's intentional activity. The teacher who wants pupils to learn and appropriate knowledge and skills that can transcend the classroom activities and influence their everyday local activities, must engage, build upon, and develop the pupils' personal everyday knowledge. Knowledge about children's motives and how to create eventful learning is important in this connection.

Radical-Local Teaching and Learning Combine Personal Knowledge with Local and Academic Knowledge through Motivating and Eventful Activities

The knowledge and skill developed by a child is determined by the child's cap-acities and possibilities in combination with the traditions of practice where significant adults and older children guide the child to participate within insti-tutional practices, thereby communicating and teaching knowledge, skills and values that are important in different institutions. Each type of institution has its own special knowledge and skills that are mediated to children participating in the institutional practice. In Western industrialized societies educational ac-tivities in families are aimed at social, emotional, and everyday skill education. Adults in this context support the child to express themselves, to show care and love to parents, siblings and other relatives, to acquire skills connected to daily household chores, food preparation, and hygienic care. In the family, the child's parents, older siblings and close relatives decide what is important implicitly through their local practice. In school the educational activities are aimed at supporting the child to learn to be literate, do mathematical calculations, acquire knowledge for a range of subject domains and adjust to the practice of the school as an educational institution. In schools and in afterschool activities, responsible adults interpret the traditions of practice and create activities that influence the local practice in which children participate and learn. The family, the school and the afterschool institution each contribute differently to children's learning and development. Learning is different for preschool and schoolchildren, because they participate in practices where the motives are different. For a preschool child, play is the dominant motive and the instruction should follow the logic of the child's play activities; for a schoolchild who has developed a learning mo-tive, teaching can follow the logic of subject-matter tasks and procedures and the activities initiated can include local as well as possible events.

Communication between adults and children usually first becomes formal-ized when a child enters school (Minick, 1993). In school, the teacher can design teaching activities that create conditions for children to establish a relation between knowledge of home and community and subject-matter knowledge. In school teaching, the teacher has to work with a group of children and has to understand how to create this relation for the whole group. This is usually pos-sible because children start school with some common knowledge acquired from shared traditions for practice in both family and community life. Furthermore, instructional tasks can create possibilities for children to cooperate in exploring their local community. An approach to designing instruction that will motivate students for this activity will be described systematically in the next chapter, where it will be characterized as a 'double move' between the formulation of teaching goals that relate subject-matter knowledge and children's already acquired competencies and motives. This double move can become an ongoing process between children's existing motives and competencies and the new motives and competencies that one wants to develop for a group of children who will work together over a time span in a classroom.

CHAPTER 6

The Double Move Approach to Instruction

We have argued in Chapter 4 that subject-matter concepts and children's everyday knowledge can be integrated by using theoretical knowledge as the frame for teaching and learning activities.

Theoretical knowledge can be seen as a tool for combining the core concepts of a subject-matter area with local and personal everyday knowledge. The tool character of theoretical knowledge becomes especially evident when formulated in core models. In this chapter we describe the double move approach inspired by the developmental teaching-learning approach of Davydov (Aidarova, 1982; Davydov, 1988). In the double move approach, we emphasize the relations among children's already acquired everyday concepts, subject-matter concepts, and local knowledge. The main point in the double move in instruction is to create learning tasks that can integrate local knowledge with core conceptual relations of a subject-matter area so that the person can acquire theoretical knowledge that can be used in the person's local practice.

The didactic implementation of the double move is based on four main principles:

1. Use of a core model of the content area under investigation to guide instruction.
2. Use of research strategies in instruction in a way that is analogical to how researchers investigate problems.
3. Creation of phases in the teaching process reflecting qualitative changes in the child's learning process.
4. Formation of motivation in the class activity through creating tasks for investigation and through facilitating communication and cooperation between children.

These principles will be elaborated in the following sections and illustrated with examples from teaching experiments conducted in Denmark, where the double move approach was implemented for the elementary school subjects of biology, geography and social history. The Danish school tradition once combined biology, geography and history into a single subject that was taught in the third through fifth grades. The experimental teaching approached this tradition by integrating these subjects into three related problem areas: the evolution of species, the origin of humans, and the historical change of societies (Hedegaard, 1988, 1990, 1995, 1996, 2002).

Principles of the Double Move in Instruction

The Function of Core Models in Teaching

In the double move approach, the teacher's planning of the instruction must advance from the abstract characteristics and general laws of a subject-matter area to the concrete reality, in all its complexity. Conversely, the pupils' learning must extend from their personal everyday knowledge to the general laws and abstract concepts of a subject-matter area.

The teacher guides the class dialogue and constructs the learning tasks from general concepts of the problem area, as formulated in a core model. A core model creates a structure for the teacher's planning of instructional tasks. The instructional mediation of general relations in the model through practical educational tasks implies that the demands and content of the tools are oriented to making the general laws of the subject-matter area visible to the children.

The two main characteristics of a core model are (a) it depicts the basic relations between complementary concepts in the subject-matter area, so that if one aspect changes then the influence of this change can be traced in the other aspects depicted, and (b) the basic relations can be recognized in the surrounding reality (the concrete complexities of real life). An example of a subject-matter area where basic relations are integrated into a core model is the problem of the evolution of animals. The concepts that form the basic relations in this core model (species, population and ecological niche) were discussed previously in Chapter 4, and this model was used in the Danish experimental teaching (where the concept *nature* was used instead of *ecological niche*, see Figure 6.1a). A change in one of the elements in this model will affect the others. A key example was used to illustrate the interdependence of the elements in the relations: the polar hare was introduced from Norway to the Faroe Islands, where there is no snow, and after some generations the population of polar hare changed colour from white to brown. This example was used in the teaching to raise the need to investigate how this could this happen. Exploring this question led to the formulation of basic principles in the theory of evolution: animals' adaptation to their environment and selection through offspring.

Formulating a core model requires a profound knowledge of the subject matter under investigation. To use core models effectively in teaching requires that the teacher has a working understanding of the model. The model is not a content to be didactically transmitted. Rather, the teacher formulates tasks, projects, exercises and questions that are based on the general relations in the core model, while incorporating the children's ways of formulating questions and their interests in the specific substance of the activities that are conducted. Teachers are expected:

1. To analyze the subject-matter area so that teaching is based on a core model of the central concept relations of a subject-matter area,
2. Have knowledge of the children's interests and background,
3. To create tasks and problems, so that the core concepts are illuminated.

Using Key Examples to Understand Core Models

The core model used in the Danish teaching project is based on a germ-cell of an individual, a group of individuals, and the environment or conditions where the group is living. This germ-cell is adapted to the three problem areas under investigation, based on an analysis of the specific relations in each content area. The models for the problem areas are shown in Figure 6.1, where the first model is an application of the germ-cell for the evolution of species (Figure 6.1a). This model is developed further and transformed into a model of the origin of

Figure 6.1a. The evolution of animals.

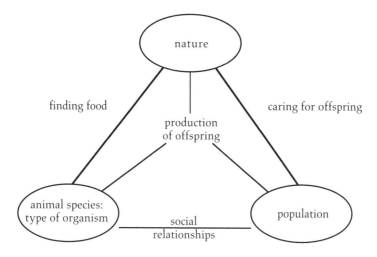

Figure 6.1b. The origin of humans.

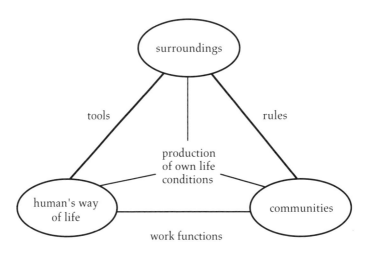

Figure 6.1c. The historical change of society.

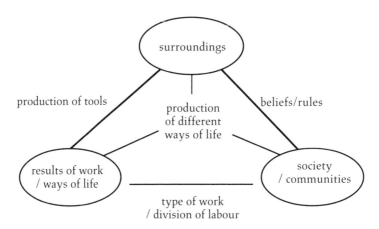

humans (Figure 6.1b), while the historical change of society is built upon the origin of humans (Figure 6.1c).

In teaching situations, the development of these models is achieved through the use of key examples, which formulate problems that require research activities for their clarification. Subject-matter concepts and their interrelations are brought forward during class discussions of these research activities, and their results are visualized in models.

Key examples for investigating the problem area – the evolution of animals – were:

(a) adaptation of the polar bear to Greenland's nature that enables the polar bear to survive,
(b) adaptation of the polar hare to changes in their life conditions that resulted from being relocated from Norway to the Faroe Islands, and
(c) the breeding of wolves into domesticated dogs.

One way the teacher helped the children to formulate the conceptual relations was by contrasting living conditions and then asking the children to reflect upon and analyze the contrasts and conflicts they could find within the different examples. For example, in their research with the polar bear the teacher brought up the question of what would happen if the polar bear was brought to the Kalahari desert (an ecology the children had investigated to find out about the desert hare's living conditions). This example, as well as the example with the polar hare, focuses on the consequences of a change in the environment for individuals and groups of individuals.

In the study of the origin of humans three key examples of tool production were used to establish relations between tool use/tool production as a mediating link between nature and living conditions. For example, a film was shown about the!Kung people's way of living, and then their living conditions were

Figure 6.2. The general research procedure that guides the teacher's planning of activities and the children's exploration.

1.	Who is investigating?
2.	What is being investigated?
3.	What do we know, and what do we not know, about the problem area?
4.	How can we formulate a model of the core relations to research?
5.	What methods will we use to investigate the problem?
6.	How do we evaluate our findings?

compared to those of Stone Age people, which were viewed in drawings in a textbook and experienced during a museum visit. Another example was the production and use of tools by Iron Age people to create living conditions suited to a cold environment in contrast to the warm climate of the!Kung people and the Stone Age people. To create an understanding of the necessity of refining tools and housing, a workshop was conducted at an outdoor museum that presented replicas of the houses and tools from the Iron Age.

USE OF RESEARCH METHODS

The acquisition of theoretical knowledge depends on exploratory activity. In school teaching, this exploration can be initiated through teacher-supported use of research procedures. In both the Danish teaching experiment and the one reported here, the basic research procedure was a variation of a social science research procedure inspired by Kurt Lewin (see Hedegaard, 1990, 1995). Our procedure contained six questions (see Figure 6.2).

The research procedure in Figure 6.2 was introduced so that the pupils would acquire a systematic way to explore the tasks whose investigation was expected to reveal the core relations of the models. To accomplish this, the teacher uses the questions in the model in three different ways in his interaction with the children.

First the teacher uses the questions in the research procedure at the start of each session (which lasted about 10-15 minutes) to guide a dialogue with the class that summarizes the previous session's research activities. The aim is that the children should (a) be able to get a connected understanding of the problems on which they worked in the class sessions, (b) the possibility to reflect upon problem solutions in relation to the core model, and (c) elaborate and formulate new relations in the model. The dialogue is directed by the following type of questions:

1. What did we research last time,
2. Evaluation of last session's activities (what did we learn and what do we not know about our research topic),
3. Formulation of appropriated knowledge into a core relation and later into a model,
4. Formulating the goal of today's session,
5. Deciding on the activities and task illuminating the problems formulated for this session.

Through this dialogue, the children's ideas and knowledge of the themes become explicit, providing a basis for the teacher and children to draw connections to the previous lessons.

Second the research procedure is used to formulate thematic problems for longer research periods that run over several teaching sessions. Thematic problems are written as the main theme on a goal result board, which is used to record the main principles being explored, and to show progress in exploring these principles. At the end of each period the teacher used the questions in the research procedure to guide a class dialogue summarizing and evaluating the class activities in relation to this theme.

Third the research procedure is used to structure the activities in each teaching session. The activities were:

1. A class dialogue at the beginning of each session that summarized and evaluated the last session
2. Writing the agenda on the black board for the tasks of today
3. Research activities
4. Class dialogue reflecting the research activity and formulation of core relations
5. Writing their results into goal result boards

STRUCTURING THE CLASSROOM ACTIVITY THROUGHOUT THE SCHOOL YEAR

In the teaching sessions the learning activities can be characterized as guided investigations. The investigations are structured into three main phases that reflect both the changing needs of the investigation and the conditions that facilitate the children's acquisition of the core models and procedures for their investigation. These phases in the teaching are constructed to reflect the three main phases of learning activity in general: (a) construction of an image of the learning goals, (b) the learning actions (learning to build and use a core model and research procedures), and (c) evaluation of the success of the learning activity. These phases also correspond roughly to the research procedure in Figure 6.2, so, in effect each class session is a unified example of the phases of investigation in a problem area.

The basic sequence of teaching strategies within the double move approach is:

1. Presenting tasks that guide pupils into constructing an image of the subject area, learning goals and problem area to be investigated.
2. Presenting tasks that guide the pupil to formulate and use a core model for investigating a problem area and to acquire procedures for active exploration.
3. Presenting tasks that guide the pupil to evaluate the core model and his own appropriation of knowledge and skills in researching the problem area.

Initially, the teacher has more responsibility for organizing and managing the discussions and activities in the daily sessions, but gradually the children become responsible for managing their own activities as they gain competence in use of the research procedure and of the core conceptual relations. The teacher's planning for the specific tasks within the overall teaching programme should adapt ideally to these qualitative changes in the pupils' competence.

Construction of an Image of the Problem Area and Learning Goals
The building of an image of a problem area is aimed at focusing children's attention on the goals of the learning activity. The children should acquire from the beginning a general idea of what the teaching is about and get an image of their learning goals and the subject area to be explored.

The construction of an image of the problem area has to be an activity in itself that the teacher facilitates through creating tasks that can guide the pupil's problem formulation. The subject-matter area should, through this first phase, become conceptualized as a problem area for exploration. To accomplish this through teaching, it is important that the teacher has some knowledge of what motivates children and what they are interested in at different age periods and in different communities. The goals and content of the teaching must transcend the children's everyday images, motives and concepts and thereby enlarge and develop their visions.

Formulating and Using a Core Model and Learning to Use
Research Procedures
For children to acquire theoretical knowledge, the teaching activity must be organized around tasks that illuminate the core relations of the subject area. As soon as the children become able to formulate a core model, they then have a tool they can use to guide their formulation and investigations of future questions.

The teaching objective in this phase is to support children to formulate their own core models. The teacher can guide this appropriation by presenting the pupils with key examples and tasks where oppositions and conflicts between phenomena are accentuated, thereby accentuating core relations. It is also important that the teacher helps the children to acquire procedures for researching problems within the subject-matter area. Often this happens by introducing tools that can be used to investigate tasks associated with the key examples. Ideally these tools are commonly found within the problem area so that they can be used to investigate both the immediate problem as well as other problems.

Evaluation of Results of Learning Activity: Core Model and Self-Progress
The core model can also be used as a guide to evaluate whether the formulated questions are relevant for the images of the subject area and the learning goals,

and whether they reflect central conceptual relations within the subject-matter area. The model itself can, when appropriated by the pupils, also become the object of evaluation. Here pupils should learn to reflect upon the core model and learn that it is also possible to change, differentiate and develop the model if the research tasks and results require this.

Exemplifying the Structure of Educational Activity
within Social History Teaching
The example presented in this section is meant to illustrate the educational activity of: (a) creating a goal image and learning goals (b) formulating and using a core model and using research procedures and (c) evaluating the core model and one's progress in the learning activity. The teaching in this example occurs during the fourth grade (the average age of pupils starting fourth grade in Denmark is 10 years old).

FORMATION OF GOAL IMAGES
In the first teaching session the children's task, using a goal-result board, is to summarize the results of their investigations from the previous year's teaching activities about the problem area 'the evolution of animals'.[20] The problem area for the coming year is to formulate the general problem of why humans live differently in different parts of the world, and why humans have lived differently through different historical periods in the land area of present-day Denmark. The image of this problem area was first outlined using questions about the evolution of animals, and class dialogue about how the evolution of humans could be different from the evolution of animals. To promote further development of the

---

20 The goal formation for that problem area started with the problems: 'Have the same kinds of animals always been on earth? Have there always been humans?' (Hedegaard, 1990). These problems were chosen because children at an early school age in Denmark often are interested in these big questions of life, and because prehistoric animals is a topic that has been presented in media, films, museum exhibitions, play material, and so on. Many young Danish school children are attracted to this material. In addition to these questions the children were presented with three different conceptions of evolution: an Eskimo myth about the creation of earth, animals and humans; a science-based description of evolution from a child's textbook on dinosaurs; and a set of explanations that other Danish children gave in a research project about children's conceptions of evolution. A class discussion was started about these different conceptions with the aim of finding out what to believe. The discussion concluded by formulating new research questions: 'Why did some animal species die, and why did some change into new species?'

goal image, the pupils are then given two different series of pictures. One series depicts types of work in different present-day societies from around the world (both industrial and nonindustrial); the second series shows the same activities as they occurred at different historical periods where present-day Denmark is located. The children are divided into groups of four and asked to sort the pictures so that different ways of living are grouped together in one pile and different forms of tool use are grouped in another pile. Then each group is asked to explain their reasons for sorting as they did. The results of this discussion raises many specific research questions that, along with an additional task that formulated methodological questions about how to investigate these research questions, become the starting point of the next phase in the teaching activity.

FORMULATING AND USING A MODEL AND LEARNING TO USE THE GENERAL RESEARCH PROCEDURE

The next phase of classroom work concentrates on developing the abstract relations in the core models. These relations are formed through many practical tasks that examine concrete relations, which are then formulated into a general form. Throughout this phase, the children are learning to use the general research procedure in solving these practical tasks.

The children were given tasks about nature, tools, living conditions, division of labor, types of society and differences in beliefs. Some of the practical tasks were connected to a visit to a prehistoric activity centre in a museum, to a film about the!Kung people of Africa, and novels about children in different historical periods in Denmark. The general formulations produced in these and other related tasks are explicated in core models (see Figures 6.1b and 6.1c). The relations in the model in Figure 6.1c are: (a) people survive in nature through different forms of tool use and production, (b) people develop different traditions in different societies for the division of labour, and (c) religions and beliefs are created differently in different societies to support specific ways of living, and the allocation of resources.

MODEL AND SELF EVALUATION

After six months, the children had formulated their own core models and through cooperation and class discussion had depicted a shared, elaborated model, showing the historical change of societies. At this point, the primary classroom activity is to evaluate their ability to use the shared model to construct and evaluate research questions. For example, a main task in this phase, which ran for several weeks, was to use the shared model to summarize the main characteristics of social life during the four historical periods they had investigated. The children are separated into four different groups and each group investigates a specific historical period (i.e., Stone Age, Iron Age, Viking Age, and Middle Ages). The children are given the task to create questions that would reflect the relations in the model they had developed for their assigned historical period including: the relation between different types of work and the division of labour, the relation between use of different tools and people's living conditions, the meaning of the division of labour for the function of society, and the meaning of beliefs and rules for distributing resources to different groups in society. After the children in one of the four groups have created their questions, they give them to another group. The other group then answers the questions, and evaluates whether the questions were good or poor. The group that constructed the questions has to rate the other groups' answers to the questions. Finally, all the groups meet in class discussion to report and discuss their evaluations of the questions and the solutions.

A subsequent task, which involved evaluation, was connected to formulating research questions in relation to an exhibition at a Viking museum. In formulating these questions, the children started spontaneously to direct their learning themselves by asking what 'good questions' were and how they could explore them. By using the core model, they evaluated their own questions. When they got tasks from the museum, they evaluated them too. The children found that their own questions about the connection between tools and living conditions and between the division of labour and the organization of society were more worthwhile than the museum's, which were more empirically descriptive, focused primarily upon appearance and functions of the objects displayed in the museum. The children recognized that the museum questions did not indicate what the objects could tell about the societies from which they came.

Play writing and performance were used as other types of activities to differentiate the relations in the model. The pupils worked in small groups to create and perform plays to explicate the division of work and the power relations in the four different historical periods they studied.

The Formation of Motivation through Communication and Cooperation

Motives and knowledge are dialectically connected because knowledge gives content to motives and motives determine knowledge appropriation. A pupil's motive for learning and acquiring specific skills and knowledge does not develop independently of instruction. Motives develop as a relation between the pupil and the activities in which he participates.

During school age the child's motives are dominated by the learning motive which both lets the child orient himself to knowledge about the world in general, and to specific skills appreciated in his community. The schoolchild becomes oriented to topics that are valued by his parents, by the community, or that the child finds new and exciting to explore. The schoolchild's social motives and play motives are still important. Acknowledgment of these motives in the Danish research led to the formulation of the following principles for motivating children within the double move approach (Hedegaard 1988, 1989, 2002):

1. Take the children's dominating motive into consideration when formulating the subject area of a teaching course. The dominating motive of early school children is orientation and curiosity towards the world around them. For 9-11 year old Danish children we formulated this as curiosity about the big questions of life (e.g., Where do we come from? Have the animals always looked alike? Why do people live differently?).
2. Give children responsibility for active research into the content of the subject area of the teaching course, and help them gain knowledge of the basic relations in this subject area so that they can formulate their own understanding (core model) and research their own problems.
3. Use the social life of the class. Children in a classroom setting often care more about the opinion of their peers than the opinion of the teacher. We benefit from this interest by supporting collaborative work on research tasks, and formulating problems that require collective effort for solution.

In addition to these general principles, specific techniques for developing motivation were:

1. Work with opposition, contrasts, and conflicts in the subject matter or in viewpoints about the subject matter.
2. Provide an overview of the programme for the year and overview for each lesson (e.g., using goal-result boards of what they have done and what they plan to do, creating posters to show germ-cell models and writing the daily agenda on the blackboard).
3. Formulate tasks for the children that require genuine exploration.
4. Use the class dialogue to make resumés, overviews and goal formulations for each lesson (e.g., the children in the Danish experiment had to make summaries of what they do know and what they do not know about the different historical periods they were exploring.).
5. Use group work with differentiation of tasks between and within the groups (e.g., the children worked in small groups to create and perform plays about

the Stone-, Iron-, Viking-, and Middle-Ages. This activity was formulated so that they had to use these plays to explicate the relations in the model they had developed).

6. Make sure that each child understands the goals of a specific task in relation to the general problem being researched.

Implication of the Double Move Approach for Radical-Local Teaching and Learning

The double move approach provides a detailed set of principles for organizing teaching situations that aim to develop children's understanding of the goals for teaching and their learning motive as part of the process of developing their theoretical knowledge and interests for different subject-matter areas. A radical-local perspective, as described in Chapters 3 and 4, puts more focus on the content from the local knowledge used in developing theoretical knowledge, and the use of that theoretical knowledge in relation to the local community. Radical-local teaching aims at helping children create an understanding between subject-matter knowledge as general theoretical knowledge, local knowledge, and the child's personal everyday knowledge of community and home practice. The double move approach provides a way to realize ideas.

Through this teaching form, theoretical knowledge and local knowledge can become integrated so that this knowledge can enrich children's personal concepts in a way that is useful in their understanding of everyday local practice. In a radical-local perspective, the teacher takes departure in children's understanding and orients children toward tasks and problems in the subject-matter area that can become meaningful for the child and thereby motivating in relation to understanding both theoretical principles and local practice and knowledge of their community.

This was the aim for the afterschool teaching project with young children from the Puerto Rican families and community described in Chapters 9-13. To realize the goal we argued that theoretical knowledge has to be related to local knowledge so that the children appropriate personal concepts that can function as tools to analyze and understand thematic problem areas in their local community.

Papote ©Jose B. Rivera, East Harlem.

CHAPTER 7

The East Harlem Community from a Cultural-Historical Perspective

When one looks at the usual statistical indicators of the social conditions that characterize East Harlem, then one is confronted with the all-too-familiar images of urban poverty. These indicators provide a picture of low family incomes (with a large percentage under the federally-defined poverty line) (Navarro, 2000), relatively high unemployment or underemployment, relatively high rates of school dropout, teenage pregnancy (Pérez, 2000, p. 11, for national data), alcohol and drug abuse, and so forth (Freidenberg, 1995; New York City Department of City Planning, 1993; Pérez, 1993).

The social indicators for the approximately 38,000 children (19 and under), who comprise a little over thirty percent of the residents of East Harlem, provide comparably disturbing pictures (New York City Department of City Planning, 1992, 2001a, Manhattan Community District 11). The relative achievement of the schoolchildren, as measured by standardized tests, suggests that these children, on average, are having difficulties with their academic subjects in school. In the United States, over 40% of Puerto Rican children live below the poverty line (Pérez, 2000, pp. 13-14).

However, if one comes past the shocking images that these statistical accounts call forth, and actually walks through the neighbourhoods of East Harlem, then one immediately experiences a functioning community. Children play in the open areas found among the high-rise apartment buildings, or along the sidewalks on the side streets. Fruit and vegetable stands are found along the major avenues that run through East Harlem. Some unused, open lots have been converted into little parks or recreational areas. Little social clubs are found throughout the area. There are churches, youth centres (including one that serves 4,000 youth from ages 5-21 and selected as exemplary by the U.S. Department of Education, Chung, 2000), restaurants, bakeries, not to mention an internationally famous medical centre, a public hospital, and the Museum for the History of the City of New York. The immediate and superficial picture that one encounters on the street is typical urban life – colourful, active, and varied, not the picture of chaos and despair engendered from the statistical descriptions.

And this is also the picture that one encounters when one meets the children of East Harlem, who are typically lively, enthusiastic, and energetic. These immediate, positive, superficial impressions that one gets in East Harlem do not negate the existence of real problems for some children in terms of their developed capabilities and orientations, but their problems reflect more about the conditions within which they are developing, than any fundamental or qualitative differences between these children and those, for example, who are growing up in a wealthy neighbourhood south of 96th street (the lower border of East Harlem). The important point is that, as a global impression, the children of East Harlem are capable of educational development, and the main teaching problem is to organize worthwhile, challenging activities to support that development. But where to start? We did not want to simply start with a new round of remedial teaching in existing subject-matter topics, but rather wanted to focus on topics that specifically addressed cultural characteristics of the children.

As discussed in the previous chapters, educational processes are viewed as having the potential to help children develop a positive relationship to their life situation, in part by gaining insight into and understanding of their community. Educational processes can also be understood as an important part of the process of community development, which was a concern for the El Barrio Popular Education Project. Therefore, it is necessary to have some analysis of the historical and cultural conditions within which the children live, both for understanding the goals of the teaching and for understanding some of the content that was used in the teaching experiment.

This chapter presents the East Harlem community from a cultural-historical perspective. First we review some history of Puerto Rico's economic and political development, with a special focus on the relations between Puerto Rico and the United States. This history provides some background for understanding how and why East Harlem developed as a predominantly Puerto Rican neighbourhood, as well as some of the ongoing relations between Puerto Rico and East Harlem and some of the structural contradictions or conflicts between the Puerto Rican community and the United States. This is followed by a brief history of the development of the East Harlem community, and a short description of the community and its the present day living conditions.

Puerto Rico Prior to United States Acquisition in 1898[21]

The island known as Puerto Rico lies between the Caribbean Sea and the Atlantic Ocean, about 1600 km (1000 miles) southeast from Florida and Galveston, Texas on the United States mainland. The island, with a land area a little under half the size of the state of New Jersey, is about 160 km (100 miles) long and 56 km (35 miles) wide – mostly mountainous, with a coastal plain in the north.

Originally the island was inhabited by a tribe of people known as Arawak (or Taíno), who came either from the northeastern part of South America, or from southern Florida in North America. The island was discovered by Columbus during his second voyage to the West Indies in 1493. The Spanish king, who had financed Columbus's voyage, claimed ownership of this territory for the next 400 years. Ponce de León started the first European colony in 1508. During this period, Spain imported slaves from Africa (starting in 1511), and permitted marriage to Taíno Indians. Therefore it is understandable that the present-day Puerto Rican population is primarily a mixture of Spanish, African, and native-American origins.

Puerto Rico had little economic significance for Spain, except for its strategic location at the eastern edge of the Antilles Islands, and the deep, protected harbour – considered the best in the Caribbean – in the main city of San Juan. For the most part, Spain did not invest many resources to develop Puerto Rico economically, so it remained largely undeveloped (from a market-economy point of view) until the late 18th century. Trade relationships, based on smuggling, between Puerto Rico and the United States can be traced back to the mid-1700s, at which time the United States was still a collection of British colonies. Sugar and molasses were sent from Puerto Rico to New York, New England, and Pennsylvania in exchange for basic foodstuffs, which Spain was not providing. In 1830 a trade association was established in New York City by merchants from Puerto Rico and Cuba to promote and facilitate trade between these countries and the United States. Coffee and tobacco plantations were also developed. By the last third of the 19th century, almost two-thirds of Puerto-Rican produced sugar and most of the molasses was being sold to the United States. But coffee, sent to Europe, was the primary source of income on the island. During this period, the United States and several European countries sold machinery needed for planting and harvesting these three export crops, which became a foundation for the island to enter into the international market economy.

21　The discussion in this and the next section is based on historical descriptions provided by Sánchez Korrol (1994), Morales Carrión (1983), Zinn (1980), and Encyclopedia Britannica articles on 'William McKinley' and 'The West Indies'.

Concurrent with these 19th century economic developments was the development of a popular struggle for political independence from Spain. The process
had started at the beginning of the 19th century, with two brief periods of
relative political freedom in the first quarter of the century, and marked especially by an ill-prepared and quickly-suppressed revolutionary attempt in the
town of Lares in 1868, which was followed by political emigrations, primarily
to the United States and to New York City in particular.[22] In New York City,
Puerto Rican exiles joined together with exiles from Cuba, and from other Latin
American countries that were attempting to achieve political independence to
publish newspapers and other materials aimed at liberating the Caribbean from
Spanish control.

   As it turned out, these liberation struggles, particularly in Cuba, did result in
removing Spanish rule from the Caribbean, but in the case of Puerto Rico, only
resulted in having Spanish rule replaced with United States control. Therefore,
to better understand the present-day situation of Puerto Rico and of Puerto
Ricans in New York City, it is useful to understand the economic, political
and ideological forces that contributed to the historical development of Puerto
Rico's relationship with the United States. It is this relationship that has had
the most significant effects on the subsequent conditions for life on the island
and for those who migrated to the United States in general, and New York City
in particular.

The United States Acquisition of Puerto Rico

A confluence of factors led to the establishment of formal political, economic,
and military relationships between Puerto Rico and the United States in 1898.
Just as there had been an independence movement in Puerto Rico, so was there
one in Cuba, which was also under Spanish domination. In 1895, Cuban rebels
initiated an armed struggle against Spanish rule, resulting in increasingly
repressive Spanish countermeasures. In Puerto Rico, matters proceeded more
peacefully, with Spain conceding political and administrative autonomy to
Puerto Rico in 1897. Meanwhile, Cuban refugees, who had come to the United
States to escape Spanish repressions, reported exaggerated examples of Spanish
atrocities in Cuba. These stories were reprinted widely, especially by two New
York City newspapers, which were competing aggressively with each other

---

22 This event, subsequently named El Grito de Lares, often has served an important symbolic
     function as evidence of some revolt or resistance in Puerto Rican history.

at the time to increase their circulation.[23] These newspaper articles are often given (or claimed) credit for creating a climate for intervention into this Spanish-Cuban matter.[24] Although it makes for a dramatic story, it seems unlikely that newspaper articles alone would send the United States into what became an imperialist adventure (Zinn, 1980). More likely, the newspaper articles were only one of several factors in the final decision for military intervention, and in retrospect probably a relatively trivial one.

A critical turning point in the sequence of events that led to the United States acquisition of Puerto Rico was a mysterious explosion that sank the battleship USS Maine, killing 268 persons, in the Havana Harbour on 15 February 1898. The United States president, McKinley, felt obligated to respond to the ship's sinking, and when Spain refused to withdraw from Cuba and recognize the island's independence, the United States Congress authorized President McKinley to use armed forces to expel the Spanish from Cuba, adding an amendment that Cuba should not be annexed to the United States. Having gained control in Cuba (where the Spanish officials were then allowed to remain in charge of the municipal offices), the United States sent during the last week of July an expeditionary force of approximately 3,500 men to Puerto Rico, Spain's last colonial territory in the Caribbean.[25] By early August 1898, Spain had signed a preliminary peace treaty in Washington, DC, with a final treaty signed in early December, to recognize Cuba's independence, cede Puerto Rico and Guam, and sell the Philippines to the United States.

This military intervention into Cuban affairs, with an eye to protecting United States interests, was not novel in the history of the United States. Over the 100 years prior to 1898, there had been at least 100 military interventions into foreign countries to protect United States citizens, property, and commerce. However, the subsequent imperialist occupation of Puerto Rico (as well as Guam and the Philippines) was largely a new chapter in the history of United States practices. Before the 1890s, the predominant political belief in the United States was that

---

23 Furthermore, the newspapers may have contributed their own stories, to supplement the ones obtained from Cuban refugees. William Randolph Hearst, the publisher of the Morning Journal, reportedly cabled his illustrator in Cuba to send pictures of atrocities. When the illustrator found none to illustrate, Hearst cabled 'You furnish the pictures and I'll furnish the war.'

24 One headline of the Morning Journal in New York City was 'How Do You Like the Journal's War?'

25 Actually, the attack was initated by General Nelson Miles without direct orders. Apparently the U.S. troops were welcomed by the Puerto Ricans, while the Spaniards fled, so that very little fighting actually took place.

the country should remain isolated from European affairs, and that it should serve as an example of democracy and peace for the rest of the world. By the 1890s, however, the main prominent features of the United States' political and economic views were the ideas of developing foreign markets for trade (because of a domestic surplus in agricultural and manufacturing production and no further expansion in the Western frontier), a military interest in acquiring foreign naval bases, and a degree of ideological rhetoric about actively spreading United States traditions and values. These were also the kinds of views that President McKinley and some members of his Republican party were expressing.[26] These economic and ideological developments made imperialist adventures more attractive, or at least within the scope of reasonable possibility.

   Against this historical background, it is not incomprehensible that Puerto Rico was acquired in the Spanish-American war, even if it had not been a direct or immediate focus of attention at the start. Indeed, it would almost appear that Puerto Rico was caught accidentally in a net of events during a brief period of United States imperialism.[27] In principle, the United States could have demanded Spanish withdrawal and independence for Puerto Rico as well, especially given that Spain had already granted political autonomy in Puerto Rico. But, despite the presence of anti-imperialist voices in the United States, including many members of the business community, the outcome was that Puerto Rico came directly under the United States sphere of influence, as a territorial dependency. The initial configuration of economic and military interests that led to the United States acquisition of Puerto Rico have remained important forces in Puerto Rico's subsequent historical development.

---

26 This is not to say that there was a general or widespread belief that advocated direct imperialist intervention. There is a case to be made that most business leaders were satisfied with an 'open door' policy that would lead to free trade, and that imperialist acquisition was not essential to realize this goal. Moreover, some Republicans were opposed to McKinley's imperialist decision.

27 The United States did not take any other territory in the Caribbean at this time, even if there were several other islands between Cuba and Puerto Rico. The common characteristic in the case of these two islands was that they were under Spanish rule.

Puerto Rico's Development under United States Rule Prior to World War II

The initial period under United States rule was marked by strong control of most aspects of societal life. After almost 18 months of military rule, the United States Congress passed the 'Foraker Act' in 1900, which enabled Puerto Ricans to elect a House of Delegates. However, all legislation from this chamber had to be approved by an eleven-member Executive Council, of which at least five had to be native Puerto Ricans, but all were appointed by the United States president, after which a United States-appointed governor had veto right. Other executive functions, such as commissioner of education and attorney general, were also appointed positions, and filled with people from the United States. There was also a possibility to elect a resident commissioner to represent Puerto Rican interests to the United States.[28] Finally, the Foraker Act granted some free trade between the island and the United States.[29] The question of granting United States citizenship was also raised during the debates before the passage for the Foraker Act, but left unresolved when the political and economic questions (e.g., should Puerto Rico eventually be made a state) proved to be too difficult to resolve, and citizenship status was seen as potentially biasing the decision.

Any idea or expectation that Puerto Rico would become an United States state was quickly abated when a 1901 Supreme Court decision designated Puerto Rico as an 'unincorporated territory' of the United States, as distinct from 'incorporated territories', such as Arizona and New Mexico, which were intended for eventual statehood.[30]

During this initial period of territorial government, the United States initiated a series of changes on the island – often motivated by a self-conception that the best political and ideological system in the world was being brought to an underdeveloped, politically immature country. The United States dollar currency was superimposed on the island's Puerto Rican peso, and eventually became the only monetary system. Health and sanitation improvements were made, thereby increasing the population. Roads and bridges were built. Schools were

---

28 After 1904 this commissioner was made a nonvoting delegate to the U.S. House of Representatives.

29 Permission for free trade was not trivial, given that the President at that time, William McKinley, had been elected on a platform of high tariffs to protect United States industry from foreign competition.

30 It should be noted that Puerto Rico's acquisition by treaty was not problematic, because other United States territories that eventually became states, such as Florida and Louisiana, were also acquired by treaty.

built and new curricula instituted that aimed to socialize Puerto Rican children into United States traditions.[31] These and other attempts of introducing United States traditions (e.g., requiring English in certain official instances, introducing United States political traditions, promoting United States holidays, while downplaying or ignoring Puerto Rican ones) met with strong resistance from Puerto Rican political leaders. After all, Puerto Rico had just achieved political and administrative freedom from Spain, after several decades of struggle, only to lose it again with the United States occupation.

A critical barrier to immigration was eliminated in 1917, when the Foraker Act was replaced by the 'Jones Act'. This new basic law replaced the Executive Council with an elected Senate, but limited Puerto Rican self-government to being able to veto the governor appointed by the U.S. president and to have Senate approval of some governor appointments to some executive departments, while the United States retained control of the police, judicial, prison, and education systems. In addition to these small steps toward self-government, Puerto Ricans were granted United States citizenship, without having to pay federal taxes. This seemingly simple step was motivated by a desire to retain control over Puerto Rico, without simultaneously acquiring too much responsibility.[32] The citizenship right enabled, however, free movement between the island and the United States, and by 1920, 45 of the 48 states had residents who were born in Puerto Rico.

---

31 For example, from 1905-1916, English was used as the language of instruction.

32 One factor, often argued as contributing to the passage of this Act at that time, was the United States entry into World War I. Even though this law permitted Puerto Ricans to reject citizenship if they wanted, and some few hundred did, it did not exempt anyone from being registered and recruited for military service. But this single event is unlikely to be the only cause for granting citizenship, especially because citizenship is not necessary for conscription when persons are living under U.S. jurisdiction (Cabranes, 1979). Among other things, Puerto Rico was seen as relevant for protecting access to the recently completed Panama Canal, as well as a refuelling station for United States warships. Granting citizenship was seen as a way of keeping Puerto Rico clearly within the United States sphere of influence, but with no intention of developing the rights and responsibilities associated with the states of the United States. Luis Muñoz Rivera, who was resident commissioner for Puerto Rico in Washington, had been fighting for years for this bill as a way to give Puerto Rico a measure of self-government and a clear political status. Muñoz Rivera testified to Congress in 1917 that he was against citizenship because it would prejudice the case for Puerto Rican independence, while the chairman of the committee hearings expressed the intention to hold Puerto Rico as a permanent possession.

A combination of factors that developed over the first decades of the 20th Century contributed to an economic migration of Puerto Ricans to the United States, with most settling in New York City, especially Manhattan and Brooklyn. A number of structural changes occurred in the Puerto Rican economy (e.g., introduction of mechanized labour processes, more efficient production processes, non-enforcement of United States anti-trust laws, increased sugar production while coffee production decreased,[33] corporate resistance to the New Deal's attempts to redistribute economic power) that resulted in the loss of jobs for significant numbers and the closing of many small farms. A plantation system of production was organized with four North American companies as the dominant producers. Within a generation, 75% of the island's population became directly or indirectly dependent on sugar production to sustain their living. With sugar as a monoculture cash crop, Puerto Rico needed to buy their staple food products as imports. Even today Puerto Rico does not have a subsistence economy, and is therefore sensitive to the fluctuations in the international markets, both for selling sugar and for purchasing staples. These structural changes in the island's economy initiated a process, similar to what happened in industrialized countries around the world, in which skilled and unneeded workers migrated from the countryside toward the cities in Puerto Rico. And some of these internal migrants eventually became external migrants to the United States when it was not possible to find adequate work in the cities.

Puerto Rico's Development under United States Rule after World War II[34]

The period after the Second World War in Puerto Rico has been characterized by economic transformation, significant migration, increased self-government, and an uncertain political future. The attraction of capital from the United States, using raw materials from the United States, and producing for the United States market, enabled an economic boom in Puerto Rico. The relative political stability was important and the Puerto Rican development was held up as a model

---

33 Puerto Rican sugar production during the last decade of Spanish rule was about 57,000 tons per year. During the first five years of American control, it rose to 200,000 tons per year, and by 1930 it was 900,000 tons per year (Perloff, 1950, p. 285). Furthermore, most of the coffee trees were destroyed in 1928 and 1932 hurricanes.

34 The discussion in this section is based on Fitzpatrick (1987), Sánchez Korrol (1994), and Maldonado-Denis (1969/1972).

for economic development in other non-industrialized countries. Today almost all of Puerto Rico's exports go to the United States, while about two-thirds of their imports come from the United States (making it the sixth largest market in the world for United States manufactured goods). Official unemployment in the 1990s has ranged from 15-18%, compared to the United States national averages of 5-8%. Agriculture accounts for only 3% of the labour force.

Despite the relative economic improvements in Puerto Rico after the Second World War, migration to the United States (and to New York City in particular) increased tremendously. Using figures from the U.S. Bureau of the Census, one can see significant and steady increases in persons either born in Puerto Rico or with Puerto Rican parents who are living on the mainland. In 1940, approximately 70,000 Puerto Ricans were living in the United States, most of them in New York City. By 1950, the total migration had quadrupled (where almost 250,000 of the 300,000 Puerto Ricans in the United States were in New York City), and during the 1950s, over 400,000 Puerto Ricans (at least 20% of the island's population) migrated to the United States. During the 1960s the outward migration continued, though half as large as the 1950s. By 1970, the number of Puerto Ricans living in New York City had reached a stable size (about 860,000), slightly over 60% of the 1.4 million Puerto Ricans recorded in the United States. Over the following twenty years, the New York City population had increased slightly, but during the 1990s decreased to a little under 800,000. At the same time, the overall mainland population continued to grow as Puerto Ricans migrated to other regions, especially cities in the north-eastern United States. At the 2000 census, the total number of Puerto Ricans living in the United States was almost as large as the total number of persons living in Puerto Rico (3.4 million vs. 3.8 million).[35]

A combination of several factors enabled and facilitated these migrations (and disputes about the relative importance and possible causal relations among them). Some of the major factors include (a) the start (and eventual failure) of the economic development policy in Puerto Rico, known as 'Operation

---

35 There are difficulties in establishing reliable migration figures, because Puerto Ricans are United States citizens and may travel freely between the U.S. mainland and Puerto Rico (see Fitzpatrick, 1987, p. 17, for a brief discussion of the problems). Furthermore, there are repeated charges of undercounting of Puerto Ricans in the census (despite the fact that Puerto Ricans, from birth, are legal United States citizens, and therefore do not need to hide from government officials) (e.g., Burks, 1972; A. Falcón, 2001; U.S. Commission on Civil Rights, 1974). For present purposes, we simply want to indicate a large and steady migration of Puerto Ricans into the United States, which these numbers, even with undercounts, easily show.

Bootstrap', that resulted in large shifts from labour-intensive agricultural production to industrial production, and further shifts from labour-intensive to
capital-intensive industries, with a resulting unemployment for many people,
(b) seasonal (half-year) unemployment for agricultural workers, especially in
sugar production which was almost 50% of the agricultural production, (c)
increases in population, especially after the 1940s, when rural health and sanitation services were initiated, (d) a pull from the post-war United States where
higher-paying (but still mostly unskilled or semi-skilled) industrial jobs needed
workers,[36] and (e) relatively cheap air travel between New York and San Juan,
with the possibility of special credit arrangements (e.g., five dollars down, and
then low monthly payments), which the Puerto Rican government helped to
arrange.

As a general tendency, life was difficult in the United States for most of the
immigrants from Puerto Rico, especially during the big migrations in the 1950s
and 1960s. Like other immigrants to the United States, they did not receive
any special treatment nor support from the municipal authorities. But it was
probably an ambivalent difficulty for many because even though many skilled
workers from Puerto Rico had unskilled jobs in New York City, and worked
long hours, the wages were better than what was available in Puerto Rico. In
other words, the consequences of structural economic developments in Puerto
Rico created a condition in which people preferred the difficult conditions of life
in New York City to the more difficult conditions of unemployment in Puerto
Rico.

Many of the problems, identified as sources for the start of the large migration after the Second World War, remain today, and while there are some
cycles of increased return migration during periods of economic downturn in
the United States, there has remained a net migration outward from Puerto
Rico. However, unlike many migrations to the United States, where the immigrants do not expect to return to their original country, most mainland Puerto
Ricans have relatives on the island and return regularly for visits. Also, there
is a significant yearly return migration (numbering in the tens of thousands)
where migrants (usually older) to the mainland return to live in Puerto Rico
(U.S. Commission on Civil Rights, 1976; Hernández, 1976; Christenson, 2001).
These practices create conditions that serve to maintain substantive cultural
links between Puerto Rico and the mainland Puerto Rican communities.

Puerto Rico's political status has remained an ongoing problem, both for the
United States Congress and for the residents of Puerto Rico. In 1952, a Puerto

---

36 At one point the mayor of New York City even travelled to Puerto Rico to tell about the
    existence of jobs in New York's manufacturing and service industries.

Rican constitution was accepted by the U.S. Congress, which made Puerto Rico a commonwealth of the United States, and finally gave considerably more self-determination about internal affairs, which had long been a desire in Puerto Rico. The people of Puerto Rico have been (and remain) more or less evenly divided between wanting statehood or commonwealth status, plus a small percentage who advocate independence. National plebiscites were held on this question in 1967, 1993, and 1998, offering a choice between commonwealth, statehood, and independence. The 1967 plebiscite was boycotted by 34% of the voters, while of those who voted, commonwealth was chosen by 60%. The 1993 plebiscite was nonbinding (i.e., the U.S. Congress was not obligated to respond); commonwealth status received 48.6% to statehood's 46.3%, with the rest of the vote given to independence. The 1998 plebiscite presented five alternatives, where the one called 'none of the above' got 50.3% of the votes and statehood received 46.5%. In other words, the disagreements and splits about Puerto Rico's political status that appeared in 1898 continue onward today.

Post-war development in Puerto Rico reflects a continuation of the historically primary focus of United States policy in relation to Puerto Rico, namely economic development turned to the advantage of United States business interests (Dietz & Pantojas-García, 1993). At the same time, the political status of Puerto Rico (from the inhabitants' point of view) remains an ambiguous situation, in that relatively few actively support separation, but there is no consensus about the preferred political future. It is striking, however, that Puerto Rico retains its commonwealth status, during a time when many former colonial territories have now gained independence.

Cultural-Historical Conditions: A Sketch of East Harlem[37]

East Harlem is located in the northeastern section of Manhattan (see Figure 7.1.). Comprising about 200 square blocks, the region is usually defined as having Fifth Avenue as its western boundary, and stretching 10 blocks eastward to the East River. The southern boundary starts at 96th street, a major thoroughfare that crosses the island from the East River to the Hudson River. Below 96th street, also between Fifth Avenue and the East River, one finds high-rise apartment buildings whose inhabitants comprise one of the greatest concentrations of personal wealth in the United States. Reaching northward from 96th Street,

---

37 Sources for this section include Freidenberg (1995) and Sexton (1965).

Figure 7.1. Map of Manhattan, showing the location of East Harlem.

over 29 city blocks, to 125th street, one finds another major thoroughfare. This northern boundary between East Harlem and what is traditionally called Harlem is more fluid, not as well-defined as the other boundaries, but this gives a reasonable description of its location. At least 115,000 people live currently within this region (New York City Department of City Planning, 1992, 2001). Almost half of these people (or their parents or grandparents) were probably born in Puerto Rico.

HISTORICAL DEVELOPMENT OF EAST HARLEM

East Harlem, also called Spanish Harlem, has not always been a predominantly Spanish-speaking area. This region was colonized by the Dutch in the mid-1600s, displacing the native Weckquaesgeks (part of the Delaware nation) who had lived there previously. The Dutch named this settlement New Haarlem, after the city of Haarlem in the Netherlands, but the Dutch had abandoned their farms in this region by the time of the United States Revolutionary War (1776), and this largely uninhabited area started to be converted into large private estates and areas for hunting and horse racing. Over the next 100 years this area developed into an exclusive residential area, with spacious estates for the wealthy, along with a small village for tenants – mostly German and Irish – who worked on the estates.

Starting in the last 19th Century, East Harlem became primarily a residential neighbourhood, often overcrowded, with mostly low-income housing. Some impression of this condition can be gained from some demographic information provided in a community study, produced by a local committee in East Harlem, which concluded that New York City does not and will not look to East Harlem for large-scale business or industry nor recreation, but rather that it will remain a site for largely low-income housing (Mayor's Committee on City Planning, 1937, pp. 11-12). In 1934, it was estimated in the Real Property Inventory that 201,000 people lived in this region. The 1920 and 1930 federal censuses showed even larger population counts, which is consistent with the fact that apartment vacancy rate by 1934 was 21.5 percent (Mayor's Committee on City Planning, 1937, p. 16). Even with this high vacancy rate, the population density of East Harlem was at least 50 percent higher than other residential areas in Manhattan.

During this period there was considerable diversity in the national origins of East Harlem residents. Starting in the 1870s, Russian and other Eastern European Jews started to move to East Harlem. Around 1890, Italians started to settle in the area, and at this time some African-Americans also moved to the northern part of Harlem, after landlords could not rent the run-down housing stock to whites. By 1910, the Italians were the second largest group in East Harlem, along with the Jews. The first Puerto Ricans started to come to East Harlem around 1917, and by 1919 most of the wealthy estate owners had moved out. By the late 1920s, most of the Germans had moved out, the Jews and Italians were starting to move out, and the Puerto Ricans were moving in, along with African-Americans. In 1937, the population in East Harlem was summarized by the community study in terms of national origin, based on census records. The largest group was still Italian (71,000), followed by African-Americans (30,000). The previous dominant groups still has some presence with Russians, Germans, and Irish Free State (15,000 each). And finally, this study claimed that it was difficult to estimate the number of Puerto Ricans in the area, because they were registered as 'native-born whites of native-born parents.' They estimated the number to be between 5,000 and up to 10,000 (Mayor's Committee on City Planning, 1937, p. 17).

These migration patterns continued such that Puerto Ricans and African-Americans have become the largest groups, but public housing built in the 1940s, 1950s and 1960s, with a non-discriminatory acceptance policy, resulted in different cultural groups coming into the area, while a small Italian neighbourhood can still be found in East Harlem. In recent years there have been notable migrations from Mexico and other Central American countries.

When the first Puerto Ricans arrived in East Harlem, other Puerto Rican settlements existed already in Brooklyn (where the steamships from San Juan docked prior to World War II), in Chelsea (on the lower west side of Manhattan, where a Spanish community was established), and on the Lower East Side of Manhattan. However, East Harlem became the cultural and economic centre for Puerto Rican life in New York City, perhaps stimulated by a large outdoor market that sold Caribbean foods and spices, clothing, and just about anything else one needed. Many Puerto Rican professionals (e.g., doctors, lawyers), Latin entertainment, and services (e.g., barbershops, pharmacists, restaurants) also settled in this area, establishing East Harlem as the primary Puerto Rican settlement in New York. Today, East Harlem is no longer the largest Puerto Rican neighbourhood in New York, as the South Bronx and Brooklyn neighbourhoods have grown; East Harlem's centrality in the Puerto Rican community is no longer as strong as it once was, and it has remained a neighbourhood that is shared with other cultural groups of people.

CONTEMPORARY LIFE IN EAST HARLEM

If you ask a child in East Harlem to give a description of their community, then you are likely to get an account of drug use, homelessness, unemployment, dirty streets, street crime, teenage mothers, poor families, and limited community resources (for one example, see Berté-Toomer, Colón, González, Ayala, Henríquez, & Pedraza, 1992-3) And from a statistical, comparative point of view, this account would be justified.

The physical condition of the housing in East Harlem is variable. One can find high-rise apartment buildings which were built in the 1950s and are still operated by the New York City Housing Authority. Other buildings, three or four story brownstones, and five or six story tenement buildings, have stood empty and dilapidated for years. There are a number of open lots where houses once stood, but now only trash accumulates. There are few green or open areas, except for some asphalt school yards, some courtyards inside the high-rise public-housing buildings, and the occasional community garden or social clubs

(Narvaez, 1974). Major traffic arteries pass through East Harlem, so there is generally a constant and busy motor traffic through the area.

East Harlem's public housing had the effect of destroying important social networks in the neighbourhood. When these high-rise blocks of apartments were built, they did not provide any commercial space; as a result, many small businesses were closed or moved away. Similarly, extended families, which had been able to live in close proximity (i.e., in the same building or a building next door), were broken up because the New York City Housing Authority used the nuclear family, the order of application, and other criteria for deciding who would get an apartment in public housing and where the apartment was located (which could be in different parts of Manhattan or even in different boroughs). Even though there is some research evidence that extended families are better able to cope with the problems of living, childcare, and so forth, the Housing Authority was not willing to modify their procedures to try to maintain some of these social networks (Mencher, 1995). It is tragic that the public housing, built with the intention of improving living conditions for residents of East Harlem should concurrently serve to undercut the social networks that were instrumental in maintaining their quality of life.

Most people rent their living place. As a rule, people live in a single family unit, though sometimes with a single grandparent. In many cases, even though the grandparents are living in the same area as the parents, the grandparents still have a separate place to live. Most Puerto Rican families in East Harlem have some relatives (e.g., brothers, sisters, aunts, uncles, grandparents) in Puerto Rico. Some families have one or more members who have lived for some period of time in Puerto Rico, and visits to relatives are common. Children of school age are usually in school; no systematic child care is available for children of preschool age.

There are many aspects of life for Puerto Ricans in East Harlem that are found in other capitalist-based urban economies. The living conditions are organized primarily around a cash economy, where most members of the community are working in legal wage labour, as well as illegal activities (e.g., selling drugs, Bourgois, 1995, gambling). Over the past thirty years there has been a tendency in New York City for jobs to shift away from the skills that people have (Falcón & Gurak, 1990), or be taken over by other groups of people who are even less powerful in the face of capitalist exploitation. There is little or no possibility to produce food, so this is bought primarily in supermarkets, greengrocers, convenience stores, restaurants, and carry-out stores. Clothing is also generally purchased in stores. There is no living tradition for producing clothing, perhaps explained partly because many women are also working outside of the home, and partly because of a social convention that values factory-produced clothing, especially in particular styles or from particular manufacturers.

Social activities in the community are based around informal gatherings. For men, this can often be in the form of social clubs (some of which re-create the tradition found in Puerto Rico). For some women, this is found in the church.

Implications

The historical sketch presented here shows that the general relations between Puerto Rico and the United States are complicated. Significant decisions, which have far-reaching consequences for people's living conditions, are being played out in corporate boardrooms and government offices. Living conditions in New York City are influenced by periodic budget crises and political decisions that extend far beyond the Puerto Rican community. At the same time, while these political and economic processes may be inaccessible to the East Harlem community, they do not preclude an attempt to clarify and understand what traditions of living have characterized Puerto Ricans in Puerto Rico and New York. Neither do they preclude an attempt to try to understand the consequences of these political and economic decisions and to reflect about the ways that one might want to respond, both personally and collectively (Pantoja, 1989). It should be clear that these kinds of responses will be facilitated by having knowledge of one's own community, and that in developing a reflective, active relation to one's situation, grounded in analytic knowledge and skill, there are better chances to develop a positive concept about one's self and one's community.

Virgin over Boat ©Jose B. Rivera, East Harlem.

CHAPTER 8

Puerto Ricans and Education in New York City

The idea of radical-local teaching and learning is to plan and implement teaching practices that serve to develop a pupil's knowledge of subject-matter content in a way that is related to the cultural-historical conditions of the children's lives. This knowledge should serve as intellectual tools that can be used to understand and act in relation to those conditions – both the specific historically developed conditions in the children's neighbourhood, and larger patterns that reflect historical epochs or general cultural change within traditions of practice. The idea of radical-local teaching and learning is motivated by a belief that this educational approach can address many of the general expectations that are attributed to education, while recognizing and developing the specific needs and interests of the individuals in relation to their life situation.

There are not readily available comprehensive models that illuminate the needs and cultural-historical conditions for Puerto Rican children in East Harlem, which can provide a starting point for constructing an appropriate radical-local approach.[38] In the previous chapter, we considered some of the general historical conditions that brought Puerto Ricans to New York City and some of the characteristics of their life today. In this chapter, we consider some of the general and historical conditions of education for children with a Puerto Rican background in New York City, as well as specific characteristics of the children who participated in the teaching experiment. For now, these analyses, based in part on our reading and in part on our practical experience in the community, are a preliminary attempt to describe cultural-historical conditions in East Harlem – the local arena of the children in the teaching experiment – in a way that would be useful for a radical-local approach. In particular, the analyses help to

---

38 This problem is not specific to East Harlem, but reflects a general condition that results from a tendency in social scientific and educational analyses to underplay the particular in relation to the general.

identify some of the content that should be drawn into the subject-matter teaching, and to motivate specific features and goals in the intervention project.

Historical Background and Contemporary Conditions

Despite the relatively few Puerto Ricans in New York City before the Second
World War, the Puerto Rican community was already active in relation to the
New York City schools. An organization of parents, *Madres y Padres Pro-Niños
Hispanos*, was formed in the late 1930s, and remained active through the early
1940s. This organization focused especially on problems concerning Puerto Rican
children who were being placed several grade levels below what they had completed in Puerto Rico because of their insufficient English language proficiency.
For example, the organization volunteered to place a parent in every classroom
to work as an interpreter and liaison to the school. Other institutions such as
settlement houses and government agencies were also involved at that time
with educational questions, often with a focus on language – either to facilitate
learning English and United States traditions, or to preserve Spanish and Puerto
Rican cultural traditions (Sánchez Korrol, 1996, pp. 83-86).

One consequence of the great migration following the Second World War
was a significant increase in the number of Puerto Rican children in New York
City schools. In 1948, almost 14,000 Spanish-speaking children (of which 5,000
were also English speakers) were enrolled in the New York City schools, and
a committee in what is considered the first systematic study of Puerto Rican
students in the United States, recommended hiring some Spanish-speaking
teachers to function as liaisons between the migrant community and the schools
(New York City Board of Education, 1947).

By 1953, the estimates of the number of children of Puerto Rican origin in
New York City schools ranged from approximately 50,000 (Finocchiaro, 1954)
to 70,000 (Morrison, 1958), and this count increased in 1957 to 122,687 pupils
(Morrison, 1958). This 1957 figure represented about 15 percent of the total
school population in New York City (where the 52,000 Puerto Rican children
in Manhattan represented almost 30 percent of the Manhattan school population). Furthermore, the demographics at that time indicated that many Puerto
Rican children of preschool age would soon be coming into the school system,
so there was a clear need to initiate programmes and activities in relation to
this population, where at least half were non-English speaking.

In many respects the New York City public schools were not prepared to
receive children who were immigrating with their families from Puerto Rico
(Castellanos & Leggio, 1983). Immigration to the United States had been re-

stricted since 1924, and the school system was not prepared to deal with large numbers of non-English speaking students. In general, school teachers could not speak Spanish (Mayor's Committee on Puerto Rican Affairs, 1951), and school classrooms were not organized to handle children who came with little or no English language.

During this period in the 1950s, one sees a pattern that is still all too familiar today. There were a series of commissioned reports and studies (e.g., Mayor's Committee on Puerto Rican Affairs, 1951; Mayor's Committee on Puerto Rican Affairs, 1953; New York City Board of Education, 1953), including a four-year (1953-1957) million-dollar Ford Foundation study into the education and adjustment of Puerto Rican students in New York City schools, which focused especially on language handicaps, language learning, and school-parent relations (Morrison, 1958; New York City Schools, 1982). These studies produced recommendations, often quite enlightened, calling for bilingual teachers, who could serve as liaisons to communicate to parents about the school's programmes and who could collect information from parents about their children's previous schooling and background. Many recommendations were never implemented, but there were many concrete achievements: curriculum materials were developed, testing methods were developed to assess non-English speaking students, in-service training programmes were developed (Cordasco, 1982), and some bilingual teachers (called Substitute Auxiliary Teachers) were hired.[39]

There were some examples of enlightened practices which indicate that some persons in the New York City educational and social service systems were aware of and concerned about the education of Puerto Rican students. For example, Finocchiaro (1954), the Supervisor of Instruction in the New York City Board of Education at the time, describes an educational perspective that focuses on the development of the whole child, a shift to a cultural pluralism, respecting the child's cultural background, and trying to adapt instruction to their needs.[40] She describes a number of efforts to improve the communication between the schools and the parents, through the use of Spanish interpreters, and parents associations. Villaronga (1954), then Secretary of Education for Puerto Rico,

---

39 Ten substitute auxiliary teachers were hired in 1949 when the position was created, which increased to 100 by 1960 (Sánchez Korrol, 1996), but they were all eliminated in a 1975 financial crisis (Fitzpatrick, 1987, p. 157). A quick comparison of the number of these teachers with the number of Spanish-speaking students suggests a clear insufficiency.

40 While this perspective may have reflected Dr. Finocchiaro's views, it is possible and likely that these views were not always found in the actual school practices. But it is interesting to note that the idea of providing education to all, according to their background and needs, was present in the educational system at that time.

describes some of the developments made in the Puerto Rican school system to better prepare children who might be immigrating to the U.S., as well as ongoing contacts with school authorities in New York City.

Dossick (1954) describes a series of summer workshops, started in 1948, in which New York City teachers, administrators, social workers got a week of orientation lectures in New York City, followed by five weeks in Puerto Rico, receiving lectures at the University of Puerto Rico from university professors and government officials about 'almost every conceivable phase of Puerto Rican life' (p. 175). One of the participation requirements was to make a before and after comparison of one's preconceptions, attitudes, prejudices and generalizations about Puerto Rico. Participants from these workshops subsequently formed an association and worked on a variety of community and educational development issues for Puerto Ricans in New York City (Puerto Rican Workshop, 1957).

Despite the good intentions reflected in these examples, we can, in retrospect, see that they were not sufficient to address the magnitude of the required institutional changes and developments; significant problems remain in New York and other United States cities for Latino students in general, especially for Spanish-dominant students (e.g., Fisher et al., 1998; Secada et al., 1998; National Commission on Secondary Education for Hispanics, 1984; Latino Commission, 1992). This pattern applies as well for children from a Puerto Rican background in particular (Margolis, 1968; Santiago Santiago, 1986; Nieto, 1995, pp. 390-391; Nieto, 1998, pp. 136-138).

According to the 2000 U.S. census, New York City's population is around 8 million persons, of which about 10% have a Puerto Rican background. Puerto Ricans are, by far, the largest group of Latinos in the city, which comprises about 27% of the city's population (New York City Department of City Planning, 2001b, p. 27). The city's school system has about 1 million pupils, where an estimated one-third have a Puerto Rican background (Latino Commission, 1992). The early engagement by the New York Puerto Rican community to address specific issues concerning education for Puerto Rican pupils in New York City has continued to the present day (e.g., Caballero, 1989, 2000; Nieto, 2000, pp. 13-24; Pantoja, 1989; Pedraza, 1997; Reyes, 2000), but many of the same problems remain.

As before, comprehensive studies are conducted (e.g., Latino Commission, 1992, 1994; C. Rodriguez, 1992), but then largely ignored, or given no resources or possibilities to implement their proposals (Pedraza, 1997; Reyes, 2000). New York City has been generally resistant towards taking active measures to provide bilingual instruction, until forced by court orders (Pousada, 1987, pp. 15-17), and even then has repeatedly tried to avoid this approach to education for its pupils (del Valle, 1998; Reyes, 2003).

The group characteristics of children with a Puerto Rican background in New York City tend to reflect the common problems of urban minority children in present-day America (e.g., higher school dropout rates, relatively lower levels of achievement as measured by standardized tests, The History Task Force, 1979; Latino Commission, 1994; Nieto, 2000, pp. 22-26). The general causes for school dropout discussed in Chapter 2 are also applicable here, but there are also some indications that there are additional problems associated with being Latino. In the United States, even when demographic factors are controlled in statistical comparisons, Hispanic students are more likely to dropout than their white and African American counterparts. For example, wealthy Latino high school students are twice as likely to dropout compared with wealthy white and African Americans students (Secada et al., 1998, p. 2). It does not seem possible to attribute these educational problems solely to an insufficient mastery of American English, because a greater percentage of American-born Puerto Rican students also have greater problems in school relative to standard comparison groups.

It may also be important to consider the reasons why children remain in school (C. Rodriguez, 1992; Wehlage & Rutter, 1986). In our view, many of these reasons are compatible with the focus of radical-local teaching and learning. Rodriguez's study of Latino high school students in New York City identified that they were less likely to drop out when the school had a good spirit and acknowledged Latino culture. The issue of self-esteem or self-concept is sometimes brought up in discussions and recommendations. Educational and psychological research has usually found a positive correlation between self-esteem (or self-concept) and academic achievement. This relationship has led some to speculate that improvement of self-esteem could lead to improved academic achievement. However, it may be necessary to develop a more nuanced understanding of the complex relationship between self-concept or self-evaluation of one's intellectual capability and one's performance and achievement in school. For example, Comas-Diaz, Arroyo, & Lovelace (1982) conducted a project in a 5th-grade bilingual class of Puerto Rican pupils in an American school. After 14 weekly sessions (1.5 hours each) of presentations about Puerto Rican history and culture, they were able to document a statistically significant change in academic self-concept from pre- to post-tests. (There were also indications of changes in total and personal self-concept that approached statistical significance, while there was no indication of change in social self-concept). Dweck's (e.g., 1991, 1999) studies of self-concept and performance have documented experimentally and in school-based studies that praise of a child's effort, rather than a child's intelligence has observable consequences on subsequent performance. In other words, it is not a simple matter of feeling good about one's self, rather it is to have a conception that one's effort will result in positive consequences.

Caring teachers may also be important (Nieto, 1998, pp. 156-59), but there is also some indication that this caring is best connected to solid subject-matter content (Torres-Guzmán & Martínez Thorne, 2000, p. 286). The observations and conclusions from these studies are consistent with the radical-local idea that it is important to work with relevant subject-matter content, in a way that is focused on developing children's capabilities to work with this material.

As C. Rodriguez (1992) noted, many of the problems identified as related to school dropout often involve aspects (drug use, pregnancy, parent's educational level, inadequate buildings and materials) that schools themselves do not have much possibility to control. Obviously, it would be preferable to make safe environments, caring teachers, better resources and the other conditions that many current studies recommend (e.g., Secada et al., 1998; Latino Commission, 1994). In relation to radical-local teaching and learning, we expect that it will be particularly useful for addressing the problem of uninteresting, irrelevant, and/or unresponsive curriculum as noted in national studies of Latinos (Lockwood & Secada, 1999, p. 82), regional studies of Puerto Ricans (Pérez & Cruz, 1994, pp. 14-15) and studies of New York City Latinos (C. Rodriguez, 1992; Latino Commission, 1994). Such curriculum is likely to contribute to alienation from the content and meaning of school experiences as can be seen in autobiographical and poetic expressions from Puerto Ricans in New York City (e.g., Algarin & Pinero, 1975; Pietri, 1973; Rivera, 1982). As noted in Chapter 2, an important factor that influences whether young people stay in school is how they experience their time in school.

Conditions and Expectations for Education Today for Puerto Rican Children in East Harlem

Judged by the overall levels of achievement (using traditional measures of reading levels or arithmetic performance) or school completion, then children in East Harlem on average are having educational difficulties. At the same time, there have been several schools in East Harlem, some getting national recognition in the United States, that have been extremely successful or have provided models for reforms in other schools in New York City (Bafumo, 1998; Fliegel, 1993; Meier, 1995b). These success cases indicate that there is no fundamental limitation in the capability of East Harlem's children to be academically competent. But when one examines the daily teaching practices and institutional organizations of typical East Harlem schools, then it is not so difficult to comprehend why many children have difficulties. Without trying to assign blame or identify the specific causes, one can report the story that is often told, with variations, about many schools in large urban areas in America: poorly-prepared teachers, large classes, inadequate materials, relatively lower levels of funding, but most importantly in our view, unambitious curricula that do not pay attention to the children's background nor formulate any structures of educational activity that would give them a possibility to develop their capabilities (González, 2002, pp. 5-8; Latino Commission, 1992; Paredes Scribner, 1999, pp 1-3).

A general expectation that education is important for societal development can also be found among Puerto Rican professionals who are working with education in New York City,[41] as well as some recognition that schools must be part of a strategy for social change that is cognizant of the need for socio-economic conditions in the community (Pedraza, 1997, pp. 82-83). However, as Pedraza also notes, there is too little attention to pedagogical forms, but he only mentions general cognitive processes ('higher-order thinking and problem-solving skills') without also considering the content upon which these skills are formed.[42] More recently, there has been a focus on language, culture, and identity (Caballero, 2000, p., 216; M. Rivera & Pedraza, 2000). Despite the relatively large number of Puerto Rican children in the New York City school system, many of whom are clustered in specific regions in the city, there is little teaching in the public school system that acknowledges this Puerto Rican cultural background. At the same time, there are some indications, at least for Latino high school students, that there is interest in learning more about their cultural background and historical roots (Latino Commission, 1992)

CONFLICTS IN LIFE SITUATION

At the beginning of Chapter 7, we described a generally positive overall impression of everyday life for children in East Harlem, at least compared to the images that can be created by statistical descriptions of school achievement and performance. However, in closer interaction with elementary schoolchildren in East Harlem, one can also detect or discover some specific signs that indicate that children with a Puerto Rican background encounter conflicts in their relation-

---

41 'Education has long been at the center of Puerto Rican efforts to achieve social justice and economic empowerment in the United States' (Rodriguez-Morazzani, 1997, p. 59). '[W]e viewed education as a vehicle for social and political empowerment' (Caballero, 2000, p. 206)

42 This general formulation 'higher-order skills' is found in other reports, often defined in opposition to 'basic skills' of reading and calculating, but it is not common to see the meaning of the term analyzed in the detail given in Chapters 4 and 6, even if these chapters did not use such terminology.

ship to the Puerto Rican community and Puerto Rican traditions (for related examples see Carrasquillo & Carrasquillo, 1979; Carrasquillo, 1985).

For example, children have some doubts about the value of their neighbourhood: A group of children from an East Harlem school were once invited to visit a school in Long Island, about 50 miles outside of New York City. After this visit, it was suggested that there should be a return visit so that the children in Long Island could see the school and neighbourhood of their East Harlem visitors. However, the East Harlem children resisted this idea. They did not think there was anything worth visiting in their neighbourhood.

From talking with school teachers in this area, we have the impression that the children tend to undervalue their academic capabilities. They show little spontaneous interest in Puerto Rican culture, or the background of their parents. There is a tendency to devalue this background, perceiving it as irrelevant to their life in New York City. In conducting educational programmes with Puerto Rican children in this area, we noticed that the children sometimes spontaneously offered negative statements about being Puerto Rican.

We can understand these local observations as reflecting a more general pattern, which has been observed in different cities, that Puerto Rican children encounter negative reactions from members and institutional representatives from the dominant culture where they live. As has also been noted for Latinos in general in the United States, they often attend a school system that tends to deny, ignore, or denigrate their culture (Bigler, 1999; Nieto, 2000, pp. 16-17; C. Rodriguez, 1992; Walsh, 1998). They may encounter teachers who have a deficit view (culturally and/or genetically) of children with a Puerto Rican background, or who come from poor socioeconomic conditions (Latino Commission, 1994; Nieto, 1998, pp. 148-152; Pérez & Cruz, 1994, pp. 14, 25).[43]

Similarly, in our previous projects with Puerto Rican children in East Harlem, they were not inclined to speak or use Spanish, even though the teacher, the project leader and the two parent assistants often spoke Spanish to each other, when the children were around. If an adult in these projects spoke Spanish to them, the children were most likely to answer in English. If they were encouraged or requested to speak Spanish, then it was only with reluctance or resistance that they would do so. We interpreted this reluctance not only as an inability, but also as a wish not to become identified as Spanish speaking and Puerto

43 This is not to say that all Puerto Rican children encounter these conditions or that all school systems and teachers are acting in this way. Our point is only that we can understand the historical origins of children's negative attitudes as reflecting the kinds of actions that have historically been observed and reported from Puerto Rican children in U.S. public schools.

Rican children when we as researchers and non-Puerto Ricans were around. This reluctance is possibly reinforced by the fact that the Spanish language is not used in official school business, and children are not usually allowed to use Spanish as part of their school work. Similar observations about the prohibitions on the use of Spanish and psychological consequences for Puerto Rican children have also been observed in other U.S. cities (Bigler, 1997; Nieto, 2000; Torres, 1997, Chap. 5; Urciuoli, 1996; Walsh, 1991; Zentella, 1997).

Why Radical-Local Teaching in a Puerto Rican Community?
Motivations for the Intervention Project

This sketch of some of the conflict situations for Puerto Rican children in East Harlem provides a historical background from which specific objectives for the educational intervention were formulated. Our immediate reaction to these kinds of stories is that something is wrong. Children should not be embarrassed or ashamed of their neighbourhood or cultural background. They should not doubt their capabilities to learn or lose their motivation for this learning.[44] They should not be reluctant to use the language of their parents and grandparents, especially when they are capable of using this language, and this language is being used around them daily (see Reyes, 2000, p. 79, for a similar view).

We believe that the children's negative view of their neighbourhood reflects a set of historical conditions, both about the maintenance of their neighbourhood (e.g., littering, graffiti, trash collection, and painting) and cultural views about what is considered a worthwhile neighbourhood to live in. Similarly, the children's disinclination to use Spanish reflects both a historical condition (where Spanish is usually seen as a weakness or inappropriate in the dominant cultural view) and a cultural condition (where the children cannot see any purpose or value for using this language in their interactions with the teacher and parent aides in the afterschool programme).

---

44 Whether these reactions are justified or not is a complicated issue. When one attempts to make a systematic, principled argument for why these are problematical situations, one discovers the need for considerable psychological, philosophical, anthropological, and political analysis – more than we will attempt in this book. For now, we are willing to accept these informal (though common) adult reactions to these descriptions as worthy of response.

Faced with this situation – particularly the lack of cultural acknowledgment and problems of academically satisfying performance – we wanted to make an educational intervention for the children that would offer both some possibility for responding positively to these conditions, and at the same time contribute to the development of a better understanding of the theoretical and practical issues involved in constructing educational programmes for cultural minorities in urban areas. We therefore developed and implemented a year-long teaching intervention programme in an afterschool programme for a group of elementary-school children with a Puerto Rican background, living in East Harlem in New York City.

We approached the design and planning of the programme from a radical-local perspective. Given that children in the programme belonged to a primarily Puerto Rican community, the idea was to make the history of their community and Puerto Rican immigration history the focus of the afterschool programme. At the same time, to strengthen their academic proficiency, we would use this content as a way to develop a general theoretical understanding about the processes of societal development. Even though the children who participated in this project are living or going to school in East Harlem, it does not mean that they have necessarily problematized the questions of where they come from, their relation to the community, or formulated a reflected understanding of their community. We thought that it was important to help the children develop a positive and critical relation to their own background, by giving them more knowledge about the community to which they belonged. Our assumption was that as the children gained insight into the historical background of their community, and came to understand that their community had many positive features that are necessary for a good community, then they would have some resources that would contribute to the development of a positive feeling for their own cultural background, an appreciation for the possibilities of their community, as well as a more critical understanding of its problems. By working with subject matter and issues that had been problematic or uncomfortable for other children in the community, we would be able to help children to develop both conceptual tools for interpreting these conditions, and a positive conception of their ability to act in relation to those conditions, built on solid intellectual achievement and understanding.

CHAPTER 9

Organization, Content, Participants and Evaluation of the Teaching Programme

The teaching programme, whose implementation is described in this and the following four chapters, was conducted within an afterschool programme that was offered by a settlement house in East Harlem. The general programme provided a place where elementary school children could come after school each day to get a snack, have help with their homework, play games, engage in artistic projects, and more generally have adult supervision during a time when many parents are away from home because of work.

Two years prior to the start of the teaching programme described here, the El Barrio Popular Education Project had started a project that focused especially on developing literacy and mathematical abilities, in part through the use of computers and telecommunications (Chaiklin, Hedegaard, Navarro & Pedraza, 1990; Pedraza, 1989). In the year prior to the start of the teaching programme reported here, we had successfully conducted some pilot activities focused on the local community and based on principles described in Chapter 6. Having some confidence in the effectiveness of the general teaching principles, we wanted to develop a radical-local teaching programme in a principled way that would build on our theoretical knowledge about educational planning and implementation, while being relevant for the children coming to the settlement house.

The teaching programme reported here was aimed principally at developing a subject-matter based teaching (i.e., social studies) where the content of the teaching addressed topics and issues motivated by and related to the local community, including its historical and cultural conditions, within which the children lived. The programme was named 'The Young Scientist's Club'.[45] The content of the educational programme focused on three research areas/projects: the conditions of life in Puerto Rico in the early 20th century (when significant

---

45 The programme continued after the completion of the teaching experiment described here (Berté-Toomer et al., 1992-3; Pedraza & Ayala, 1996).

economic immigration first began); living conditions in New York for these immigrants; and conditions in the present community in East Harlem.

The way in which we used this content was inspired by the following radical-local considerations:

– motivation and self-respect can be created through the use of subject-matter content that has both objective meaning and personal sense for the children. Learning about one's own history acquiring knowledge of the positive aspects and potentials of one's own community, and acquiring procedures for investigating these conditions, was the medium through which we expected this could happen.
– connecting local knowledge of family and community life with subject-matter knowledge should improve the children's concept and skill development. Literacy as a skill also has a content and by working with a content that is both objective meaningful and has personal sense, we expected this would both promote literacy and motivation for school work.

Fifteen children between 8-12 years old participated in the programme. The grade level ranged from second to sixth grade. The pupils and parents had to register for participation, at which time the programme was explained briefly. From September through December the children met three days a week from 4 p.m. to 5:15 p.m. in the computer classroom at the settlement house. After December, we decided to eliminate one weekly session because the attendance was not so stable. Parents wanted the children to have time to do their homework.

The classroom had 16 Macintosh computers. The computers were seen as a tool that became subordinated to the content of the research study. The children used the computers in every session but only for the last 15 minutes to summarize their research or for solving a task either by writing or drawing.

PLANNING TEACHING SESSIONS

Each week the research group, including the teacher, met to plan the upcoming teaching sessions. The researchers and teacher used the general core model in Figure 9.1 as a tool for planning specific activities (see Chap. 6 for details about and function of core models). The plans were formulated by considering both the goals and content of teaching as well as evaluating the results of the previous teaching sessions. The idea was to follow the theoretical outline of three phases sketched previously in Chapter 6.

During the first three months the planning was guided mostly by the researchers. Each planning meeting started with a written outline that was prepared in advance. The plan included goals, concepts in focus, materials to be used, and suggestions for the children's activities. This plan was then modified based on the teacher's practical experience (which she used to evaluate potential pitfalls with the plans) and from group discussion that further clarified the substantive goals of the teaching. After three months, the plans became less and less specified before the meetings. Instead, the plans were formulated by the teacher and researchers together at the planning meetings. Our analysis of the implementation of the teaching programme shows that the children contributed a lot to formulating the content of the teaching and the teacher integrated their contributions into her instruction.

Teaching Local Social History as Theoretical Knowledge

The goal of history instruction is to help children acquire an integrated image of the central concepts of history which can become a tool for their understanding and analysis of historical and present day societies. The objectives in our experiment were to give the children an understanding of the connection between differences in living conditions, resources and social characteristics of two different historical periods and in two different locations (i.e., Puerto Rico and New York City). Furthermore, we wanted the children to understand that neither their community in particular nor society in general is always the same society, but that it has changed historically and that it will change in the future.

PROBLEM AREA INVESTIGATED

The domain of social history used in the afterschool teaching project was formulated into a research area with the following questions: What are our roots? What are the characteristics of the society we live in today? And, How do we relate to this society as a member of a Puerto Rican community? These questions focus on the living conditions in the community and how these conditions are formed in relation to the larger society of New York City of which the Puerto Rican community in East Harlem is a part. We created tasks for the children to explore these problems by examining the Puerto Rican tradition for family life and the resources found in their community for a good life.

In exploring these problems, the activities were designed to investigate the relations between family life, living conditions, resources and community.

Figure 9.1. The core model that structured the planning of tasks presented in the teaching.

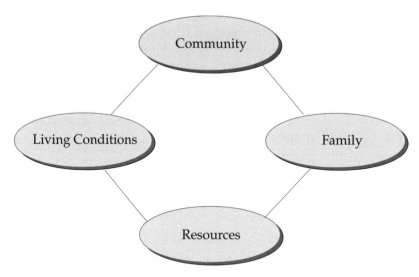

Concepts around which the Teaching Was Structured
Family life, living conditions, resources and community were chosen as the basic conceptual relations for the core model guiding the teaching.

These concepts were investigated in relation to Puerto Rico and New York City at the beginning of the 20th century and their own East Harlem community in relation to the present-day New York City. These concepts were formulated into a core model shown in Figure 9.1.

The model in Figure 9.1 was not presented directly to the children. Rather it was used as a starting point for the creation of learning tasks that required the children to explore the conditions of their community, thereby creating the possibility to formulate these relations explicitly in the classroom.

The concrete problems investigated in the learning tasks were:

1. The children's location in the world and their ancestor's location (by using maps).
2. Puerto Rico at the turn of the century before large-scale immigration to the U.S.
3. New York at the beginning of the 20th Century when Puerto Ricans started to immigrate.
4. East Harlem community today, its location and characteristics in relation to New York.

These relations were introduced through a variety of forms. For example, we used pictures of life in Puerto Rico at the turn of the century to contrast with life in New York, interviews with parents, and films. We conducted several teaching activities that investigated the relations between family life, living conditions, resources, and community to give the children content which could be helpful for them to form their own conceptual models of these relations (see Figure 9.2).

PROCEDURES

The children's investigations of the concrete problems were facilitated by the use of a general research procedure (see Figure 6.2), which they learned to use, as well as specific procedures (interviews, computer drawings, and graphs). We used the procedure (a) so that children would learn to conduct a joint investigation of a problem area, and (b) so that the daily class activities could develop the children capacities for being self-guided.

We followed two general teaching strategies to support the children's acquisition of the general research procedure. At the micro-level, each teaching session was organized to reflect the research procedure. The main elements of a teaching session were (a) a resume of the previous session's activities, (b) formulate the goal for today's activities, (c) conduct the activity, and (d) review what was accomplished and learned. At a macro-level the programme was divided into phases progressing from (1) goal formulation, (2) model formulation, where we had two distinctive sub-phases: (a) formulation and use of core relations in investigating the goals, and (b) model formulation, and (3) model use and model revision. At the beginning of each phase the teacher took more responsibility for organizing and managing the educational activities, but the children gradually took over managing the research activities as they learned the procedures and the particular core relations.

Each phase of the macro-level plan was characterized by a dominant activity. The dominant activity of the first phase was goal formation and the objective was to create a common understanding of the main goals for the whole course of teaching. This does not mean it was the only activity the children participated in at this specific phase or that goal formation was not a topic for later concern in the class activity, but it means that the other activities were subordinated to the goal formation activity. The next phase – the formulation of core relations – was seen as a first step in children's formulation and acquisition of a core model. This activity resulted in model formulation as a second step in a coherent understanding of the research area. In the third phase, this core model was used to guide the research activity, and the results of these new investigations were used to refine the model.

Figure 9.2. Overview of the phases and sessions of the teaching-learning activity.

Phase	General Content	Sessions – Main Content
Goal formation	Introduction to research activity Exploring origins	1. Formulating questions about their origins
		2. Steps in doing research
		3. Formulating research theme: living conditions, family life Viewing pictures from Puerto Rico in the old days
		4. Living conditions in Puerto Rico in the old days
		5. Exploring computer menus
		6. Location of their families in Puerto Rico
		7. Resume of goal formation activity
Model formulation: subphase 1: building core relations	Researching family life and living conditions in the early 20th century	8. Preparing interviews about living conditions and family life
		9. Interviewing Mr Fernando B. about Puerto Rico in the old days
		10. Chart making of living conditions and family life
		11. Family life in two historical periods
		12. Drawing pictures of family life and living conditions for the charts
		13. Living conditions in two historical periods
		14. Film about Puerto Rico and New York City today
		15. Living conditions and family life in Puerto Rico and New York City today
		16. Film about Puerto Rico in the early 20th century
		17. Rich and poor in different communities and time periods
		18. Objects from Puerto Rico
		19. 'Moving' people from Puerto Rico to today's New York City
	Christmas break	

Phases	General Content	Sessions – Main Content
Model formulation: subphase 2: starting model formulation	*Researching the history of their city*	20-21. Children's model making
		22. Explicating research procedure
		23. Planning museum visit
		24. Visit to New York City Museum
		25. Preparing and interviewing each other about the museum visit
		26. Interview of Mr Fernando B. about New York City around 1925
	2-week break	
Model formulation: subphase 3: model use and refinement	*Researching their community*	27. Model formulation that includes a historical dimension
	4-week break	
		28. Discussion: What a family need to be happy
		29. Locating East Harlem
		30. Preparing community research
		31. Community walk
		32. Discussing what they saw at the community walk in relation to the core relations
		33. Registration of the different types of places on the community walk
		34. Making a model of what a family need to be happy living in a community
		35. Making bar graphs to represent the types of places found on their community walk
		36. Making bar graphs of statistics for New York City and Manhattan and East Harlem
		37. Making bar graphs for different dimensions in East Harlem

Data Collection

Each session was recorded by a participant observer who wrote field notes throughout the session about what was happening. Mariane Hedegaard and Jorge Ayala were observers for the whole programme. The observers tried to write down as much as possible of the communication and physical interaction between the teacher and children and among the children. Sometimes the observers also helped the children when they saw they had problems and none of the other adults were available. Thus, both the observers and the children became acquainted with each other. By participating in the class activity, it was obvious if the children were engaged, and this engagement was also recorded in the fieldnotes. The observations were interpreted using the same procedure as described in Hedegaard (2002, Chap. 7) with a focus on the social interaction, the children's motivation, the problems, and the children's appropriation of competence.

The products of the children's work (e.g., printouts of the drawings and texts that they produced on the computer), and the models, posters, and charts that the teacher produced, were collected. To avoid creating a school-like condition that placed emphasis on individual test performance, we did not test the children individually.

Evaluating the Teaching-Learning Programme

A teaching experiment will often give positive results in relation to the existing practice that is being modified. Additional resources are usually put into such experiments, both in relation to supporting the teacher's planning and having more adults involved and present in the classroom. Both the teacher and the children are presented with information about being involved in something special and promised that an interesting activity is going to happen. Therefore it is less interesting to make a general evaluation of the effects of the teaching-learning activity. Rather it is important to analyze whether we can implement the specific techniques that are proposed, such as the use of a general research procedure, the formulation of core models, and so forth. This kind of analysis requires that we examine the specific interactions that took place in the teaching-learning situation.

At the same time, the teaching plan has formulated general goals for the acquisition of specific conceptual knowledge, together with an ability to use this conceptual knowledge in relation to local situations. Therefore, we would like to examine the characteristics of the children's learning in relation to these goals.

The results presented in the next four chapters describe the progress through four phases in the teaching-learning process (see Figure 9.2). Each chapter focuses on a single phase, starting with the goals for that phase, and an overview of the concepts introduced. Then, session for session, the teaching-learning activity is presented in a condensed, narrative description, so that it is possible to form an image of the dynamic development of the teaching programme (i.e., what tasks are given, how the children respond to them and the concepts that are introduced, and how they solve the tasks). This description is followed by an evaluation of the children's motivation for participating in those class activities (as judged by their communication and the engagement shown in relation to the given tasks), and a summary of the main teaching-learning problems that turned up.

In Chapter 14 we evaluate and discuss the material presented in Chapters 10 through 13. One theme is a discussion of the programme in general. The other theme is an evaluation of the new competences and motives that the children developed from participating in the teaching programme.

In Front of Saint Cecilia's ©Jose B. Rivera, East Harlem.

CHAPTER 10

The Goal Formation Phase

Exploring Origins: Who Are We? Where Do We Come From?

At the start of the goal formation phase the teacher made her own outline of the learning goals. She used this outline as a guideline planning her interactions with the children. Thereafter through the planned activities, the teacher and the children created common goals in a language and fashion that reflected the children's understanding. Two themes structured this phase: – (1) introduction to the research question and working as a researcher, and – (2) learning to use the computer on the problem area 'Puerto Rico in the old days'.

GOALS

The two main goals were to: (a) help the children understand that they were to have an active part in formulating and exploring the problem area, and (b) let the children together with the teacher formulate the content area as questions of research. The questions that reflected these goals were of the following kind: Where do we come from? Who are our ancestors, and how did they live? How different are the background and roots of the people (including the teachers) in this project? How is the way of life in the society we live in today? Is our way of living much different from the way our ancestors have lived? How do we think a good way of life should be in our society? Can we think of a good life for ourselves in this society? Is there any way of working for this?

Conceptual Problem Areas

(a) Introduction of a procedure for exploring problems (i.e., to make research).

(b) General problem formulation for the whole learning sequence.

(c) Introduction of the computer as a tool for making drawings and writings to be used for illustration and for solving problems.

TEACHING-LEARNING ACTIVITY

The first phase runs over 7 sessions (see Figure 9.1) The content was: (a) introduction to the research questions and to the Young Scientist Club, (b) computer training and (c) conducting interviews.

Introduction to the Research Questions and Working as a Researcher
In the *first session* the teacher formulates three questions: Who are we? Where do we come from? How did people live in Puerto Rico in the old days? In the last part of this session the teacher reads a story from a picture book about a girl in Puerto Rico, and asks the children to comment on the pictures. The session ends with each child being asked to choose a single book from a selection of picture books about Puerto Rico. The children appropriate quickly the idea that they should take the role of doing research. This appropriation was manifested in the *second session* when the teacher asked 'What are we researching?' The teacher extends the children's conception of doing research in this session by focusing on three steps: (a) who is doing the research, (b) what are they researching, and (c) how are they getting information. In the last part of the session the children draw pictures of their ideas of where their ancestors come from. Their ideas are oriented more towards the origin of humans than to life in Puerto Rico in the past. *Session three* starts with a discussion of their drawings with a focus on their ancestors. Then the children get the task to fill in a prepared sheet about 'What are we exploring?' The questions on this sheet were constructed to reveal the principles of doing research (see Figure 10.1).

Figure 10.1. What I want to explore.

Name of scientist
Gabriel

What are you going to explore?
Who I am

Who will you interview?
Grandparents

What questions can you ask?
What did they do? How what it in the old day. How children ancestor live.
How was it in the old day? What did you do for fun? What did the cars cost then?

The children are shown three pictures of childhood activities in Puerto Rico before the 1920s. One shows a child bathing outside a small wooden house. The second shows two children carrying water from a stream (see Figure 10.2). The third picture shows a child sleeping in a hammock inside a wooden house without other furniture in the room.[46] These pictures show scenes from daily life (a family eating, a street made of dirt surrounded by small wooden houses) and different types of work.

In the *fourth session* the dialogue focuses on living conditions and being poor in Puerto Rico in the old days, especially in relation to the pictures seen in the third session. Other pictures of activities from the 'old days' in Puerto Rico are discussed and hung up on the classroom wall in sessions four. The teacher writes down on a chart the children's description of living conditions in the old days. She writes:

Living conditions in Puerto Rico in the old days:
poor clothing
houses look like garbage cans
lanterns used for light
women sew by hand
working in the field

---

46 We borrowed some historical pictures from around 1920 from the Library at the Center for Puerto Rican Studies, Hunter College, City University of New York.

Figure 10.2. Archive photos from Puerto Rico in the 1920s: Children fetching water from a river, a child bathing.

Figure 10.3. Joseph's drawing of science workshop.

The children then discuss what topics a scientist can research, and are given the task of drawing a scientist at work. See Figure 10.3 for an example.

In *session five*, looking at new pictures that have been hung on the wall illustrating cigar-rolling, farming and basket-weaving, they discuss the different types of work in Puerto Rico in the old days. The discussion is followed by an introduction to the class computers and most of the session is used to explore appropriate basic options in the computer's software applications.

In the *sixth session* the teaching is still focused on creating ideas about the problem areas of research in the 'Young Scientist Club'. In this session the research activity is to find the location of known places in Puerto Rico and New York City and locate these two places on the world map. Looking at a map of Puerto Rico, the children try to locate the places where their relatives and their teacher's relatives live. Then the children are given maps of New York City where they have to locate their own homes, after which the teacher presents a world map and the children locate New York City and Puerto Rico on this map.

In the *seventh session* the main activity is to make a summary of the activities from the previous six sessions. The teacher asks the children to show the pictures they drew of their ancestors in the second session and explain how these pictures were to be used. Several of the children answered in relation to the general purpose of the learning activity. For example, Gabby said: 'We drew our picture to trace where our family comes from'. In answering this question Gabby is able to formulate the general purpose of the programme and not just the special task. The teacher then asks the children about the photos from Puerto Rico and about the location of relatives on the maps. She makes it very explicit that the point of the tasks they have worked with earlier has been to explore living conditions and family life.

Computer Training
The computers are introduced first in the fourth session. Technical problems prevented their use from the start. At this introduction the children are allowed to explore and familiarize themselves with the computer, assisted by the parent teachers, the teacher, the researchers, and each other. In the fifth session the teacher gives a short lecture about the different menus and drawing functions in the computer software. In the sixth session the children all get the same task – to draw their living place (see Figure 10.4). From that session onwards the computer is accepted as a tool for class work and not only as something to play with.

Figure 10.4. Sharome's computer drawing of living places.

Interview Technique

In the third session interviewing was introduced but it was not named as a research method.

Extract of Observation from the Third Session

The children have the sheet containing questions about doing research. The teacher initiates a discussion about the questions. The first question on the sheet is about their name. The second question is asked by the teacher: What they are going to explore?
A child answers: Who we are.
Second child: Who I am.
Teacher: Who would you like to interview? She asks them to make a selection from the sources mentioned earlier.
Some of the children's responses were: people here (rejected by the teacher), parents, and family.
Teacher: Why not grandparents or great grandparents?
Children accept and tell about their choice.
Teacher asks somebody to read the next question: What questions can you ask?
Nobody answers.
Teacher then repeats and extends: What questions can you ask, so that you can learn more about your ancestors?
Child: What did they have in the 50s? What did they do? and, What was it like in the old days?
Teacher suggests that the children ask where their parents come from and formulates the questions: Where are you from? What was it like in the old days? What kind of jobs did my grandparents have?
Teacher then tells a story about her grandfather who used to collect honey from beehives. Several children then tell about the kind of work their grandparents had.

By the sixth session the children have not yet succeeded in interviewing their grandparents. One child had asked what a chocolate bar cost in the old days.

In the seventh session, interviewing is introduced formally as a technique for obtaining information and the first exercise is to prepare written questions to be used for interviewing a family member.

The next sessions are devoted to helping the children acquire skill in interview technique.

CHILDREN'S MOTIVATION IN THE GOAL FORMATION PHASE

In the first session the children are not certain about what it means to do research about where they come from. Nonetheless they participate and contribute actively in discussing this question when the teacher reformulates it in terms of finding information. They also contribute to clarifying the concepts of society and ancestors. After some time they start to get restless. The teacher then pulls out the books she brought with her and starts to read one of them asking the children questions to clarify the content and pictures. They are still restless; it is first when they are allowed to choose a book themselves that they seem to become really interested in the book activity.

The children are interested in the question of relatives in Puerto Rico in the second session, and they become particularly eager when they start to ask the adults about their relatives in Puerto Rico. They also contribute seriously to the discussion of the three pictures with children from the old days in Puerto Rico.

The children became noisier in the third session when they still cannot get to use the computers and the task is the discussion of pictures. In the fourth session the children participate eagerly in the class dialogue about their an-cestors and several preempt the teacher by formulating questions and tasks. For example, Maria asks if they should draw their ancestors, and also when they can come to use the computers. They are motivated for using the compu-ters. Maria and Gregory do not have patience to talk about the pictures, but the teacher keeps them to the task and they become interested in the other children's descriptions and then contribute their own. The topic is about being rich or poor.

In the fifth session some of the children work in pairs at the computer, as proposed by the teacher, while others work alone and draw houses, mostly trying the different software functions. The drawing activity is not *content* motivated. The children become eager in the sixth session to find their ances-tors' home on the map of Puerto Rico, and later locating New York City on the world map. Max says directly during the summary that: 'We found out where our family lives, it is really nice to use a map'. The children are eager to draw on the computers and several try to draw the task of the day: their own living place and their family members.

In the seventh session the children are both eager to learn computer skills and to listen to the teacher. They are all eager to tell what they are drawing and to contribute to the summary in the class dialogue.

PROBLEMS

In the first session the introductory class discussion becomes too long, and the teacher's book reading is too school-like; it does not communicate to the chil-dren that they should be active in searching for information. In the end this is compensated for, however, when the children are allowed to choose their own books and to read about the country where their ancestors lived.

At the start of the second session the children expect to use the computers. Korin comments on this and Gabby asks if they can make their drawings on the computers. This expectation is understandable with all the computers in the room, but perhaps it is also stimulated by the teacher's introduction to the children about being young scientists.

The introduction of the interview activity in the third session is a little unorganized so the interviewing activity becomes mingled with the activity of discussing what a scientist does. When it comes to the drawing task the children are not clear as to whether they have to make a list of the questions to be asked at home or if they have to draw their ancestors, because both tasks have been formulated. Furthermore it is starting to become a problem that the computers are not introduced; the children expect this activity, but practical problems delay its start.

In the fourth and fifth sessions the children are disorganized in their computer work, they do not work on a specific task even though they plan to draw something about their ancestors. It is the first time, and some of the children have never tried to use computers so it is difficult to get all of them started, though some of the children who know how to use the computer demonstrate for the others.

The fifth session is very much teacher-guided, without the children being able to get an overview of what they have to work with today. The teacher formulates all the summaries and subgoals around living conditions, jobs, and climate in Puerto Rico.

By the sixth session the children had not yet asked their parents the questions they had prepared last time. The teacher comments on this by saying that they had some problems making interviews, but then goes on to reviewing the photos from last time and handing out the maps. In the map activity in the sixth session the researcher brings up the problem of what those children who do not have ancestors from Puerto Rico should work on. Gregory answers: 'You can give them sheets of paper and talk about how to do interviews'. The teacher takes up this idea and gives all the children sheets of paper on which to write what they will ask about in an interview.

The seventh session is too teacher directed; she instructs the computer lessons, makes the summaries so that the children can only give short responses, leaving little room for their personal comment or initiative.

Main Features of the Goal Formation Phase

In the first three sessions of the goal formation phase the class dialogue centred on the role of being a researcher, that the children were members of the Young Scientist Club, and that they had to work as young researchers at these meetings. This content characterized primarily the first three sessions in October, but the content of this phase became a standing theme in the following phases as well. The research questions became differentiated, however, and the capacity for research activity became more refined throughout the entire year.

In the four following sessions the teaching was still focused on identifying and formulating the problem areas for investigation. This was primarily done through discussions of pictures showing daily life and different types of work in the 'old days' in Puerto Rico, and locating on maps their family in Puerto Rico and themselves in East Harlem.

The skill of computer use was introduced in the last sessions and became a regular part of the programme which would take place in each session related to their research activity.

Interviewing was introduced as a technique for obtaining information. The next several sessions were devoted to helping the children acquire skill in interview technique.

The children liked to participate in the class dialogue. They all contributed and were engaged but did not want to talk too long about the topics. They became especially engaged in discussing the pictures from the old days in Puerto Rico and the activity of the location of relatives on the map of Puerto Rico.

The activities in this first part were centred to a very great degree around class dialogue, and to a lesser degree on activities that the children themselves had to realize, but fortunately we succeeded in changing this in the following phases.

CHAPTER 11

Researching Family Life and Living Conditions in Early 20th Century Puerto Rico

Building Core Relations and Appropriating Research Procedures

Entering the phase of building core relations and appropriating research procedures the children have some ideas and images about what the general research theme is. These images or ideas are the basis for research activity during this phase. The main activities were: (1) interviews about Puerto Rico in the old days; (2) conceptualizing the relation between living conditions and family life from a historical perspective; (3) conceptualizing subcategories of this relation – being rich or poor – from a historical perspective and a societal perspective (being rich or poor in Puerto Rico in the old days and in New York today), (4) objects from the old days in Puerto Rico; and (5) explication of the conceptual relation: living conditions–family life.

GOALS FOR THE CORE RELATIONS PHASE

The main goals in this phase were:
- To give the children an idea of how to research a problem area. The first task contributing to this goal was to let the children learn to do interviews and reflect and conceptualize the results of their interviews.
- To start formulating core conceptual relations of family life and living conditions. The goal was for the children to acquire a basic understanding of the interdependence of these two aspects of life, such that a change in one aspect influences the other. In particular, the children should understand that social and material conditions influence family size, family relations

and family traditions, while family size and structure can influence social and material conditions. This first relation was extended in the last part of this phase to include the aspect of work.

Conceptual Problem Areas

The conceptual tasks are:

(a) to differentiate the core relation, living conditions–family life, into the categories shown in Figure 11.1, and

(b) differentiate types of society and relate them to family life.

Two types of society:
The simple commodity-producing society in which the whole family helps to work and directly produce the products for living.

The complex commodity-producing society in which there is a division between production and consumption so that the producers do not consume but exchange their products for money, and only one or both parents provide the means for living, whereas the children typically do not contribute.

Figure 11.1. Core relations between living conditions and family life.

Living conditions	Family life
Material conditions – Things available in daily life – Poor-rich material life – Food traditions	Division of work – Quality of family life in different kinds of families
Social life – Traditions in the community	Power relations – Who decides in the family about what

Interviewing about Puerto Rico in the Old Days

TEACHING-LEARNING ACTIVITY

The *eighth session* begins with the children spontaneously mentioning that they had 'interviewed' their family members, but the questions were still about relative prices: how much a chocolate bar or a shirt cost in the old days. The teacher then asks what task they are doing on the computer. A child tells that they are drawing how we live and how they live (people in the old days). Then the teacher introduces the two categories: family and living conditions, and asks the children to define them. The day's task: the practice of interviewing.

The teacher demonstrates how to interview by interviewing one of the parent helpers about her family and living conditions. The teacher points out that the general topic of the interview has to be living family and living conditions, and that she has formulated a question about each: Who lives in your house? How much free time do you have?

The children are given prepared questions on a sheet of paper and grouped in pairs so they can take turns interviewing each other in the way the teacher had just demonstrated. One child in the pair interviews about family and the other about living conditions. The children are deeply engaged and concentrated while doing these interviews (see Figure 11.2).

In next session the children are supposed to interview a guest who has lived both in Puerto Rico in the old days and now lives in New York City. The children are given the task of writing as many questions as they can about living conditions and family in the old days in Puerto Rico. These questions will be used in the interview. Each child writes his or her questions either on a sheet of paper or on the computer.

In the *ninth session* the children concentrate on interviewing Mr Fernando B. about the old days in Puerto Rico. The children are asked to take turns in asking one of the questions they prepared the previous day. The teacher had printed each child's question and glued them onto a sheet with the heading 'Family' and another with the heading 'Living Conditions', so it was easy for the children to orient themselves in the questioning process. They are supposed to take notes, but only one boy really succeeds (see Figure 11.3).

Extract from Observation of the Ninth Session
Our guest Fernando arrives. He is 89 years old. He speaks Spanish so Pedro[47] has to translate the whole session. He is a very lively man and starts to talk at once. He tells that he comes from a town, Salinas, in Puerto Rico.
Pedro tries to find it on the map.
Fernando tells that he was born in 1900 and he came to New York City in 1925. All the children are sitting ready with their questions.
Pedro invites the children to ask their questions.
Max: What did you do when you were young?

---

47 One of the researchers.

Figure 11.2. The question sheets.

Interview about family Carlos

1. Who does the cooking?
his mother Ms Green

2. Who cleans the table after each meal?
his mother

3. Who does the food shopping?
his mother

4. What's your family's favorite meal?
rice and beans

5. Who cares for the children?
his mother

By Bebe

Interview about living conditions Sascha

1. What type of building do you live?
She lives in a building, the color is dark red, a lot of staris cases
and two elevator.

2. What electric appliances are there in your house?
She has four T.V, five radio, the tossters, a mixer and a blander,
the iron.

3. Where does the heat come from in your house?
The heat come from, the stem, and oven.

4. How do you get fire on your stove?
She gets fire on your stove maches and pilets

By Madelin

Figure 11.3. Max's question sheet and records of answers.

My interview questions

1 - What did you do when you were young?
2 - What was the weather over there?
3 - Do you have a son?
4 - What kind of building?
5 - Who pays the rent?
6 - Who lives in your house?
7 - What is your house made of?
8 - Who cooks in your house?

Answers*

1. He went to school unto 4 grade because his family was poor, and had no shoes, so he had to work at 9 years old.

2. He was't born but he noes that there was one that broke buiding, And there was a earthquake in 1917 that broke building.

3. He din't need to pay the rent because they work for him.

4. His mother, his father, and sisters, and his brother.

5. His mother use to cook.

6. He had a leaves [palm leaves] and wooden building.

7. It was always hot.

8. He is 89 years old.

* The childreen took turns presenting their questions so the answers Max wrote down are not directly related to his questions.

Fernando tells that he went to school until the fourth grade, when he was 10 years old, but as he did not have any shoes he stopped going to school and started to work.

Gabby: Who lived with you when you were young?

He tells about his family.

Tyhem: What were the houses you lived in like?

Fernando tells that he lived in a sort of Indian house. The walls were wooden, the roofs were straw. They didn't have any water in the house. They had to go to the river to get water. It was the woman's job to go to the river. In order to take a bath they had to go to the river too. The women also washed clothes in the river.

The observer tries to signal to Pedro that the children should ask their questions.

Fernando goes on to tell that they used lanterns for light. He used to live in the country. In the town they had lanterns in the street and a man had to go and light all the lanterns when it became dark. The same man also cleaned the streets.

Tyhem gets his turn and asks how much the rent was. He concentrates very hard on reading his questions, supported by the teacher (just like the other children were).

Fernando: They didn't have to pay rent. They worked for the landowner and for their work they were allowed to live on the land and they also got some money for their work.

Tyhem writes the answers down supported by the teacher. Some of the other children write as well (at least Max tries to write down all the answers too).

Efrain tries to gain attention so that he can ask his question, but Fernando continues his story.

He tells that they had land on which they grew crops, and had animals. The landowner paid them two dollars a week for their work.

Efrain: Did they have cars?

Fernando tells about the cars they had in those days (though his family did not have any). He mentions the problem of starting them with a crank and the noise they made.

Ishanty: Who went shopping?

Fernando: The father went shopping. On Saturdays he would get his horse and put a basket and a saddle on his horse and go to town to buy what they needed. It was not so much because they grew food on the land itself and had animals.

Somebody asks what he could buy for two dollars.

Fernando tells that they could buy the things that they could not raise themselves (e.g., codfish).

At the *tenth session* some guests from Puerto Rico attended the class. The children and teacher talk about the interview with Mr Fernando B. The teacher made a chart of the answers (see Figure 11.4). To demonstrate for the guests they all used their questions from yesterday to interview the teacher and the parent helpers about living conditions and family. The computer task was to write the answers on the computer.

Figure 11.4. Chart developed by the teacher and children to summarize the results of their interviews.

THE CONCEPTS IN THE CHART

LIVING CONDITIONS

The present		Old days
New York City		Puerto Rico
	houses	
	heating	
	electric appliance	
	water	
	production of cloth	

FAMILY

The present		Old days
New York City		Puerto Rico
	number	
	cooking	
	cleaning	
	shopping	
	cares for the children	

CHILDREN'S MOTIVATION FOR INTERVIEWING ABOUT PUERTO RICO IN THE OLD DAYS

In the eighth session the children spontaneously tell about questions they have asked at home concerning Puerto Rico in the old days. They participate in the class dialogue and all practice interviewing. Afterwards they seem eager to write questions for the interview in the next session. During the ninth session the children were concentrated on asking their questions and interested in Mr Fernando B.'s answers. In the tenth session the children liked to demonstrate for the guests their capability in interviewing and using the computers.

PROBLEMS

In the eighth session the children do not know how to report the results of their interviews with each other; Madelin is a little shy and does not want to have her interview answers shared. The teacher demonstrates with Max and Ricki's interviews how they can report their interviews. Most children can handle the writing of their questions for the interview on the computer; only two (Crystal and Ephran) have difficulties and therefore do not start to write directly, but they are helped and eventually write their own questions.

In the ninth session Mr Fernando B. starts himself to tell his story, and it is a little difficult in the beginning to get him to wait for the questions the children have prepared. After a while he succeeds in interacting around the children's questions.

The tenth session is only a repetition and demonstration of capabilities. This does not challenge the children's competences, but because a new child is attending it could be relevant.

Conceptualizing the Relation between Living Conditions and Family Life from a Historical Perspective

TEACHING-LEARNING ACTIVITY

In the *eleventh session* the children and the teachers summarize the interviews they did with the teacher and the parent helpers. The teacher writes the results on the chart of family and living conditions. The teacher then makes a new chart, presenting two different families using copies of computer drawings of a boy, a girl, a man and a woman. Each family was given its own column on the chart. One family has two children; the other has five children. The teacher told the children that the small family should symbolize the families in New York City today; the big family should symbolize the families in Puerto Rico in the old days. In the middle of the chart the teacher writes the interview questions about family so that there is room on the one side for answers about family life in the old days in Puerto Rico, and on the other side for answers about family life in New York City today. Another cardboard chart is filled out in the same way for living conditions. The teacher asks the children to remember the interview questions. As the children come up with the questions the teacher writes them down, sometimes after having suggested a reformulation.

Extract from Observation of the Eleventh Session
Teacher: I am making up families.
Isalia: A huge family.
Teacher: Yes I am putting more children in this.
Teacher continues and says that the children can discuss at the same time as she is doing this.
Teacher makes two families: one parent with two children, another with five children.
Teacher asks what a symbol is.
Gabby: It's like a flag.
Child: It's like a rule telling you something
Isalia points to the family and says this is the symbol of a family.
Teacher makes a summary and concludes that a symbol stands for something.
Teacher asks which of the two family symbols will represent Mr Fernando B.'s family and which will represent yours?
Teacher: Don't raise your hands just tell us. Korin says the big one represents Mr Fernando B.'s family, and the children talk about how many siblings he had.
Gabby tells how many he has and says that the other (family symbol) could be mine.
Teacher supports, remarking that she is pleased that he says it is like his family, because the pictures of the families are symbols.
Korin asks which one represents Pedro's family. She suggests the big one.
But Pedro says it is in the middle because they were not five siblings.
Max supports that it must be in the middle, but this is ruled out by the other children.
Teacher tells that Pedro's family was like that in the old days but, as they have learned, the size of families can change.
Teacher asks the children which side of the cardboard should represent the old days. She had put the two family types in two different rows with the interview questions in the middle.
Gabby does not think the symbol of the families can represent the old days. He says that we should draw some houses.
Teacher asks the children which period of time is covered in the interview of Mr Fernando B., and points to the result board containing his data, including the year of his birth.
Max suggests that they should draw dinosaurs as a symbol for the old days but this is ruled out by the other children.
Teacher puts the pictures of the two families on the columns and writes old and new days. Then she asks what questions were asked to Mr Fernando B. She suggests they take the ones about families first.

Max comes up with the question: What did you do when you were young?
Teacher takes it and redefines it, saying that they should just try to remember the questions.
Isalia then says: How many were in your house?
They discuss which category this question should go into, living conditions or family.
Korin says: How many ancestors did you have?
Teacher asks if she had put this question to Mr Fernando B. and gets a "no", thereby it is ruled out.
Child: What did the houses look like?
Teacher writes this down on the cardboard.
Child: What were the schools like?
Teacher: No one asked this question. Then the suggestions come: who did the shopping, who did the cooking, and T. writes it on the cardboard.
Isalia: How many families were there?
Teacher did we ask this question? Should we put it in anyhow, she is doing this and reformulates it to how many families were in the community.
The children do not know whether to put it under family life or living conditions.
Teacher says a star can be put on it, if it can be in both places. She puts it under living conditions and puts a star on it.
The children become eager and several say together now: Who pays the rent? Who takes care of the children?
A child suggests that the computer task for today is to make drawings that illustrate the answers for the old days in Puerto Rico and for today in New York. The teacher accepts this as the day's computer task.

In the *twelfth session* the opening summary concentrates on the interview questions and the illustration of the different ways families live which is supported by the children's memory of the interview with Fernando. The children go on with illustrating their ideas by making drawings on the computers about the different ways of family and living conditions in the old days in Puerto Rico and in New York City today. Thereby the two concepts become conceptualized in the two different societies.

The *thirteenth session* starts with the teacher presenting those drawings that the children made in the last session and which she had succeeded in printing out.[48] She asks the children to relate the pictures to the concepts on the chart of family and of living conditions in the old days and of today. The children take turns sharing and describing their computer-picture and they discuss in which category it should be placed on the chart. The teacher, through this class

---

48 There had been a problem with the printer the last time.

dialogue, connects to the interview with Mr Fernando B. and his description of the old days in Puerto Rico. The teacher then asks one of the pupils to read the questions asked to Mr Fernando B. about how many people lived in an apartment in the old days. They begin to guess the answers, so she asks them to try to remember what Mr Fernando B. actually told them. Shawn says they can ask Mr Fernando B. again. Then the teacher says: 'Let us do it scientifically and ask how many live in our own community'. Madelin starts to figure out how many live in their apartment building. Max joins Madelin in calculating how many people live in the apartment building where they live. They do this by calculating first the number of people on their own floor, and then multiplying this with the number of floors in the building. Several of the other children join this activity, calculating the number of people in their apartment building. The teacher stresses that a community is more than one block, so they start to discuss what a community is, with Gabby saying 'it is stuffed with people'. The teacher draws an empty box into which can be written the number of people the children have calculated to be living in their community. She then starts to assign the computer task, which is the drawing of living conditions, primarily from the old days.

CHILDREN'S MOTIVATION FOR CONCEPTUALIZING THE RELATION BETWEEN LIVING CONDITIONS AND FAMILY LIFE FROM A HISTORICAL PERSPECTIVE

In the eleventh session the children are eager and excited when contributing themes and questions to the charts of families and living conditions in both the old days and present-day society, and it seems a good way to summarize the interview with Mr Fernando B. Later, when the teacher suggests that they should use computers to write the questions – which can then be glued onto the chart – all the children, except Jaquanda, became very excited. Jaquanda writes interview questions instead.

In the twelfth session the children are really eager to contribute to the class dialogue about how people in Puerto Rico lived in the old days and how it is different from today. First the teacher writes down their answers, but because the children are so eager she realizes it is a good idea to give each of them a turn to write down the answers on the chart. The children all contribute to spelling the words that are written on the chart, to be sure they are spelt correctly.

In the thirteenth session Tyhem has to go and fetch some of the children who are still in the homework room. The teacher makes some effort to motivate the children by saying that she has several things to give them (i.e., the pictures she has printed out). The children seem motivated as soon as they start and eagerly discuss if the pictures contain aspects of living conditions in the old days. They contribute spontaneously, introducing new aspects. For example, when the teacher asks if anyone can draw a boheo (a type of hut characteristic for Puerto Rico in the early part of the 20th century) and a fireplace, Shawn fetches the picture of a boheo that he had drawn. When the teacher introduces physical conditions, Korin tells how much a candy bar cost in the old days (she has asked her grandmother). The calculation of the number of people in the apartment houses where they live is started spontaneously by Max and Madelin, and the other children join in so that it develops into a shared activity. Later it looks as though Madelin is not that motivated, because she does not respond to the teacher's suggestions for a drawing task. She eventually draws a fireplace, a task that the teacher had proposed as a possibility during the class discussion half an hour earlier.

PROBLEMS

In the eleventh session the children who did not attend the last time are mo-tivated to discuss the interview they held with Mr Fernando B. Max asks if they can discuss this, but the teacher has forgotten the sheet with the children's interview results. She solves the problem by making the children practice interviewing, using the questions they made. They interview the teacher and the two parent helpers and use the answers to make a chart about living con-ditions and family life, which also initiates a discussion of the interview with Mr Fernando B.

   In the twelfth session some of the children have problems drawing the topics they discussed and often do not have enough confidence to complete the task. Sometimes they erased what they had started. (e.g., Carlos, Madelin).

   The missing problem formulation at the beginning of the thirteenth session is a recurrent problem. Another problem this time is that the teacher suddenly starts to characterize living conditions as physical conditions, without really introducing this concept or distinguishing between the two. Buildings and community are characterized as physical conditions.

Being Rich or Poor – from a Historical and a Societal Perspective

TEACHING-LEARNING ACTIVITY

In the *fourteenth session* the children are introduced to the MacPaint computer programme. Most of the session is occupied by a film about a 13 year old Puerto Rican boy living in New York City which shows his daily life and his visit to

Puerto Rico. The teacher points out the differences in the physical conditions of the two places in the film.

In the *fifteenth session* they talk about the film, which they had seen about the Puerto Rican boy living in New York City. They talk about his living conditions in New York City: that there were drug dealers in the basement where he lived, and what he wanted to be when he grew up. They talk about his family, and that they spoke Spanish. The teacher makes a chart of the physical characteristics and writes 'New York City' and 'Puerto Rico' as column categories. She writes 'concrete' for New York City, as opposed to 'green grass' for Puerto Rico. Max wants to go back to the chart about living conditions and to add something to this. The teacher accepts this, and instead of talking about physical characteristics they work on the chart with living conditions. Katharina mentions that people are poor in Puerto Rico but that there are homeless people in New York City. Max joins in saying it is easier to get a job here (in New York City), and Gabby says people work as slaves over there. The teacher asks each child to contribute with something from the film. When they talk about the boy who goes back to Puerto Rico, Gabby repeats that they can get jobs here and do not need to work as slaves. As an example of work, Shawn mentions that the Jamaicans sell things on the street (cheap jewels, and they ask for quarters). This comment turns the focus of the children's discussion onto negative characteristics of New York City connected to crime, homelessness and traffic jams.

Sixteenth session: The teacher starts to talk about Christmas in Puerto Rico, but leaves the topic after a very short period and asks: 'Why are we looking at the film?' Some answer 'We are learning about Puerto Rico and what they do there'. The teacher corrects and says: 'It is because we are scientists and are doing research about family and living conditions'. She points to these two categories on the chart. She points to what is missing and asks what still needs to be filled in under 'New York City today' and 'Puerto Rico in the old days'. Then, with reference to the categories still open on the chart, the children start discussing what they know about the respective characteristics of living conditions and family life in Puerto Rico and New York City.

The next activity is an old black and white movie made in the 1940s about a farmer in Puerto Rico who is working for a patron. It is a fictional movie in Spanish and Pedro has to translate the main points into English. He introduces the movie and tells that it is a film about living in Puerto Rico 50 years ago and that the children should pay special attention to living conditions and family life. During the movie there are many comments from the children, and the teacher and Pedro clarify aspects of the movie that the children do not understand. The children notice that the whole family is working in the field and that there are no radios or TV, but that there is a man playing a guitar. They comment that there is

Figure 11.5. Nancy's conceptualizing of an event in the film.

This boy went to get water.   by Nancy Bonet
He went to the lake and carried
the water in a can.

He gave the water to his mother and she could wash the
clothes. She washed the clothes by hand and outside.

no electricity and ask how they get light in the boheo. The children also mention
that the tobacco in the field belongs to the patron but that the 'protagonist' does
all the work. Afterwards the children comment that the children in the film have
to work in the fields and carry water for their mother and that they do not have
shoes. Korin mentions that they harvest and that the children ask their mother
and father to dance with them. The children are given the task of drawing the
family's living conditions on the computer (see Figure 11.5).

In the *seventeenth* session the teacher starts by asking the children to tell some
of the things they saw in the movie and then make a list of the characteristics
of living conditions. From the beginning the children compare the two families
and call them the rich and the poor family. They start by characterizing the
differences in their houses and then they describe the characteristics of tobacco
crops. Following that the money aspect appears when they say that the rich man
receives money for his work, while the poor man does not. Then Korin mentions
that everyone in the poor family worked, that the children also worked and that
they needed shoes and clothes, but that the rich family had everything. Carlos
points out that the radio used batteries. The teacher recapitulates twice what
the children have described about living conditions, the second time recapitu-
lating the children's descriptions more broadly. She uses the headings: clothes,
electricity, farms, work, transportation and entertainment as categories. Then
she contrasts the rich and poor people, where the poor people worked on farms

Figure 11.6. Rafael's conceptualizing of a building in the old days in Puerto Rico and nowadays in New York City.

owned by the rich people. The children discuss the differences between the rich and poor. Some mention that it is not fair, but Sascha says they have different experiences and another child comments that we all have different experiences and it influences the way we think. Gabby makes a comparison between the rich people today and the rich people in the old days in Puerto Rico and says they are all alike because they all have 'a lot of stuff'. They do not use their hands to wash clothes and they use money to buy things. The teacher stresses this comparison and furthermore points out that in the past the rich did not work, but now everyone works for money. Somebody says that the rich give money to the poor; Korin says that they should all share.

They draw pictures for the charts. Carlos draws two houses one for the rich and one for the poor family. Rafael draws a building for present days and one from the old days (see Figure 11.6).

THE CHILDREN'S MOTIVATION FOR ANALYSING BEING RICH OR POOR – FROM A HISTORICAL AND A SOCIETAL PERSPECTIVE

In the fourteenth session the children did not run into the classroom, but the new activity of seeing a film and discussing the living conditions became engaging and they were eager to write and draw something that reflected the physical conditions they saw in the movie.

In the fifteenth session Max asks spontaneously to use the categories for living conditions, so the children finish the chart on this theme before moving on to a new dimension. All the children contribute to this and are excited, with the exception of Jaquanda. They eagerly follow the teacher as she writes down their answers about living conditions. When they begin to talk about work they almost throw themselves across the table to see her writing, but the teacher asks them to return to their chairs and sit down. The teacher tries to keep order in the class, saying that they are too excited and must slow down so that she has a chance to write their suggestions on the chart. She solves this by taking a round where each child can make a suggestion. But this is not working so well. Katharina says she does not know what they are talking about and that she does not want to make suggestions when everybody is looking at her, Katharina then whispers and Gabby repeats her comments loudly. Jerome does not want to say anything, but the rest contribute. The children become restless after the round, perhaps it took too long, so when they should formulate their computer task not all of them manage to get one formulated. This resulted in the task being less focused and concentrated. Gabby spontaneously tries to stop the noise, and Carlos points out that he will draw something for the chart of living conditions.

In the sixteenth session the children press the teacher to see the movie when she proposes to postpone it. After seeing the movie they have many comments and are eager to discuss the different aspects of living conditions. In the seventeenth session the children also show great eagerness in describing the characteristics of the living conditions they saw in the film about life in Puerto Rico in the old days. Several are quite indignant about the differences in the living conditions of rich and poor. Korin complains that this is not fair. Carlos jokes about it by saying it is fair but quickly adds that it is not fair. He then says that the poor people cannot buy the same things as the rich ones. The children are interested in using the computers to draw the differences they have been discussing.

PROBLEMS

In the fourteenth session the children do not get a general introduction to how living conditions and family life relate to the task they work on. The concept of 'physical conditions' is still not stressed as being different from living conditions.

In the fifteenth session the teacher becomes disquieted about the children's eagerness, and is irritated that they are not sitting in their place. They speak loudly, and in their eagerness interrupt each other. The teacher's way of solving the problem is to take a question round asking each child to make a suggestion, but because the children have to wait their turn it did not work out that well as they became shy or bored.

In the sixteenth session the teacher draws explicit attention to the teaching objective and the children keep in mind the categories in their answers. But the role play that they are working as scientists is not commented on or used by the children.

In the seventeenth session the teacher starts by asking the children to write a list of the characteristics of the 'physical conditions' for the people in the film, but she then forgets about this task and never gets back to it after the discussion of the characteristics of the 'living conditions' applying in Puerto Rico in the old days, as shown in the film. Another problem is that money and work were not differentiated but mingled in the teacher's recapitulation of the living conditions for rich and poor.

Objects from the Old Days in Puerto Rico

TEACHING-LEARNING ACTIVITY

Eighteenth session: One of the parent helpers has brought a lot of things from Puerto Rico: a kerosene lantern, a shell for eating, about ten different ceramic versions of the small frog typical for Puerto Rico (coqui), a coconut cup, a monkey for taking money, a donkey before a cart. The teacher decides that each child can, in turn, take an object and ask the parent helper to tell about it. Ephran comments on the different objects several times (the monkey and the donkey) and is really eager to have his turn. The teacher starts to ask questions about what the cup is used for, and explains the most common food, plantains. Then the teacher and parent helper start to talk about spices. Jaquanda comments about this, saying it is like they cook all day. One of the parent helper's small frogs disappears and everybody starts to look for it, but without success. The teacher then wants to formulate the task for the computer, but the children in their eagerness run to the computers before they have been given a task. Although this activity was not very organized in the beginning, the children ended up focusing on the theme they had worked with before, i.e. living conditions in the old days in Puerto Rico.

THE CHILDREN'S MOTIVATION FOR THE HANDS ON ACTIVITY

The children show great eagerness about being allowed to pick up an object, but are not good at asking questions about these things. Even though the teacher criticizes what some of the children are doing, they continue to work on drawing pictures from the old days. Jerome has drawn a picture of somebody paying rent in the old days. The teacher tells him they did not pay rent then, but Jerome had not participated when Mr Fernando B. told the children about the old days in Puerto Rico. Jerome, Katharina, Nancy, Jenny and Korin make relevant pictures for the chart about living conditions in Puerto Rico in the old days.

PROBLEMS

It is a problem that this activity with objects from the old days in Puerto Rico – which in itself is a relevant activity – was not connected to the general research question. Another problem was that the teacher had difficulty in delegating her authority, which meant that the parent helper was not given sufficient opportunities to answer the children's questions.

Explicating the Conceptual Relation: Living Conditions – Family Life

TEACHING-LEARNING ACTIVITY

The *nineteenth session,* the last session before Christmas, starts with the children gluing the pictures that they have drawn on the computer onto the chart of family and living conditions in New York today and in Puerto Rico in the old days. In collaboration with the children the teacher starts to identify what topics they have already covered in their drawings. Then the teacher asks the children to name the jobs they know of in present-day New York City. The central question of the day's discussion is 'What would happen if the families from the old days came to live here in New York City?'. The children all respond that it would not be a good idea. Sascha says: 'They will have problems'. Madelin adds: 'They won't know what is going on; they will have to use electricity and will not know how to use it.' Carlos says: 'They will be laughed at when they go shopping because of their clothes.' Rafael comments that it would be a problem that they have no shoes, because it can snow in New York City. Joseph thinks they will be confused, and Rafael is afraid that an accident could happen. Gabby utters that 'they will be called *nerdo*'. The session ends with the children using the computers to finish their pictures about living conditions and family life, so they can be glued onto the charts.

MOTIVATION FOR ANALYSING THE RELATION BETWEEN FAMILY LIFE AND LIVING CONDITIONS

There is some tension at the beginning, but all the children contribute to the discussion when the question is raised about moving a family from 'old day' Puerto Rico to present day New York City. They go eagerly to the computer to draw and write something about the old days in Puerto Rico, so the chart can be finished.

PROBLEMS

The children seem to be tired of the class discussion where they again should summarize the characteristics of life in 'old-day' Puerto Rico. Perhaps there has been too much repetition, but their interest is re-awakened when the question of moving people from Puerto Rico in the old days to New York City today is brought up.

Main Features of the Phase of Building Core Relations and Appropriating Research Procedures

Throughout the period the children attended the sessions regularly, and were absent only when they were ill.

What characterized the sessions for the first part of this phase until Christmas was that the children became engaged in the topic 'Where do we come from', Puerto Rico in the old days, and also in the procedure of doing interviews. The computer became an important tool, which they used in the last part of the session, either to write interview questions or to draw the results of the day's investigations.

The interview activity with Mr Fernando B. seemed to be very motivating for the children. They became competent at formulating questions, asking and waiting for answers, and conceptualizing the results.

The children were excited and very eager to contribute when they conceptualized the interview questions into the charts about family life and living conditions. The relation between living conditions and family life became a topic they could work with and discuss. The children became able to use the concepts they had differentiated, making the charts of living conditions and family life when they analyzed the two films. They talked about and confronted the theme of being rich or poor under different historical conditions, and they also discussed their images of how it would be for a poor family from 'old-day' Puerto Rico to come to New York City today.

The activity with objects from Puerto Rico should have initiated a discussion about aspects of Puerto Rican life. But the activities these objects were connected to did not become related to the central concepts of family life and living conditions. Therefore this activity became a little loose and did not become so useful in illustrating Puerto Rican life.

During the last session before Christmas the children became tired of summarizing living conditions and family life and it was obvious that they were ready to move on to the next phase of teaching and learning. However, this change was a task that was not so easy for the teacher and researchers to accomplish, as can be seen in the next chapter. Research procedure and modelling were the themes to be worked with in the next phase.

CHAPTER 12

Researching the History of their City and Starting Model Formulation

With the introduction of this theme the teaching is still within the second phase, where the focus is on helping the children to formulate the basic conceptual relations of the core model. The basic conceptual relations are still family life and living conditions, but now they become related to community. The concepts of community and work had appeared already in their discussions in the last sessions before Christmas about family life and living conditions in different communities (Puerto Rico and New York City). After the Christmas holidays the activities were aimed at developing the children's research competence and to make them use what they already knew about family life, living conditions, community and work when formulating a model of their research activity. The idea was that they should be able to conceptualize their research area as a whole and start to make models, even though we did not yet expect them to formulate clear conceptual models. The research area now became New York and the children's own community. We planned the following three activities related to their local community.

The first activity was to draw a model of what they knew about their community in relation to the core concepts. If the children could not describe relationships between communities, family life and/or living conditions, then it was all right if they just started by making a list that characterized the life in their community. The teacher's task was to ask the students about the relationship between family life and living conditions in their own community, as a step in relating these three concepts into a conceptual model. The second activity was related to the historical aspects of their community, which should help the children to understand that what they find in their community today had not always existed this way. The third activity involved the children in doing research about their community in order to gain inspiration for extending their first modelling attempt.

The expectation was that after the children had started to work on building their models, certain issues, questions and topics would undoubtedly come up which they would like to know about, and these could be the basis for forming the questions they want to investigate.

GOALS FOR THE RESEARCH AND MODEL FORMATION PERIOD

– The first goal for this period was to get the children to formulate topics that they would like to investigate about life in their community, in terms of the basic relations: family life – living conditions – work.
– The second goal was that the children should acquire an ability to use the six-step research procedure (see Figure 9.2) as a tool for exploring and analyzing a problem area.

Conceptual Problem Areas
1. Making a model of their community

2. Investigating the history of their community by:
   a. Formulating questions about New York City from the perspective of the questions of their previous explorations: 'Who are we, where do we come from?'
   b. Formulate questions about living conditions, family life and work, and interview an elderly citizen who was among the first Puerto Rican emigrants to New York City, about his meeting with the city.
   c. Trip to the Museum of the City of New York and conceptualizing what they saw along the lines of the concepts in the basic relations.

Using the Basic Relation for Modelling their Neighbourhood

TEACHING-LEARNING ACTIVITY

In the *twentieth session* and continuing into the *twenty-first*, the children are given the task of drawing a model of their own neighbourhood, using the computer, which shows what is characteristic for the area. Bebe's model includes several themes (see Figure 12.1). In the picture one can see dwellings, a park, and a man mailing a letter, a subway, a school, and Bebe's home.

Figure 12.1. Bebe's neighbourhood model.

For the *twenty-second* session the teacher brought six cartoons along, each with one of the questions from the research procedure (see Figure 12.2). She hangs them up on a string.

The children take turns reading the questions on the cartoons. The teacher wants the children to share their models of their neighbourhood. Madelin and Sascha are a little reluctant to show their model. Christel cannot find hers but Sascha finds it for her. When it is Gabby's turn, the teacher is a little cross because he only points at objects in his model, saying 'houses, trees, streets' (see Figure 12.3). The teacher explains to Gabby that it is not 'researching' our neighbourhood by merely pointing at things. She then addresses all the children and asks what they will research in their neighbourhood. She writes their suggestions

Figure 12.2. Teacher's drawings of the research procedure.

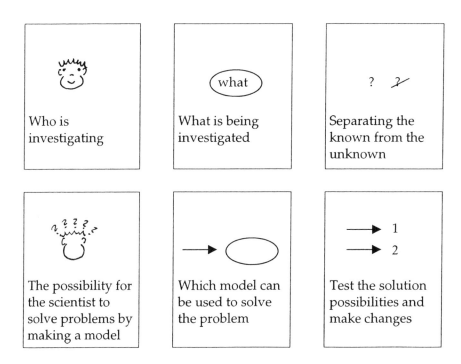

down as they mention them. Korin says she wants to find out about people on drugs. The other children follow up on this.

Extract from Observation of the Twenty-Second Session
The teacher asks what they will investigate and is prepared to write the children's answers on a piece of paper.
Korin says she wants to find out about people on drugs.
The teacher asks if it is enough to say that only New York City is being investigated.
The teacher asks if drugs can be related to crime.
Madelin mentions that drug people drive cars and smoke.
The teacher points out again that they should be looking at their own community.
The children do not agree with Madelin's description.
Teacher: This is fine because not all researchers agree.
Teacher: What could we do to explore this?
Sascha suggests asking people questions.
Gabby says it is interviewing.
Teacher: What can we do otherwise?

Figure 12.3. Gabby's neighbourhood model.

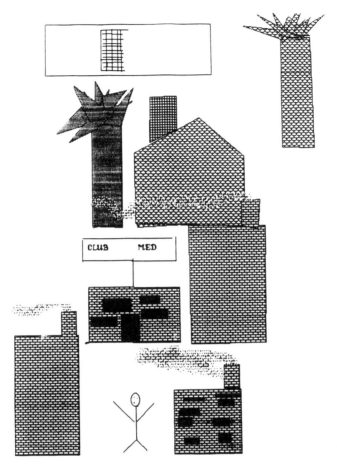

Gabby: Investigate.

The teacher tries to get the children to formulate their view on what they will investigate.

Somebody says that there are no drug people in Long Island. Not all agree with that, however. They then formulate that they can take a trip and look.

Teacher: How can we get proof?

Cristel: Some drug people are crazy. We can go and look if there are any needles on the ground [in the yards].

MOTIVATION

In the twenty-first session, the children, especially Korin, were eager to show and explain their drawings of their neighbourhoods, and several children 'shared' their drawing. Later at the computers, however, the mood began to change and there was very little enthusiasm for drawing. The computer task was not explicated, so several children were just sitting without doing anything.

In the twenty-second session, there was no enthusiasm in sharing the drawings of their community. The teacher got upset about that, so the modelling of the community was put aside for several weeks. Enthusiasm returned in the January session, when they started to discuss what and how they could research in their neighbourhood. But it is difficult to know if it was the topic discussed – drugs – or if it was the activity of doing research that made the children eager in this discussion.

PROBLEMS

The tasks the children worked on the computers with in January were not very clear to them, so those who were drawing, actually drew buildings they *thought* belonged in a community. The children were not clear about what the model should conceptualize. Instead they should have been asked explicitly to make a model about living conditions – family life – community, because these were the concepts the children had been working with in the previous sessions.

In the twenty-second session, the teacher becomes angry. She does not understand that the instructions given to the children have not been clear enough. Although the task did not become better explicated in this session, Gabby ended up making a model of living conditions comparing old and new days, reflecting the themes of the conceptual categories the children had worked on during several sessions. This model is a relational model of key concepts for a community model and is the first step in making core models (see Figure 12.4).

Another problem, connected to the problem of modelling the community, was that the children did not get much guidance to conceptualize to do research about their community. Their research into the topic of drug users was indeed the opposite of what we wanted, as this subject could not give the children a positive basis for identification with their community. But the discussion about this problem showed that the research procedure started to become conceptualized. The children formulated that by doing interviews, making observations at special places and using the news, they could find out about drug use.

Figure 12.4. Gabby's model of living conditions.

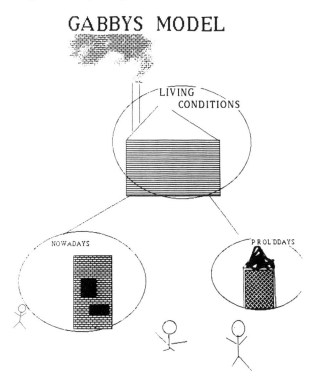

Researching the History of their Community

Teaching-Learning Activity

The *twenty-third* and the *twenty-fourth sessions* have the theme 'The historical change of the city and the community we live in'. The twenty-third session is devoted to planning a trip to the New York City Museum, which is located in the neighbourhood. The trip took place the following day. The children and adults walk to the museum where they see a film about the development of New York City from the first settlers in the 1640s through to the 1950s. The film was shown in a room featuring different model buildings from New York City in 1925. Afterwards the children visited the other rooms in the museum, one of which contained dolls houses. At the following session, *the twenty-fifth*, they discuss the visit. First they have a class dialogue about what they saw at the museum and then the teacher instructs them to work in pairs, interviewing each other about what they saw and then writing down their answers on a sheet of paper (see Figure 12.5).

The next activity is to prepare questions for a new interview with Mr Fernando B., the elderly man whom the children interviewed previously about the old days in Puerto Rico. This time they plan to interview him about the old days in New York City. The teacher stresses that the questions [and answers] should help in gaining an understanding of the transportation, hospitals and other places in New York City at the time when Mr Fernando B. arrived in 1925. Carlos proposed questions about black and white people at that time, and Gabby formulated this suggestion into a question, which asked if there were any black people in New York City in 1925. The questions were to be computer written. Carlos said he had many questions to write. All the children concentrated on writing questions (see Figure 12.6).

In the *twenty-sixth session* the children continue to prepare interview questions for half an hour before the arrival of Mr Fernando B. The children ask him questions about living conditions and family. By using their questions they obtain information about how he lived when he first immigrated into New York City.

Figure 12.5. Examples of the children's interview questions to each other about the museum visit.

1. What did you like about the museum?
She liked the houses [models of houses], the movie, and the toys.

2. What did you like the most in the museum?
The houses, the movie, and the museum.

3. What was the movie about?
What happen in the movie is, there was wars, and they were showing about the Standbair building, and they were showing about the presentent [President] of the United States of America.

Figure 12.6. Carlos' questions.

CARLOS QUESTIONS

1 – Were you born when the black could not be with the white?

2 – How were school in the old time?

3 – Did you like the old times?

4 – Was you in wars?

5 – Did you work hard?

6 – Did you have friends?

7 – Was life nice in those days?

8 – Did thins cost alot in those days?

9 – Did you work hard?

10 – Did you have a job?

11 – Did people have clothes like now?

12 – Did you like the thins in those times?

13 – Did you live in a big house?

Extract from Observation of the Twenty-Sixth Session
Gabby asks what it was like in New York City when Mr Fernando B. first arrived.
Mr. Fernando B.: These first days were terrible and depressing and for about two weeks he wanted to go back. But everything got better when he found a job.
Madelin asks if he used to help his mother
Mr. Fernando B.: Yes.
Sascha asks if he got friends.
Mr. Fernando B. differentiates between "amigos" and "conocidos", and argues that "amigos" are like brothers.
Korin: How were things when he arrived in New York City?
Mr. Fernando B. explains that by 1925 he was living in Brooklyn, in a building with no hot water, no bath inside, and no electricity, and that each floor had a common toilet that was outside the apartments.
Sascha asks: Could anybody see you.
The teacher explains that there was a little room.
Maria says like a "latrina" (some laugh).
Mr. Fernando B. continues and says that the building had no electricity. They used gas for cooking and light.

Jorge asks Mr Fernando B. about the job he had when he first came to New York City.

Mr. Fernando B. says that for two years he worked in a factory in Long Island that produced rope. He worked eight or nine hours a day for five-and-a-half days per week, and was paid $16 per week. After this job he worked at a refinery for four years until it closed. He then worked alone, painting and repairing things for 12 years. Later, until his retirement, he worked for St. Lucas Hospital.

MOTIVATION

During and after the visit to the City Museum and in the following session, the children were eager to talk about what they had seen at the museum. Everyone felt it had been a great day. The children were filled with expectation and joy over the movie, the dolls houses, and the other things they had seen at the museum. The children liked interviewing, both interviewing each other after the museum visit and interviewing Mr Fernando B. about the old days in New York City. While they were eager to go into teamwork in interviewing each other about the museum trip, they did not succeed in taking turns in preparing and answering the questions.

PROBLEMS

The children had trouble in the classroom preparing the interview questions about the museum trip. It was difficult for the children to understand at first that two of them should work together as a pair in preparing questions, while another pair should answer the questions: one pair constructs the questions, another pair answers them. However, after the teacher explained the procedure again, Gabby and Korin succeeded in formulating some questions and later allowing others to answer. Sascha, on the other hand, still wanted to produce and answer her own questions, even after the procedure had been explained again.

   After the interview with Mr Fernando B., he commented that the children should learn to be a little more focused in their interviews; perhaps because he had hoped to relate something that the children had not asked about.

Main Features of the Phase of Appropriating Research Strategies and Model Formulation

After Christmas (in January) the children's attendance starts to vary. There were two reasons for this: The afterschool was in the process of appointing a new director, which resulted in some general instability in our project, and illness among the researchers meant that some meetings had to be cancelled.

The children's community model making did not go well, because the modelling activity was not planned and outlined sufficiently. It was not clear to the children that the models they were to make should relate to the concepts that they had been working with, i.e. 'living conditions' and 'family life'.

Through the following research activities: Visiting the City Museum and interviewing Mr Fernando B. about work and life at the start of the century, the children gained an understanding of changes in their community on the dimension of living conditions and places of work and services, which was relevant for their further conceptualization of their community.

The children's engagement in the research activities changed the picture of attendance. The disintegration which resulted from the January sessions disappeared when they began to explore community history. Both experientially and motivationally they gained a better basis through these activities for doing the modelling, as can be seen in the next chapter. But some new activities and experiences were needed for the children to develop a model that included the conceptual content of a historical change in their community. The goal for the next phase of teaching was to formulate a conceptual model of the relations between community, living conditions, family life and work.

Fun House ©Jose B. Rivera, East Harlem.

CHAPTER 13

Community Modelling and Model Use

The teaching was moving to a new phase. The central theme for this third phase was that the children should create their own theoretical model of community which they could use to research and understand relations between living conditions, family life, work and resources in their own community. To create this model, several steps had already been taken. One was to let the children formulate their understanding of the concept of society and community which they started to discuss in the thirteenth session when they evaluated differences between peoples' living conditions now and in the old days in Puerto Rico. The concept of community had come up earlier in discussions relating community to the concepts of living conditions, family life and work. A second step had also been started in earlier teaching periods researching the history of two different communities – Puerto Rico and New York City in the old days. The third step came in this period, where they had to use these conceptual relations to make research about their own community and to make a model of the concepts they had already acquired to become able to conceptualize this research. An objective of the model construction was that the children should connect the different parts they have worked with, so as to acquire an integrated understanding of the areas they have researched: Who are we? Where do we come from? and, What is needed for a good life in our community?

The research started with the activity of locating the community in the city and in the country. This was followed by activities of differentiating the community into places for services and work, and of collecting material about these places. The third type of activity was a statistical analysis of their community and comparison with New York City and Manhattan.

Goals for the Community Modelling Phase

The goal was to use the relation the children had worked with, family life – living conditions, to form a model where this relation was extended to relations with the concepts of community, work and resources.

Conceptual Problem Areas

The relations between family life, living conditions and society were formulated into a model where resources become a separate category. This model could encompass three different types of society based on different forms of production:

(a) the simple commodity form of production: people consume the products they produce;

(b) the feudalistic form of production where the producers take part of the products needed to reproduce themselves and give the rest to a patriarch, and

(c) the capitalist form of production, where the producers do not get their products but are paid and there are legal relations between the producers and the owners of the production system.

The themes of the teaching period were: (a) to make a model of the community that could guide children in their research into their own community, (b) to work with the concept of resources, and (c) to differentiate between the two economic types of societies (Puerto Rican feudal society in the early 1900s and the New York capitalist society of today) on a historical timeline. The historical timeline was incorporated in a model of the relation between family life, living conditions, work and community.

There were two teaching pauses because of classroom renovation. The first pause was during the last two weeks of February; after that there was a single session, and then another – new – teaching break occurs because the renovations had not been finished. In the single session early in March (in the twenty-seventh session) before the second break, the children and teacher created their first model on a piece of cardboard and hung it up in the classroom. Meeting again after the second break in April, a revised model was formulated and put up in the classroom. This revision was caused by several factors, but a dominating factor was that under renovation of the classroom of the 'Young Scientist Club' their posters and cardboard material had disappeared. The second model was kept for the rest of the teaching sessions for use in class discussions.

Model Making of the Community

TEACHING-LEARNING ACTIVITY

Twenty-seventh session: There had been a break for two weeks where no teaching had taken place. But when the children and the teacher meet again, they continue as if there had been no pause and they talk about the museum visit. Important conceptual areas are covered in this session: A historical timeline and a first draft of modelling the concepts the children had worked with so far was formulated; then working places are explicated conceptually. The session starts with the teacher asking Korin and Sascha to take the role of teacher and explain what they did last time and why. Korin talks about the different types of stores and workplaces in the old days that they saw at the museum. Sascha tells about a carriage pulled by horses that she had seen at the museum, and about a sugar factory – also referring to the work Mr Fernando B. had described. The teacher asks why they have collected this information. They formulate that they wanted to investigate the old days and the present in New York City. The teacher then introduces the timeline drawing on a poster (see Figure 13.1) and asks what a timeline can help us to understand. Korin answers that a timeline can help us to understand when things have happened. The teacher draws a timeline for New York City and one for Puerto Rico. First the teacher asks the children to mention something that can be shown on the timeline for these two places. When they mention something, she wants them to ask each other where it should be placed on the timeline, and she then writes their answers on the timeline.

The teacher writes an outline for a model with five boxes and explains to the children that they are going to make a model that they can use to explain to others what they are doing. They fill out the boxes while they are talking (see Figure 13.2).

Figure 13.1. Illustration of timelines.

New York City	1900	1925	1990
		Mr. Fernando B.'s arrival	
Puerto Rico	1900	1925	1990

Figure 13.2. The model they create on the poster.

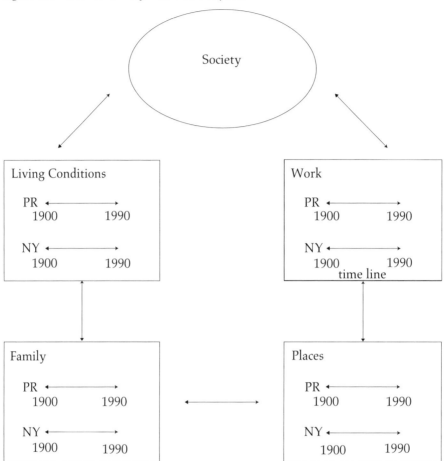

Extract from the Observation of the Twenty-Seventh Session

The teacher recapitulates that the timeline helps us to understand things, to put them in order. By way of "boxes" she shows the children an outline for a model of the relations between living conditions, work, family and places. The boxes are empty.

Teacher: How can we tell people what we are studying?

Sascha: In the old days there were rich people and poor people who worked for them. The rich made money.

Ephran: That's not fair.

The teacher comments that they are talking about the topic of work, and that they have done research about that, comparing the old days with the present day. She asks how this can be shown.

Sascha responds: A timeline.

The teacher then draws this timeline inside the boxes on the poster (see Figure 13.2). Sascha mentions that people were not as rich as today.

Teacher: When we are talking about rich and poor we are talking about the topic of living conditions.

Then the children suggest a timeline for living conditions.

The teacher also draws this timeline.

Ephran points out that from the "family" box we go over to the "work" box, and that "places" are almost "living conditions".

The teacher agrees, saying that everything is related, and draws arrows from box to box.

She asks then if family and places are related.

Sascha: Yes, because families live in places.

Korin points out that work is also at places.

The teacher argues, however, that not every place is a working place.

MOTIVATION

The children, especially Sascha, asked questions to the teacher about difficult problems. For example, Sascha asked about the timeline and then about the relation between living conditions and places. Sascha, as well as the other children, were absorbed in what they were doing. Although it was on an abstract plane, the children could discuss and give content to the concept of society.

PROBLEMS

Sascha's problem was to understand the meaning of the timeline. The teacher solved this problem by letting the children place all the things they had mentioned on the timeline. She made the children point to where they think something should be on the timeline and then she wrote it on the line. The teacher concluded for the children that the timeline helps one to organize things. A problem for some children in this session was to relate the concept of places to work and living conditions. This problem is rooted in the teacher's model, because 'work' should have been a subcategory to 'places' so that work and places were part of the same concept. This was something the teacher did not clarify enough.

Family Life, Community and Location of their Community in New York City

TEACHING-LEARNING ACTIVITY

Twenty-eighth session: The classroom was closed for four weeks because of renovation and painting. It meant that when we met with the children, there had been a break of four weeks, and for some children it had been six weeks. Also, two new children have joined the session. Because of the long break since last session, we decide not to work directly on the model building, but instead the teacher tries with the activity she introduces to connect family – living conditions – and work places as general concepts. The first activity is to let the children recall what they remember of family life and living conditions. She shows a picture of a large family with eight children, the parents are sitting on green grass with the four youngest children, while four older children are playing with a ball. There are palm trees in the background, giving a clear association to Puerto Rico. The question the teacher starts with, therefore, when showing this picture is: *What do they need to be happy?* Sascha replies: *jobs*, but then the teacher modifies the question to: *What does this family need to survive.* The children mention most of what they have written down before, but the concepts of God and love are brought up by one of the new children. Then they mention firemen, ambulance, cars, police, education, prison, and president. They actually anticipate the next activity which is connected to places for services and work in a community. The children have to write their suggestions on a piece of paper. After this the teacher spreads out the drawings of different places in a community. These drawings show: a fire department, a police station, a drug store, a bakery, a hospital, a school bus, a post office, a flower shop, a bank, a garage, terraced-houses, apartment buildings and single-family houses. The teacher starts a competition between the children and herself to see who can mention the most types of work associated with these places. In the end the children win, and then the rest of the time is spent with the children colouring the different drawings. The teacher also shows pictures of people in different types of work connected to these places.

In the *twenty-ninth* session the teacher proposes that the children should make a book about their community, and to illustrate her idea she has come with an example of how some other children have made such a book. Then each child is given a folder into which all their subsequent work – glued on special sheets with a header prepared by the teacher – should be put. Each child was first given a map of New York City where the task was to locate Manhattan, and then the children were given a map of Manhattan where they had to locate East Harlem. After locating their community on the maps, the teacher asks the children to guess the next question she is going to ask. Ishanty guesses 'where do we live'. The teacher then gives them a street map and they are given the task of locating the settlement house on the map. The teacher also asks which streets they know and makes them locate these streets. After this they discuss how far East Harlem stretches on the map and then the children have to mark the border on their map. After they finished the tasks the maps were put into their book folder. The teacher then asks what they should do on the computer, with several of the girls responding 'draw a map'. They discuss if they should draw buildings, so it ends up with the children drawing houses on a street instead of a map of a community (see Figure 13.3).

MOTIVATION

Following a resumé of previous assignments at the beginning of the session, the children participated eagerly in the class discussion. And, inspired by the pictures of a family and the different places of work and services in a community, their eagerness continues during the discussion of what a family needs. The competition made everybody excited and the children seemed to enjoy colouring the fire station, school and other work-places. They did not get to use the computers because time did not allow, but no one objected, even though they are usually very eager to use the computers.

Figure 13.3. Gabby's drawing of his street.

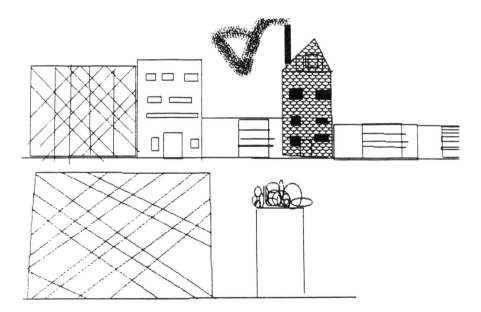

The children liked the map activity, and eagerly studied the maps, asking questions and finding places they know. Those children, who do not live in the apartment building where the afterschool is located,[49] found the location of their own street. However, Gabby was the exception in this regard as he lives in the Bronx, and there was no map of the Bronx. He repeats several times that he needs a street map of the Bronx, so he can draw the area.

PROBLEMS

The potential problem of the long break seems to have been solved with the activities the teacher presented. The teacher had a problem introducing the activity about the family. The idea was to discuss family life in relation to community and this was not done very directly in the first activity. The activity about services, work places, and types of work, was also unclear when introduced because services and families' needs were not related, but these relations became explicated more in the following sessions.

The children participated eagerly but it was not an easy task for them to draw the borders of their community on the map. With help from the adults (parent helpers, observer, and teacher) they all finished this task, and also with some help they located on the street map the building where their afterschool is situated.

Community Walk and Registration of Places: Formulating a Model for what a Family Needs Living in a Community

TEACHING-LEARNING ACTIVITY

In the *thirtieth session* the children are given the task of counting the buildings in their community and reporting the different types of work places and other institutions they find. The pictures they coloured last week have helped in preparing them to notice the different types of places. They are prepared also with a sheet of questions they are supposed to answer (see Figure 13.4).

---

49 The afterschool was located in a community centre on the first floor of an apartment building in which most of the children's families had their homes.

Figure 13.4. Question sheet.

Researching my community

Take a walking trip of your community. Make a street map of the blocks you visit ... make note of the buildings, business, parks, subways, bus routes, empty lots and anything else that is on that particular street. Record all your data by drawing your street map. Use this information to answer the following question.

1. What streets did you visit?
2. How many different businesses did you observe?
3. How many buildings did you observe where people live?
4. How many were both, a residential and a business building?
5. How many families do you think live on one of the blocks that you observed?
6. Do these families have everything they need to survive) (If the answer is no, then please write what they are missing).
7. Did you enjoy doing this kind of research where you makes visits? Why or why not?

Thirty-first session: On the day of the walk the children are split into three groups, each with an adult. Each group covers a different street next to the afterschool site. The teacher has prepared a street map so that each group can mark the different types of places, and when they return to the afterschool the groups can compare what they have seen.

In the following session (*thirty-second*) the children recapitulate first what a family needs to be happy, a discussion they had 14 days ago. They use the chart on which the teacher had written their answers from this discussion. Then the three groups that had walked together report on the places for services and work they had found. After their report the teacher asks if a family can be happy in their neighbourhood, to which Sascha gives a positive response. The teacher then asks the children where dead people are put (since this was not found on the trip), to which the children answer 'in cemeteries and funeral homes'. Then each group is asked to organize their research on a poster showing each of the streets they made reports from: Madison Ave., Park Ave. and Third Ave. The research is transformed into numerical counts of the number of houses, the number of stores, and so on. The teacher draws this into a block diagramme on a poster.

The *thirty-third session* starts with a review of the children's research concerning how many different types of places could be found in their community. Sascha mentons that they registered the different types of stores they had seen, for instance flower shops, and they counted the number of each type, because there was not enough room to register each place on the map of the streets. The teacher extends her answer by saying that they had looked at places for services, and she asks the children to name different examples. The teacher summarizes the goals of the community walk with the following formulation: 'We gathered information about our community and put it into a graph, and to do this we had collected information during our walk which was placed on the maps we had drawn'. The teacher asks why the information has been put in graph form. Manuel suggests it is because the maps were rather large, while in graph form the information can be hung on the wall and people can read it. The teacher agrees, adding that it is a tidy way to show information.

The next activity concerns the question: What did we find when we went out in the community to do research? In answering this question the children contributed verbally to the teachers drawing of a chart, which included the different findings of the three 'research groups'. The poster (Figure 13.5) was the result of this activity:

The teacher then questions what could be missing. Manuel suggests that something to make people happy is missing. The teacher asks how people could be happy if they did not have bus stops, for example. Sascha replies: 'People could build what is missing. They can get bricks and water and make the building necessary'. This led the teacher to reformulate the question into something more general about how a person or a family could acquire what they needed if it was missing in the community. Indirectly the problem of resources has

Figure 13.5. The chart about resources in the children's community.

Park Avenue	Madison Avenue	3rd Avenue
Transportation	Bus stop	TV studio
Social club	Mail box	Cleaner
Subway	Playground	Flower shop
Chinese restaurant	Parking lot	Pizza restaurant
Hair style place	Pizza shop	

been brought up in this discussion. The teacher asks: 'What if the people do not have any money'?. The children discuss the possibilities for survival. Their answers were:

- They could make things.
- They can move to another place (like Mr Fernando B. did).
- They could make things to sell (Sascha says sew and sell coats and stuff like that).
- Make a placard saying 'I need money'.
- A child remarks: 'Go to school and get a diploma'.

The teacher then asks if money is all that counts. Sascha says money was not really important, what counts is food.

The computer task is to draw the answers they brought up (See Figures 13.6, 13.7, 13.8 13.9).

In the *thirty-fourth session* the children and teacher formulate together a model of what a family needs for living in a community. The teacher brought four cartoons formed as circles. The categories – community, family, living conditions and resources/exchange – were written respectively in one circle. The teacher glued the circle with 'family' on a piece of cardboard and asked the children where she should put the other circles. The children make suggestions and help the teacher to glue them on.

Figure 13.6. Jaquanda's list of what a family needs.

WHAT PEOPLE NEED:
about their homes

They live in houes and all the things we are going to tell you about they have to cook and clean up the miss and they need air and water and fire they really need money they need clothes and we have to go shopping to feed the family and always go to cherc for god be good for the lord get a job for your home

By Jacquana

Figure 13.7. Korin's model of a family.

Figure 13.8. Sharome's model of a family.

a model of the family

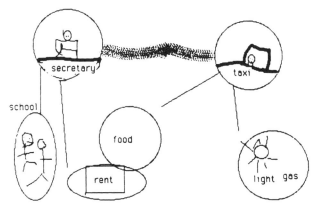

Figure 13.9. Raphael's model of what a family needs.

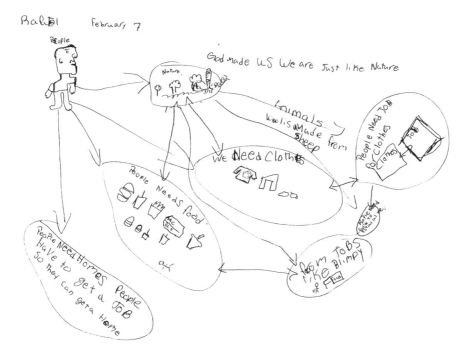

The teacher then asks what all of this depicts. Korin: 'Four aspects of the model'. In response to the teacher's request about the relation between community and family she explains: 'Families are like people. They take care of themselves. They love each other and when they get sick they take each other to the hospital'. Then she goes on and tells about 'our ancestors' in the 1950s. The teacher corrects her by saying that they had researched their ancestors from around the year 1900. The teacher writes a reformulation of Korin's explanation into the circle of the family. Korin continues, telling about living conditions at that time, and then about families in the old days. The teacher again formulates the relations by writing 'community determines living conditions' in the circle for living conditions on the poster. The teacher then asks about resources, but Korin stops here and no other child comes up with anything. The teacher suggests that they talk about resources. She points to the model they made 10 days earlier (the thirty-third session) about what a family needs, and reads aloud what they had written into this model as resources. The teacher also reminds them that they had been out researching the streets and registering places of service and work in the community. The children respond by naming the places they had registered during their community walk (i.e., family houses, stores, restaurants and so on). The teacher points again to what they have put on the model for a family to be happy (what they need to survive).

Extract from the Observation of the Thirty-Fourth Session
The teacher asks if a man comes from Puerto Rico and cannot get a job but he can make tables, how can he get what he needs.
Korin suggests the man makes the tables and gives them away.
Ishanty and Carlos say he can ask for money for his tables.
The teacher rejects the solution.
Korin: Give them to a furniture shop.
The teacher asks again how he will survive.
The children are focused and tried to solve the problem.
Teacher: All you guys are money minded. How can you get food without money?
Ishanty: Have a friend or go to the supermarket and pay it later.
Jaquanda: Yes, but what if you do not have the money later?
Carlos: You can get animals and milk them.
The teacher summarizes that they are suggesting credit, and also milking animals to survive, but then asks once again how a person can obtain food without money.
Korin tells a story and mentions "buying", but letting her father pay.
Ephran: The only way to get food is to get a job.
Korin tells about begging.

Figure 13.10. Korin's picture of exchange.

The teacher refers to Mr Fernando B. and reminds them that if he did not have any milk, he could exchange a chicken for milk. She asks if that gives any ideas.

Teacher: If you have a lot of tables.

Jaguanda: If a lot of people get a job and get money they can give other people food.

Korin tells a story about trading tapes (cassettes) for a table.

Teacher: Couldn't a man with a lot of tables trade them for a coat? The children agree. She then mentions trading bananas and other sorts of food for tables.

She reformulates the children's answers into the relation "living conditions and resources".

Later, during the computer task, Korin draws a man who exchanges a table for food (see Figure 13.10).

MOTIVATION

The children contribute in a concentrated way to make the graphs and describe the differences between the three streets they have researched. At the model-making session the children enjoyed putting the categories for the model up on the wall and Korin was really eager to tell about the model. Later they become engaged – but also frustrated – in the discussion of how to acquire resources to survive, if one does not have a job.

PROBLEMS

The teacher's intention was to start the thirty-second session with the question 'What do people need in our community to be happy?', but the children did not know how to talk about this problem. So the teacher reformulated the question to 'What do people need to survive?'. The children did not have any trouble discussing this question and after working with it they could discuss what people need to be happy. Although in the thirty-fourth session there was a drawing of a timeline for Puerto Rico and New York City in the classroom, as well as a chart with Mr Fernando B.'s data indicating that he came to New York City in 1925, we can see that Korin did not really know the time period they were researching. For her the 'old days' were the 1950s. The children not only had difficulty in understanding 'resources' as anything but money, but also in formulating something other than money as necessary for survival. The problem is whether the children actually gained a good understanding of resources from the discussion of how to survive without getting a job.

Statistics about Resources in their Community

TEACHING-LEARNING ACTIVITY

Thirty-fifth session: The teacher asks Korin again to explain what the activity is about. Korin explains the model on the wall and says it is a model about what a family needs to survive. The teacher asks why charts have been made of three avenues. Gabby informs it is because they are doing research about the community. The children take turns explaining the meaning of the bars on the graphs, which are on the poster they had made earlier (in the thirty-second session). After this they have to make a graph covering the three avenues so they can directly compare which avenue has the highest number – and which has the lowest number – of different services and place types. They work in groups to make these graphs. They then take turns counting and describing which avenue has the highest number within the different categories.

Thirty-sixth session: The teacher presents statistics for New York City, Manhattan, and East Harlem so the children can make bar graphs. The categories are: population, households, high schools, income and employment.

The teacher uses some numbers for Manhattan for the class activity in which she draws bar graphs explaining the categories to the children. She wants the children to make the statistical material for their own community; therefore the children are given the task of writing down some questions to ask their parents. Working on the computer, they all copy these questions:

- How many families go to this centre?
- How many of these have a high school diploma?
- How much do these families earn?
- How many people work?

Thirty-seventh session: The teacher brings some statistics about Manhattan and New York City with her. She starts to repeat the categories she used last time and asks what each one means. 'Population', Sascha says, means people, while 'total households' means families. Then income, employment, and education, are mentioned. The teacher repeats that the chart tells us about the number of people in our community, in Manhattan and in New York City.

The task is now to make some graphs for East Harlem. The teacher has prepared graphs where each unit corresponds to 1000. The teacher draws while the children read the number of different categories. The next activity is to record the numbers the children have brought from home, but only a few children have done this task.

The teacher then says 'we can make an educated guess'. First she asks how many families they have in the class. A child mentions 'eleven', since Jaquanda and Katharina are sisters. The teacher asks if the graph can show 'eleven'. Gabby: 'No, it is in thousands, that's too much'. Teacher: 'So what will we need to change to have our new graph show a smaller number of families?'. 'We can change the thousands to one', Ephran answers. Teacher: 'That's what we will do. Each thousand will just become one'. She asks Ephran to fill in the graph to show they have eleven families. Before deciding on a colour, however, he first looks at the graph of New York City and Manhattan and then chooses the same colour as used for the graphs of the 'family' column. After questioning each other and making some rough estimates of numbers, they count families, high schools, income, and employment for East Harlem. When they have finished the chart for East Harlem, the teacher asks how the number of people in Manhattan compares to the number of people in East Harlem. The children count and the teacher asks rhetorically about each category. Then the children are given a piece of paper where the categories are written: population in East Harlem and in Manhattan, and employment in East Harlem and Manhattan. Their task is to make a bar graph so they can compare Manhattan and East Harlem.

Then they count the differences between the bar graph for Manhattan and that for East Harlem, and the teacher writes the difference on a chart, which is to be hung in the classroom.

MOTIVATION

During the sessions in May the children concentrated on making the graphs, and at the last session the children all concentrated on making the comparisons between East Harlem and Manhattan. They seem to have enjoyed doing graphs and comparisons.

PROBLEMS

A general problem during the thirty-sixth session was that the model was now formulated as a model for the family, while earlier the same model was formulated as a model for the community. The model covers both aspects but this should have been explained to the children.

At the thirty-seventh session several of the children had not done their homework, but the teacher manages to proceed with the task of comparing living conditions in East Harlem and Manhattan, and even though the numbers were only estimated for East Harlem, the children were engaged (or perhaps it was the activity with the graph itself which engaged them).

Main Features of the Phase of Community Modelling and Model Use

In the thirty-third session the model became formulated as a general model including the following aspects: Community, family, living conditions and resources. The concept of work is left out in this final model. In the previous model, formulated in the twenty-seventh session, work was part of the model. Work would certainly have become integrated in the model if the teaching had lasted longer.

Parallel with the model making the children collected information and made overviews and comparisons of the resources in their community with the resources in Manhattan. They came to understand that the unit for measurement could be negotiated and they could decide themselves, and that the graphs reflected their choice.

In general the teacher took the lead in formulation of the model but the children joined her without any difficulty and cooperated in contributing to the completion of the model and explaining the categories. Contrary to our expectations the children became active and engaged in this mathematical task of making and comparing graphs.

CHAPTER 14

Discussion of the Teaching Experiment

The previous four chapters present a narrative description of teaching-learning activities that were organized by principles of the double move in teaching and learning, analyses of the children's motivation in relation to specific teaching content and tasks, and the relevant problems encountered in realizing those tasks. This chapter assesses the teaching experiment in relation to the ideal of radical-local teaching and learning, which focuses on the comprehension of local knowledge through theoretical concepts. Given that the double move was used as a general methodological approach for integrating theoretical concepts and everyday concepts, there is first an evaluation of the realization of the double move approach, where radical-local content was being used. Then there is an assessment of the children's learning and development from participating in this teaching experiment, with a particular focus on the development of theoretical knowledge and research methods.

Realisation of the Principle of the Double Move Approach in the Teaching Experiment

The three main aspects in the double move approach are that tasks used in teaching-learning should (a) change qualitatively through three different phases, (b) be organized around models of core relations, and (c) provide the opportunity to develop a general research procedure for investigating problems. The full content and the teaching procedures are not specified completely before the start of the teaching programme, but developed during the course of the programme in relation to each new problem area, using the general principles described in Chapter 6. This kind of development is expected whenever the double move approach is implemented, because it is necessary to incorporate specific themes and topics that arise as part of the children's investigation of a problem area. The development is done as a cooperation between the researchers and the teacher. In what follows, we consider the extent to which these three aspects were realized in the teaching experiment, and some of the main problems that arose in their realization. We conclude that it was possible to realize the principles of the double move procedure in this teaching experiment.

PHASES IN TEACHING

In the double move approach, a teaching programme is conceptualized in three main phases. Each phase is realized concretely through tasks directed at specific themes in the problem area under investigation. In the goal formation phase, the tasks should lead to construction of an image of the problem area and the learning goals. In the model formulation phase, the tasks should aim at identifying and relating core concepts in the subject-matter area, while giving pupils research procedures that help them investigate core relations in the subject matter. In the third phase the tasks should give pupils the opportunity to evaluate their learning progress and the usefulness of the formulated models as tools to guide their investigations of the problem area.

Figure 9.2 gives an overview of the observed phases through which the teaching proceeded over the course of the experiment. The first two phases of the double move approach were realized: goal formation and model formulation/research activity. As often happens in the double move approach, the model building had three subphases: building core relations and learning specific research methods, model formulation (based on research of their city), and model refinement and model use (so the model became a community model and a model for the good life). The final phase – evaluation of the core model and of learning progress – was not initiated in any significant way. In the final sessions of the programme, some initial steps toward model evaluation were begun. Had the programme run for a longer time (or had not been interrupted for longer periods), more tasks of model evaluation and self-evaluation could have been introduced. In short, it was possible to implement a teaching approach that proceeded through different phases where the purpose of the educational tasks change from goal formation, to model formulation and research methods, and to model use that guided research activities.

TEACHING CORE RELATIONS AND MODELS

The core model used in the teaching experiment was based on relations between living conditions, family, community, and resources (see Fig. 9.1). The teacher succeeded in using tasks to establish a core relation between living conditions and family life early in the programme and to relate this dimension to historical periods (sessions 3-13). These relations were developed through the use of contrasting examples. The historical dimension and the differences between communities in the old days and today in Puerto Rico and New York City were accentuated through tasks that contrasted the two communities (through the interview with Mr. Fernando B. in session 9 and through films[50] in sessions 14 and 16). Tasks in relation to the film about Puerto Rico in the old days also introduced the concept of resources. The relations between resources, family, and living conditions were established in session 19. The task of imagining how a Puerto Rican family from the old days would survive in today's New York City was a way to contrast living conditions and resources in a village from the early part of the 20th century to a modern metropolitan city. The concept of resources was introduced and related to historical periods, but there was no explicit analysis of resources in relation to the other core concepts. Before Christmas the core concepts had been part of different tasks and we expected that children could start to build models after Christmas (sessions 20 and 21). This task could not be achieved adequately, so new tasks were introduced to help the children become aware of the conceptual relations. The model formulation task had several longer breaks in the teaching (see Fig. 9.2). In session 27 the children together with the teacher formulate their first model, which they used subsequently for their community research. In session 34 the model was refined (see Figs. 13.2 and 13.6).

TEACHING THE GENERAL RESEARCH PROCEDURE

The general research procedure is presented in Figure 6.2. The intention is that children should acquire this procedure, in part through using it to structure a discussion at the beginning of the teaching session and in part from using it to summarize the investigation of research questions, which always ran over several teaching sessions. To what extent could this procedure be used in these two different ways?

As planned, the teacher started each session with a class discussion, where her intention was to use the six questions in the general research procedure to structure the discussion. The teacher was able to discuss consistently the question of what was learned last time (i.e., what do we know) and what we want to do research about, but several times she forgot to relate the specific theme more explicitly to the more general problem that was being investigated and to ask what we do *not* know, so that the children could understand the goal to which the day's investigation was supposed to contribute.

---

50 One about a Puerto Rican boy and his family in New York City today and the other about a Puerto Rican family in the old days in Puerto Rico.

The teacher was also able to use the general research procedure to summarize the results of an investigation of a research question. At the end of each research activity, a chart was prepared with the children that summarized the results of their investigation, where the presentation on the chart was structured by the general research procedure. These charts were hung in the classroom. One indication that these charts were meaningful both for the children and the teacher is that they often pointed to them when it was relevant for something they were talking about.

Children's Learning and Development in the Teaching Experiment

In the previous section, we demonstrated that it was possible to realize a double move approach in this teaching experiment. Now we want to consider the children's learning and development as a consequence of participating in this teaching experiment, where radical-local content was a focus.

The intention of radical-local teaching is to support child development. Development reflects qualitative changes in the child's relation to the world. In an educational situation, this refers to the acquisition of concepts, methods and motives that enable new possibilities for action, investigation and reflection about aspects of one's life. In this particular teaching experiment, data collection was focused on the content of interactions in the classroom among the teacher and children. As a result, it is possible to assess the class's appropriation of significant intellectual methods, in particular theoretical knowledge and research methods that are likely to contribute to development.

Motive development is dependent in part upon conceptual and procedural learning, because acquisition of theoretical knowledge and methods of investigation open new possibilities for action. Of particular interest in relation to primary school children is the acquisition of a motive to learn (i.e., where the process of subject-matter learning itself can become an objective for one's actions). It is not possible to assess development for individual children, which would require that they were followed and assessed more directly.

CHILDREN'S DEVELOPMENT OF A CAPABILITY TO USE SUBJECT-MATTER CONCEPTUAL RELATIONS TO ANALYZE LOCAL KNOWLEDGE

In a radical-local perspective, education for school children should be organized around theoretical dialectical knowledge with the aim that this knowledge should become tools for children in their concrete everyday activities. A main aim of radical-local teaching is to relate subject-matter knowledge and local knowledge so that it contributes to the development of children's everyday concepts, and in this way helps them to develop the capacity to think theoretically-dialectically in relation to their local and historical life conditions.

In Chapter 4, we distinguished three general forms of knowledge: empirical-paradigmatic, narrative-dialogical, and theoretical-dialectical. Theoretical-dialectical concepts give the possibility to integrate subject-matter knowledge and local knowledge; in this way theoretical concepts serve as tools for analyzing specific matters of concrete events and places. In the following we evaluate the children's learning in relation to their appropriating theoretical concepts and research procedures as personal knowledge.

At the beginning of the teaching experiment the children came to work with the relation between living conditions and family life and the categories of 'the old days in Puerto Rico' and 'today in New York City'. Within the first month they became able to use this conceptual relation to characterize empirical descriptions of life in Puerto Rico at the beginning of the 20th century and of life in New York City (sessions 8-19).

Within the first three months of the programme the children became able to work with all the relations between the different concepts in the core model (Fig. 9.1), and showed signs that they understood the meaning of the general concepts in the model and the implications of their relationships for analyzing specific, concrete problems related to their local community. This could be seen in their discussions of how differences in living conditions influence the conditions for family life and their relation to resources in a community, such as when they discussed the different ways of life that could be seen in the two films about life in Puerto Rico and New York City today (session 14), and in Puerto Rico in the old days (session 16). They discussed what it meant to be poor and rich (i.e., resources) under the different local and historical conditions (i.e., communities). Another example is from session 19 in which the children discussed what it would be like for a poor family from a village in Puerto Rico in the 'old days' to come to New York City today. In this discussion, they referred to general conceptual relations about how different communities were characterized by differences in family life and living conditions.

The understanding of resources was not developed sufficiently in the first three months, but later the role of this concept in the general model became clarified. For example, this was seen in the discussion of the model of what a family/child needs to survive (session 28). Another example occurred when the investigation came to focus on East Harlem as their community and a goal was formulated to analyze resources in their local community. The children had no trouble comparing graphs of resources in East Harlem with resources in Manhattan and New York City (sessions 35-37). They came to understand that the unit for measurement could be negotiated and they could make graphs reflecting their choice. These choices indicate that not only did they have an empirical understanding of the resources they had identified, but they also had a theoretical understanding of how to measure resources.

Integration of local empirical and narrative knowledge was also observed in the teaching experiment. An example that illustrates how local theoretical-dialectical relations became related to empirical knowledge in the children's learning activity was seen after the interview with the elderly citizen, in which he had described how he lived in Puerto Rico before coming to New York City. The children were subsequently able to interpret this local empirical knowledge in relation to the general concepts of living conditions and family life, discussing this empirical information in relation to the specific conditions that actualized them (sessions 9-13). An example of how local, narrative knowledge became integrated with theoretical concepts is seen in the children's discussion of events from the film about life in the old days in Puerto Rico, taking the perspective of rich and poor people. They were relating different perspectives on the same event to concepts in the core model.

CHILDREN'S APPROPRIATION OF A CORE MODEL AND CAPABILITY TO USE THE MODEL TO ANALYZE THEIR COMMUNITY

The double move approach oriented the children towards the building and use of core models of conceptual relations. As noted before, in this particular teaching experiment, building and use of core models was accomplished in three subphases: building core relations; model formulation; and model use and refinement. The formulation of the first core relation (family life – living conditions) was started in session 10. Halfway through the programme the children were asked to make their own models (sessions 21-22). At first, the children did not have the teacher's understanding of a model as a depiction of the relations among the concepts with which they worked. Instead they drew iconic models depicting the concrete places where they lived (e.g., Gabby's model in Fig. 12.4). Later they became able to discuss general core conceptual models (sessions 27-34) and draw their own versions of core models as has been illustrated by Sharome and Raphaels's models (see Figs. 13.8 and 13.9).

The children's formulation of conceptual models can be seen as a development of their everyday concepts to contain theoretical knowledge. At the same time, for some children, they came to understand that the idea of *model* can include both a conceptual meaning and an iconic meaning as seen in Gabby's conceptual model of living conditions (Fig. 12.4) and his iconic model of the street where he lives (Fig. 13.3). This enrichment of the understanding of different kinds and ways of constructing models is seen as an important intellectual development that can be used more generally for investigating different problem areas.

CHILDREN'S APPROPRIATION OF A SOCIAL SCIENCE RESEARCH METHOD AND THEIR DEVELOPMENT OF COMPETENCE TO USE THIS METHOD TO ANALYZE THEIR COMMUNITY

The idea of interview as a method for collecting information was introduced already in session 3. We had expected that this method of questioning would be easy for the children to use, because they had seen interviews before in television and films. However, the task to make interviews about the old days became a problem. In the beginning of the programme the children could not realize independently an interview of their parents or grandparents; they did not remember or know what to ask about. This problem motivated the decision to put the interview activity as a learning goal in the teaching programme because interviewing was seen as a general research method in the social sciences and a relevant tool for the problems that the children were investigating. It became clear that the children needed some concepts to guide their questioning, both to become able to ask about something and for the task to be interesting for them. These concepts were achieved gradually through the discussion of pictures about living conditions and family life in Puerto Rico in the old days (sessions 3-5). Their insight about the interview as a general method for making investigations came during the first interview of Mr. Fernando B. (session 9); because they could see that it was not simply a classroom exercise but served a useful purpose in relation to their learning goal.

The children developed their competence in this area over the course of the programme. In the first interview with Mr. Fernando B. he leads the dialogue even though the children had prepared questions. In the second interview his complaint that the children did not wait for him to explain enough showed that the children could take the lead in the dialogue through the presentation of their interview questions. The children had started to take more responsibility for the topics of the interview, connected to the questions they had prepared around the core concepts.

CHILDREN'S ENGAGEMENT AND DEVELOPMENT OF A LEARNING MOTIVE

The children's engagement and motivation for the activities throughout the programme can be seen as a source for developing a learning motive. The children's engagement throughout the programme can be used as an indicator of the development of a learning motive.

In the first three sessions of the goal formation phase the class dialogue centred on the role of being a researcher. The idea of 'The Young Scientist Club' was well received by the children. The children were engaged from the very beginning in the activities of doing research. Participating in the class dialogue also engaged the children, though in the beginning they did not want to talk too much; instead they wanted to get a task that they could do with the computer. An activity that did not engage them was the story reading in the first session. This is understandable from a 'young scientist's view' because this activity is not related to doing research, and did not have anything to do with their ancestors. The children were enthusiastic whenever the content of the classroom activities had some relation to their families, such as using a map to find where their relatives live in Puerto Rico and where they live in New York City, or when they had to draw their neighbourhoods.

The first subphase of model formulation, the class discussion and shared activities of chart making and interviews are the motivating activities. In the second subphase of model formulation, the drawing of models of their community (session 22) did not engage the children; perhaps they had difficulty to imagine what was expected of them. When they started to discuss how to make research about their community history (session 23) the engagement came back. The visit to the City Museum and the discussion and interview construction also engaged them. In the third subphase, when they came to make a model for what a family needs to survive, they had enthusiasm for this task in contrast to the earlier model-making task. They participated eagerly in the community walk and the graph activity.

The children's engagement and their shared motivation led them to be engaged in tasks that were related to school activities. Through the research activity the children engaged in such academic activities as writing and spelling for the charts about family and living conditions, writing questions for the interviews on the computer, using maps to locate their family, relatives and their community. Over the experimental period this engagement gradually turned into a learning motive, as reflected in the steadiness and engagement in the research of their own community, where they studied, registered and calculated resources, ending up eagerly engaged in graph making of their findings.

Conclusion

In the teaching experiment the main idea of a double move approach – qualitatively different phases in teaching of a subject area, use of core models and a general research procedure – together with a radical-local focus in the choice of topical content, were realized in a way that influenced the children's competence to work with theoretical-dialectical thinking modes in relation to their community and their own life. By incorporating the history and culture of the immediate community in this teaching programme, the children in the programme developed their knowledge about the Puerto Rican community in general and in East Harlem in particular. By bringing the methods of investigation from subject-matter disciplines into the classroom as a working approach, the teacher, in collaboration with the children, developed specific substantive results in relation to the children's local community, while developing general intellectual concepts and procedures such as conceptual models of communities, and conceptually-motivated interviews. This knowledge contributed to their understanding for and appreciation of their local community and their relation to it.

An afterschool programme can be an ideal place to experiment with radical-local teaching and learning bridging local knowledge of family and community traditions with subject-matter knowledge because the practices of afterschool activities are not formalized by laws and curriculum plans, and the children cannot fail the programme. An afterschool programme can also be a place, in addition to school, where it would be meaningful to use a radical-local approach.

McDermott (1993) brought a new dimension into the picture of learning by showing that a child's competence and learning disability is dependent on the demands of the situation. He describes a child who has been characterized as being learning disabled because he has difficulties in reading. In describing this case McDermott shows how the child's cognitive ability is relative to the context in which the child uses his ability. The case illustrates that both a child's motivation and cognitive competence to read can change radically between a school and afterschool setting, depending on the demands of the situation. An important factor in this change is connected to children's anxiety to fail in school (see also Mehan, Villanueva, Hubbard & Lintz, 1996; Paradise, 1998).

In the United States, afterschools (in recreational and community centres) and summer schools take over more and more responsibility to enrich or remediate what children have learned in school (Adler & Adler, 1994). Activities at these places can give the children extracurricular competencies or support their school competencies (e.g. at the Casita afterschool centre the children could do their homework) (Chung, 2000). Other examples of enrichment can be found in projects that have used computers in afterschool settings (e.g., Cole, 1996; Garner & Zhao, 2000). The teaching experiment reported here was located in an afterschool setting. This gave us the possibility to work with subject matter that could potentially be included in a school curriculum, while integrating this content with tasks that motivated children. In this situation, the children's anxiety for academic failure could be substantially reduced, because the individual child's performance was not evaluated and the children had no expectation that the quality of their performance would be judged.

The approach to designing radical-local teaching programmes that we have presented here is one example of how this can be done. The principles that we draw upon in the teaching experiment can be realized in many other forms of teaching but the basic criterion is that there has to be an integration of general conceptual relations with everyday knowledge using research methods and models in this integrative activity.

CHAPTER 15

Radical-Local Teaching and Learning and Educational Practice

The preceding chapters have introduced the idea of radical-local teaching and learning, both theoretically and in practice. This perspective on planning educational practices for children is motivated by interconnected interests to acknowledge the diversity of children's cultural-historical background, while contributing significantly to the development of the quality of their life in society. In this final chapter, we review briefly some main features of a radical-local perspective and consider potential problems and limitations both with the radical-local idea itself and with its possibilities for being implemented under contemporary societal conditions. This critical review helps to better understand some of the consequences and implications of a radical-local perspective on teaching and learning. Finally, a radical-local perspective is considered briefly in relation to constructing appropriate educational approaches for children from cultural minorities.

Main Features of Radical-Local Teaching and Learning

A distinctive feature of the radical-local teaching and learning perspective is an explicit focus on the role of subject-matter teaching to support children's development in relation to the societal conditions within which they live. Given this focus, it should be clear that radical-local teaching and learning is not meant to be a comprehensive perspective for organizing a school or for addressing the diverse social and societal conditions that must also be considered in creating adequate conditions for children to participate in classroom teaching. However, once children are assembled in the classroom, and one wants to start teaching-learning practices, then a radical-local perspective becomes meaningful.

We conceptualize education as involving relations between societal knowledge, personality development and teaching-learning, such that teaching-learning of societal knowledge supports personality development. The main idea of radical-local teaching and learning is that school knowledge has to be related to the child's lifeworld such that school knowledge can qualitatively transform children's everyday concepts. In this theoretical conception, the children's appropriation of theoretical-dialectical subject-matter concepts elaborates and transforms their everyday concepts so that they can acquire wholeness in their conceptualizations of themselves and the world around them. A teaching programme should aim to develop children's capacity to think theoretically-dialectically in relation to their local and historical life conditions, and in this way to give children intellectual tools to understand and relate to their living conditions in their community (i.e., local knowledge). For everyday concepts to be integrated with theoretical-dialectical concepts, both subject-matter concepts and children's everyday local knowledge have to be taken into consideration when planning educational tasks.

This focus on local topics does not necessarily result in a dilemma or contradiction in which the teacher must choose between academic relevance and personal relevance. By bringing the methods of investigation from subject-matter disciplines into the classroom as a working approach, the teacher, in collaboration with the children, can develop specific substantive results that can be related to the children's local community. In this way, it is possible for children to acquire knowledge and skills for understanding and developing better relationships to their life conditions.

This book has introduced a theoretical perspective that can be used to analyze how to combine subject-matter concepts with themes central in children's community life, as well as showing a specific teaching approach, 'the double move', that can be used for these purposes. The double move approach should be considered as one among several possible approaches for realizing a radical-local perspective to teaching programmes. The double move approach was inspired by Davydov's theory of theoretical knowledge and developmental teaching-learning. In our further development of Davydov's approach, children, family and community background, as well as children's personal knowledge and interest, were given a more prominent position. In the 'double move' approach the goal is that subject-matter knowledge, structured in models of core relations, can become analytic tools for children.

Radical-Local Teaching and Learning: Is It Possible?

The teaching experiment presented in this book is one indication that it is possible to create a teaching programme motivated by radical-local principles. We have argued that children's development takes place through participation in several different institutions at the same time, and children learn through their activity in all these institutions, at home, in daycare, in school, in afterschool and at work. But we have also argued (e.g., in Chap. 5) that learning in school is qualitatively different from learning in other institutions. This raises a question about whether a radical-local approach could be used as part of a regular school programme, given that the teaching experiment was conducted in an afterschool programme.

In school, children should be presented for subject-matter content that is structured around core concepts so that a subject-matter area can be seen as a conceptually related whole. Learning academic concepts both builds upon a child's everyday concepts, but also leads to changes in these concepts. In the teaching experiment we gave children research tasks connected to themes of their community and introduced core concepts and models that they could use in their research of these themes. Moreover, the double move approach – used in this teaching experiment to integrate subject-matter concepts and children's everyday concepts – has been used successfully in other teaching experiments in Danish schools (Chaiklin, 1999; Hedegaard, 1990, 2002, 2004). And finally, from a practical point of view, the teaching experiment, conducted under the difficult conditions of the afterschool programme, where children are free to stop attending if they wish, emphasizes that exceptional conditions are not needed to realize a radical-local perspective. In short, the idea of radical-local teaching and learning seems to be both coherent (given its theoretical account of the relations between teaching, learning, and development and the use of subject-matter content to relate general concepts with local knowledge), and viable (given that there are now several examples of successful educational programmes that were organized by the double move approach and have been oriented in relation to local knowledge).

Further Development of Radical-Local Teaching: Open Questions and Likely Barriers

MUST ALL SUBJECT-MATTER LEARNING BE RELATED TO LOCAL KNOWLEDGE?

At first glance, it would appear that the main argument of this book is that all school teaching must involve local knowledge. We have not tried to investigate or analyze this question systematically but a few comments are appropriate. Whether local knowledge should always be a part of all school teaching seems like an open question. If it were a requirement, then it seems like a strong criterion for, and potential barrier to, including various topics and themes in a teaching programme. Are some topics important to learn about, but cannot be addressed as local knowledge? What about theories about the origins of the universe (e.g., big bang) or other topics in astronomy and astrophysics? Historical studies of ancient Greece and Rome? Must everything pass through the (possibly egocentric) filter of local knowledge? Is it possible to relate everything to local knowledge? Is it desirable? These questions are important to consider in the further elaboration of a radical-local perspective.

From one point of view, it could be important to include local knowledge in relation to all topics of teaching. This does not mean that the content of topics are limited to the interests of local knowledge; rather, in the study of the diverse topics found in school teaching, it is important to include opportunities to reflect about and analyze the significance and relations between academic topics and one's local situation. This can be done in many ways and for different purposes (e.g., to be used as contrast cases). In other words, it is not a matter of choosing topics because they are relevant to local knowledge. Rather the focus is to develop the ability to understand and relate all kinds of academic knowledge to one's local situation. It is an intriguing idea. Maybe it is impossible to realize in practice, but it might serve as an important ideal and challenge for school teaching to justify the reasons for its choice of content and how it is used.

MUST ALL EDUCATIONAL PROGRAMMES BE RADICALLY LOCAL?

The focus in this book has been on primary education. Given that a major goal of primary education should be to help children acquire theoretical thinking, a motive for learning, and knowledge about their local world, then it is meaningful to speak of a radical-local perspective. In considering secondary and tertiary education, it may also be meaningful to speak of a radical-local perspective, if an appropriate referent for *local* is chosen. For example, in the case of professional education, there is a local practice for which persons are being prepared, and it is meaningful to consider how to relate general conceptual knowledge within a discipline in relation to the specific practices for which people are preparing. In other words, it is likely that a meaningful radical-local perspective can be formulated for other educational practices besides primary education.

LACK OF SUBJECT-MATTER ANALYSIS

One of the main barriers to the further development of a radical-local perspective is having adequate analysis of subject-matter areas in terms of theoretical concepts whose relations are formed into core models that can be used to analyze and interpret different problems and phenomena within the subject matter. This conception of subject-matter analysis, formulated more fully and introduced in educational research by Davydov (1972/1990), has not been used widely as an approach. Some models have been constructed for some problem areas within arithemetic (Davydov, 1966/1975), language (Aidarova, 1982; Markova, 1974/1979), history (Hedegaard, 2002), and biology (Lompscher, 1984), however there are still many other problem areas within these subjects, and many other subject-matter areas that need analysis.

The main idea of radical-local teaching and learning is predicated on the use of subject-matter models as the way to relate local knowledge to theoretical-dialectical models of the subject matter. It is a problem that there are so few examples of good subject-matter analyses. This is an important area for further research and development, especially because of the need for cooperation with subject-matter experts.

LACK OF LOCAL KNOWLEDGE ANALYSIS

A second barrier to the further development of a radical-local perspective is having adequate analysis of children's local knowledge. There are two aspects to this problem. First, there is not a tradition for documenting local knowledge in relation to the life world of school children. The 'funds of knowledge' approach is one important exception (e.g., Gonzáles & Moll, 2002), but this kind of approach has not yet found widespread general use in many different communities. It is still rare to find material collected together in relation to local historical conditions. For example, Morales and Tarr (2000) developed a course for preservice teachers that focused on social action, especially for Latinos, in relation to New York City. They comment on the lack of useful materials for helping the students to investigate societal problems. Second, even if one is able to find sources of local knowledge, it is still necessary to relate this knowledge to theoretical concepts in subject-matter traditions. And given the lack of adequate subject-matter analysis for many disciplines, it is clear that, for now, attempts to use a radical-local approach will require that one is able to assemble and analyze local knowledge in relation to subject-matter traditions.

TEACHER PREPARATION

Theoretical knowledge and thinking is not normally taught in primary schools. Moreover, it is not a typical approach to teacher training. A third barrier to the implementation of the double move approach for radical-local teaching and learning is that many teachers are not familiar with the idea of using theoretical concepts in relation to elementary school children, and do not have experience themselves in working with theoretical concepts. They are not usually prepared to work with models of conceptual relationships, using them as tools for planning educational tasks, and helping children to investigate these tasks as a way of forming these models as tools that are used to construct explanations for the problems under investigation and formulating new questions. The teacher in the teaching experiment reported here commented once that it was sometimes difficult for her to allow the children to investigate problems, because she did not feel like a teacher if she was not telling them things. Even if the problems mentioned in the previous section, about having relevant local knowledge and adequate subject-matter analysis of conceptual relations, were resolved, there will still be the significant problem of helping teachers to understand and use conceptual models both for planning teaching tasks and in teaching interactions.

Radical-Local Teaching and Learning in Relation to Cultural Minorities

To conclude, we consider briefly radical-local teaching and learning in relation to contemporary educational practices for cultural minorities. Three topics are addressed:

— What is the relation of radical-local teaching and learning to other educational approaches that are oriented to cultural minorities?
— How do we avoid the 'cultural trap' in which children are caught in a specific cultural stereotype by teaching that draws on knowledge of their local community and history?
— How can the idea of radical-local teaching be used in classrooms where the children come from families with different cultural backgrounds?

There has been increasing focus over the past decade on the idea of culturally responsive pedagogy (e.g., Irvine & Armento, 2001; McIntyre, Rosebery, & González, 2001; Scribner & Reyes, 1999). As a first impression, it seems like many of these approaches are comparable to a radical-local perspective, because they often draw subject-matter content from local sources. However, the examples that we have seen do not formulate an explicit analysis of forms of knowledge (such as found in Chap. 4), and have not considered how to use the local content as part of developing general subject-matter knowledge. This aspect of understanding local knowledge in relation to general subject concepts is a critical point in the radical-local perspective, because we do not want to create a situation which gives the impression that it is the 'real' (i.e., societally-valued) content of schooling that is separate from the culturally relevant content.

Many examples of culturally responsive pedagogy either seem to uncritically presuppose the content and performance of the dominant educational form as the desired objective (where cultural sensitivity is a mediating action for realizing those objectives), or as a replacement for this content. That is, they either are teaching standard procedures, while using local content for motivation and/or self-validation, but then not relating this content to the child's concrete life situation, or they are focusing on important local content, but not relating it to general subject-matter concepts, thus forming a ghettoized version of special topics that are not related to the other tasks of school. Even in cases where a sophisticated analysis is presented about the relation between culture and schooling practices, one is only presented with a general list of desirable characteristics (e.g., academically rich curriculum, active learning, culturally appropriate) without elaborating on the connection between the subject-matter content and the life conditions of the pupils (García & Dominguez, 1997).

In short, while there are often many points of agreement between the general goals stated in culturally responsive pedagogies and a radical-local perspective, significant differences usually appear when one considers the content chosen for teaching and the ways in which this content is used.

We originally formulated the teaching experiment as being aimed at a special group of children defined by their cultural background; we gradually came to the conviction that we should focus on the children's everyday life in a community rather than construct an ideal cultural identity, binding or restricting the children to a special cultural category. To know one's history is important, but to be bound by one's history is another matter. Culture is something to be lived, not something to be asserted as a category to characterize children in school or as empirical facts about children's background. We see children in relation to their community and not as representative of a permanent social category of people. If schooling practice (e.g., teachers's assumptions, instructional material) are organized in relation to cultural categories, then it can contribute to holding children in definite, often limiting, developmental trajectories. As we have argued here, and consistent with the values of liberal democracy, education should help children to develop a theoretical understanding of societal life, where cultural traditions and differences are understood in relation to historical developments, rather than essentialist sources.

In the case of the teaching experiment reported here, the core of the programme was the children's relation to their local community and through this relation to the children's Puerto Rican background. Children's knowledge of their cultural background is important but it should be related to the children's everyday life in their community and their future possibilities for education.

The main idea in the programme then became to relate school knowledge and subject-matter concepts to children's everyday life so that they get new perspectives and intellectual tools to understand their life and make a future.

In Chapters 2 and 8, we argued that cultural minority children do not always have an easy time in school both because they have trouble with the subject-matter teaching and trouble with their own self respect, feeling inferior in relation to a dominant cultural tradition. It is too simple to say that cultural differences can explain the problems that children encounter in learning and appropriating academic knowledge in school. Cultural differences can contribute to the conditions, but many other factors are also involved (García & Dominguez, 1997). It is not the child's cultural background in itself, but the social relations and interactions and the possibilities to appropriate competencies and motives that can give the children a position and an identity in the society in which they live.

Recent literature (e.g., Davidson, 1998; Fordham, 1988; Gibson, 2000; Nieto, 2000; Ogbu & Simons, 1998; Phelan, Davidson & Cao, 1991; Valdes, 1996; Vasquez, Pease-Alvarez & Shannon, 1994) report cases in which cultural minority children, against the expectations, actually do well in school. But this research also shows that many children who succeed often do so in opposition to their cultural background and community. Family traditions and local peer groups create expectations for what future these children and young people can and should orient themselves towards. Children in these studies express feelings and experiences of being isolated. This problem is related to the tradition of categorizing people according to their ethnic or cultural origin as a minority in relation to a majority society. Through their minority status, and the discrimination that follows with this status, cultural minority groups often grow into an opposition against the majority society (see Malik, 1996, for a discussion of this problem).

Radical-local teaching and learning shifts the focus away from specific characteristics (cultural background, socioeconomic status) as defining features of the content of education. This is not to deny that these characteristics have significance, or to avoid culture entirely; rather it emphasizes an understanding of culture as traditions for practice that change through people's participation in the practice.

The idea of radical-local teaching gives us the possibility to acknowledge the cultural background of the children in minority families and make their background become a relevant aspect in the organization and content of the teaching, without having to be trapped in essentialist notions of culture as the defining perspective. Educational tasks should be oriented to a child's development in relation to these characteristics and not because of them. This view makes it possible to make culturally-sensitive teaching within a classroom of children with different cultural backgrounds.

When we conducted the teaching experiment, one of the children in the project lived in the Bronx, not in East Harlem. Another child's family came from the Dominican Republic, not Puerto Rico. At several points in the teaching experiment, these children expressed interest in doing tasks (e.g., locating their family and relatives on maps) in relation to their background, and not the dominant focus on East Harlem and Puerto Rico. This particular problem reflects a more general problem found in contemporary school classrooms where children often come from different cultural-historical backgrounds. How is it possible to make radical-local teaching under such circumstances?

Here is one concrete example of how this problem was handled in a radical-local perspective. In a research project in a Danish community, the children came from a variety of immigrant and refugee backgrounds. The subject-matter teaching was geography, and reading and writing Danish. The themes in the teaching were 'being a child and being young in three different continents, Africa, Asia, and Europe', and then making comparisons with 'being young in Denmark'. The idea was to take the children's family background as a guide to finding relevant material and then relating this material to issues that motivate the children in relation to the local community in which they live. In this way, the diversity in the class is taken into consideration, while engaging the children in a way so they also become oriented towards learning subject matter. To both have knowledge of one's own community and subject-matter competencies the children come to understand their own position in society and get tools to be active in relation to this position.

As sketched in Chapter 2, we do not expect that education – radical-local or otherwise – will be sufficient by itself to create conditions for a good life. At the same time, the content and focus of education does not have to be irrelevant or immaterial for a child's life in society. We have tried to develop the idea that the development of intellectual capabilities and motives in combination with particular content are an important part of having a good life in society, both to understand the conditions under which one lives and to see possibilities for action. The main focus of the radical-local perspective is on how to conceptualize and create educational programmes that realize these educational goals. At the same time, the radical-local perspective shifts focus from global properties to considering the relations between a child's life conditions and the content of education. In this respect, a radical-local perspective is meaningful and appropriate for all children.

References

Adi-Nader, J. (1990). 'A house for my mother': Motivating Hispanic high school students. *Anthropology and Education Quarterly, 21,* 41-57.

Adler, P.A. & Adler, P. (1994). *Sociological Quarterly, 35,* 309-328.

Aidarova, L. (1982). *Child development and education* (L. Lezhneva, Trans.). Moscow: Progress. (Original work published 1982).

Algarin, M., & Pinero, M. (Eds.). (1975). *Nuyorican poetry: An anthology of Puerto Rican words and feelings.* New York: William Morrow.

Alvarez, M.D. (1992). Promoting the academic growth of Puerto Rican children. In A.N. Ambert & M.D. Alvarez (Eds.), *Puerto Rican children on the mainland: Interdisciplinary perspectives,* pp. 135-166. New York: Garland.

Antrop-González, R. (2003). This school is my sanctuary – The Dr. Pedro Albizu Campos Alternative High School. *Centro: Journal of the Center for Puerto Rican Studies, 15*(2).

Anyon, J. (1981). Social class and school knowledge. *Curriculum Inquiry, 11*(1), 3-42.

Arias, M.B. (1986). The context of education for Hispanic students: An overview. *American Journal of Education, 95,* 26-57.

Ascher, C. (1993). *Changing schools for urban students: The School Development Program, Accelerated Schools, and Success for All* (Trends and Issues 18). New York: Eric Clearinghouse on Urban Education. (ERIC Document Reproduction Service No. ED 355 313).

Bafumo, M.E. (1998). The Basic School: Building a framework for curriculum. *Principal, 78*(2), 5-6, 8, 10.

Banks, J.A. (1994). *Multiethnic education: Theory and practice* (3rd ed.). Boston: Allyn and Bacon.

Banks, J.A., & Banks, C.A.M. (Eds.). (1995). *Handbook of research on multicultural education.* New York: Macmillan.

Bartolomé, L. (1994). Beyond the methods fetish: Toward a humanizing pedagogy. *Harvard Educational Review, 64,* 173-194.

Berger, P.L., & Luckmann, T. (1966). *The social construction of reality: A treatise in the sociology of knowledge.* New York: Doubleday.

Berté-Toomer, D., Colón, I., González, W., Ayala, J., Henríquez, A., & Pedraza, P. (1992-3). Voices from the Young Scientist Club. *Centro: Journal of the Center for Puerto Rican Studies, 5*(2), 82-95.

Bigler, E. (1997). Dangerous discourses: Language politics and classroom prac-
    tices in Update New York. *Centro: Journal of the Center for Puerto Rican
    Studies, 9*(1), 8-25.

Bigler, E. (1999). *American conversations: Puerto Ricans, white ethnics, and
    multicultural education.* Philadelphia: Temple University Press.

Bloom, H.S., Ham, S., Melton, L., & O'Brien, J. (2001). *Evaluating the accel-
    erated schools approach: A look at early implementation and impacts on
    student achievement in eight elementary schools.* New York: Manpower
    Demonstration Research Corporation. (ERIC Document Reproduction Ser-
    vice No. ED 460 971).

Bourgois, P. (1989). In search of Horatio Alger: Culture and ideology in the
    crack economy. *Contemporary Drug Problems, 16,* 619-649.

Bourgois, P. (1995). *In search of respect: Selling crack in El Barrio.* Cambridge:
    Cambridge University Press.

Bowles, S., Gintis, H., Osborne, M. (2002). The determinants of individual
    earnings: Skills, preferences and schooling. *Journal of Economic Literature,
    39,* 1137-1176.

Bowles, S., Gintis, H., & Osborne, M. (2002). The determinants of individual
    earnings: Skills, preferences and schooling. *Journal of Economic Literature,
    39,* 1137-1176.

Brookover, W.B. (1987). Distortion and overgeneralization are no substitutes
    for sound research. *Phi Delta Kappan, 69,* 225-227.

Brown, G.H., Rosen, N.L., Hill, S.T., & Olivas, M.A. (1981). *The condition of
    education for Hispanic Americans.* Washington, DC: National Center for
    Education Statistics.

Bruner, J.S. (1974). *Beyond the information given.* London: Allen & Unwin.

Bruner, J.S. (1986). *Actual minds, possible worlds.* Cambridge, MA: Harvard
    University Press.

Bruner, J.S., Goodnow, J., & Austin, G.A. (1956). *A study of thinking.* New
    York: Wiley.

Burks, E.C. 1972. Puerto Ricans say census cuts political power here. *New York
    Times,* (October 2), pp. 1, 32.

Burstyn, J. (Ed.) (1996). *Educating the tomorrow's valuable citizen.* Albany:
    State University of New York Press.

Caballero, D. (1989). School board elections: Parents against the odds. *Centro:
    Journal of the Center for Puerto Rican Studies, 2*(5), 86-94.

Caballero, D. (2000). The Puerto Rican/Latino Education Roundtable: Seeking
    unity in vision and organizing for educational change. In S. Nieto (Ed.), *Puerto
    Rican students in U.S. schools,* pp. 203-221. Mahwah, NJ: Erlbaum.

Cabranes, J.A. (1979). *Citizenship and the American empire: Notes on the
    legislative history of the United States citizenship of Puerto Ricans.* New
    Haven: Yale University Press.

Calitri, R. (1983). *Minority secondary education in New York State and New York City*. New York: ASPIRA of New York.

Carr, R. (1984). *Puerto Rico: A colonial experiment*. New York: New York University Press.

Carrasquillo, A.L. (1985). *Hispanic children and youth in the United States*. New York: Garland.

Carrasquillo, A., & Carrasquillo, C. (1979). *The Neorican: Unwelcomed in two worlds*. New York: Ediciones Puerto Rico de Autores Nuevos.

Carter, R.T., & Goodwin, A.L. (1994). Racial identity and education. In L. Darling-Hammond (Ed.), *Review of research in education*, Vol. 20, pp. 291-336. Washington, DC: American Educational Research Association.

Carter, T.P., & Chatfield, M.L. (1986). Effective bilingual schools: Implications for policy and practice. *American Journal of Education, 95*, 200-232.

Castellanos, D., & Leggio, P. (1983). *The best of two worlds: Bilingual-bicultural education in the U.S.* Trenton: New Jersey Department of Education, Office of Equal Educational Opportunity. (ERIC Document Reproduction Service No. ED 243 316).

Cazden, C.B. (1982). Four comments. In P. Gilmore & A.A. Glatthorn (Eds.), *Children in and out of school: Ethnography and education*, pp. 209-226. Washington, DC: Center for Applied Linguistics.

Cazden, C.B. (1983). Can ethnographic research go beyond the status quo? *Anthropology and Education Quarterly, 14*(1), 33-41.

Chaiklin, S. (1999). Developmental teaching in upper-secondary school. In M. Hedegaard & J. Lompscher (Eds.), *Learning activity and development*, pp. 187-210. Aarhus: Aarhus University Press.

Chaiklin, S. (2003). The zone of proximal development in Vygotsky's theory of learning and school instruction. In A. Kozulin, V. Ageyev, B. Gindis, & C. Miller (Eds.), *Vygotsky's educational theory in cultural context*, pp. 39-64. Cambridge: Cambridge University Press.

Chaiklin, S., Hedegaard, M., Navarro, K., & Pedraza, P. (1990). The horse before the cart: A theory based approach to the use of computers in education. *Theory into Practice, 29*, 270-275.

Chasin, G., & Levin, H.M. (1995). Thomas Edison Accelerated Elementary School. In J. Oakes & K.H. Quartz (Eds.), *Creating new educational communities* (Ninety-fourth yearbook of the National Society for the Study of Education, pp. 130-146). Chicago, IL: The National Society for the Study of Education.

Christenson, M. (2001). *Evaluating components of international migration: Migration between Puerto Rico and the United States* (Working Paper Series No. 64). Washington, DC: U.S. Census Bureau, Population Division.

Chung, A.-M. (2000). *After-school programs: Keeping children safe and smart*. Washington, DC: U.S. Department of Education.

Civil, M. (1994, April). *Connecting the home and the school: Funds of know-ledge for mathematics teaching and learning.* Paper presented at the annual meeting of the American Educational Research Association, New Orleans. (ERIC Document Reproduction Service No. ED 370 987).

Cole, M. (1996). *Cultural psychology: A once and future dicipline.* Cambridge, MA: The Belknap Press of Harvard University Press.

Comas-Dias, L., Arroyo, A.L., Lovelace, J.C. (1982). Enriching self-concept through a Puerto Rican cultural awareness program. *The Personnel and Guidance Journal, 60,* 306-309.

Comer, J.P. (2001). Schools that develop children. *The American Prospect, 12*(7), 30-35.

Comer, J.P., & Haynes, N.T. (1999). The dynamic of school change: Response to the article, 'Comer's School Development Program in Prince George's County, Maryland: A Theory-based Evaluation', by Thomas D. Cook et al. *American Educational Research Journal, 36,* 599-607.

Comer, J.P., & Joyner, E.T. (2004). *Six pathways to healthy child development and academic success: The field guide to Comer schools in action.* Thousand Oaks, CA: Corwin Press.

Cordasco, F. (1982). Puerto Rican children in American mainland schools. In F. Cordasco & E. Bucchioni (Eds.), *The Puerto Rican community and its children on the mainland,* pp. 260-281. Metuchen, NJ: The Scarecrow Press.

Corson, D. (1993). Restructuring minority schooling. *Australian Journal of Education, 37,* 46-68.

Cummins, J. (1989). A theoretical framework for bilingual special education. *Exceptional Children, 56*(2), 111-119.

Cummins, J. (1994). The socioacademic achievement model in the context of coercive and collaborative relations of power. In R.A. DeVillar, C.J. Faltis, & J.P. Cummins (Eds.), *Cultural diversity in schools: From rhetoric to practice,* pp. 363-390. Albany: State University of New York Press.

Davidson, A.L. (1998). *Making and modelling identity in schools: Students' narratives on race, gender and academic engagement.* Albany: State University of New York.

Davydov, V.V. (1975). Logical and psychological problems of elementary mathematics as an academic subject (A. Bigelow, Trans). In L. Steffe (Ed.), *Soviet studies in the psychology of learning and teaching mathematics: Vol. 5. Children's capacity for learning mathematics,* pp. 55-107. Stanford: School Mathematics Study Group. (Original work published 1966).

Davydov, V.V. (1988a). Learning activity. *Multidisciplinary Newsletter for Activity Theory, 1*/2, 29-36.

Davydov, V.V. (1988b). Problems of developmental teaching. *Soviet Education, 30*(8), 6-97.

Davydov, V.V. (1990). *Types of generalization in instruction: Logical and psychological problems in the structuring of school curricula* (Soviet studies in mathematics education, Vol. 2; J. Kilpatrick, Ed.; J. Teller, Trans.). Reston, VA: National Council of Teachers of Mathematics. (Original work published 1972).

Davydov, V.V. (1998). The concept of developmental teaching. *Journal of Russian and East European Psychology. 36*(4), 11-36.

Davydov, V.V. (1999). A New Approach to the Interpretation of Activity Structure and Content. In S. Chaiklin, M. Hedegaard & U. Juul Jensen (Eds.) *Activity Theory and Social Practice*. Aarhus: Aarhus University Press.

Davydov, V.V., Lompscher, J., & Markova, A.K. (Eds.). (1982). *Ausbildung der Lerntätigkeit bei Schülern*. Berlin: Volk und Wissen.

Davydov, V.V., & Markova, A.K. (1983). A concept of educational activity for schoolchildren. *Soviet Psychology, 21*(2), 50-76.

De La Rosa, D., & Maw, C. (1990). *Hispanic education: A statistical portrait 1990*. Washington, DC: National Council of La Raza.

Delgado-Gaitan, C. (1991). Involving parents in schools: A process of empowerment. *American Journal of Education, 100*, 20-46.

Delgado-Gaitan, C. (1994). Sociocultural change through literacy: Toward empowerment of families. In B.M. Ferdman, R.-M. Weber, & A.G. Ramírez (Eds.), *Literacy across languages and cultures*, pp. 143-169. Albany: State University of New York Press.

Delpit, L. (1988). The silenced dialogue: Power and pedagogy in educating other people's children. *Harvard Educational Review, 58*, 280-298.

del Valle, S. (1998). Bilingual education for Puerto Ricans in New York City: From hope to compromise. *Harvard Educational Review, 68*, 193-217.

Depew, J. (1985). Narrativism, cosmopolitanism, and historical epistemology. *Clio, 14*, 357-377.

Diaz, S., Moll, L.C., & Mehan, H. (1986). Sociocultural resources in instruction: A context-specific approach. In *Beyond language: Social and cultural factors in schooling language minority students*, pp. 187-220. Los Angeles: Evaluation, Dissemination, and Assessment Center.

Dietz, J.L., & Pantojas-García, E. (1993). Puerto Rico's new role in the Caribbean. In E. Meléndez & E. Meléndez (Eds.), *Colonial dilemma: Critical perspectives on contemporary Puerto Rico*, pp. 103-115. Boston: South End Press.

Dossick, J.J. (1954). Fifth Workshop field study in Puerto Rican education and culture. *Journal of Educational Sociology, 28*, 174-180.

Dweck, C.S. (1991). Self-theories and goals: Their role in motivation, personality, and development. In R.A. Dienstbier (Ed.), *Perspectives on motivation: Current theory and research on motivation*, Vol. 38, pp. 199-235. Lincoln, NE: University of Nebraska Press.

Dweck, C.S. (1999). Caution – praise can be dangerous. *American Educator, 23*(1), 4-9.

Edmonds, R.R. (1979). Effective schools for the urban poor. *Educational Leadership, 37,* 28-32.

El'konin, B.D. (1993). The crisis of childhood and foundations for designing forms of child development. *Journal of Russian and East European Psychology, 31*(3), 56-71.

El'konin, D.B. (1988). *Legens psykologi* (J. Hansen, Trans.). Moscow: Sputnik. (Original work published 1978).

El'konin, D.B. (1999). Toward the problem of stages in the mental development of children. *Journal of Russian and East European Psychology, 37*(6), 11-30.

Erickson, F. (1993). Transformation and school success: The politics and culture of educational achievement. In E. Jacob & C. Jordan (Eds.), *Minority education: Anthropological perspectives,* pp. 27-51. Norwood, NJ: Ablex.

Falcón, A. (2001). *De'trás pa'lante: The future of Puerto Rican history in New York City.* New York: Puerto Rican Legal Defense and Education Fund, Institute for Puerto Rican Policy.

Falcón, L.M., & Gurak, D.T. (1990). *Features of the Hispanic underclass: Puerto Ricans and Dominicans in New York City* (1990 Working Paper Series 2.09). Ithaca, NY: Cornell University, Population and Development Program.

Fashola, O.S., & Slavin, R.E. (1997). *Effective dropout prevention and college attendance programs for Latino students.* (Hispanic Dropout Project Paper No. 4). Washington, DC: U.S. Department of Education, Office of the Under Secretary. (Available at http://www.ncela.gwu.edu/miscpubs/hdp/4/).

Fashola, O.S., Slavin, R.E., Calderón, M., & Durán, R. (1997). *Effective programs for Latino students in elementary and middle schools.* (Hispanic Dropout Project Paper No. 2). Washington, DC: U.S. Department of Education, Office of the Under Secretary. (Available at http://www.ncela.gwu.edu/miscpubs/hdp/2/).

Fernández, R.R., & Shu, G. (1988). School dropouts: New approaches to an enduring problem. *Education and Urban Society, 20,* 363-386.

Fillmore, L.M., & Meyer, L.M. (1992). The curriculum and linguistic minorities. In P.W. Jackson (Ed.), *Handbook of research on curriculum,* pp. 626-658. New York: Macmillan.

Finocchiaro, M. (1954). Puerto Rican newcomers in our schools. *Journal of Educational Sociology, 28,* 157-166.

First, J., Kellogg, J.B., Almeida, C.A., & Gray, R., Jr. (1991). *The good common school: Making the vision work for all children.* Boston: National Coalition of Advocates for Children.

Fisher, M. with Pérez, S.M., González, B., Njus, J., & Kamasaki, C. (1998). *Latino education: Status and prospects. State of Hispanic America 1998.* Washington, DC: National Council of La Raza. (ERIC Document Reproduction Service No. ED 427 129).

Fitzpatrick, J.P. (1987). *Puerto Rican Americans: The meaning of migration to the mainland* (2nd ed.). Englewood Cliffs, NJ: Prentice-Hall.

Flaxman, E., & Inger, M. (1992). Parents and schooling in the 1990s. *Principal, 72*(2), 16-18.

Fliegel, S. (with J. MacGuire) (1993). *Miracle in East Harlem: The fight for choice in public education.* New York: Times Books.

Foley, D.E. (1991). Reconsidering anthropological explanations of ethnic school failure. *Anthropology and Education Quarterly, 22*, 60-86.

Fordham, S. (1988). Racelessness as a factor in black students' school success: Pragmatic strategy or pyrrhic victory. *Harvard Educational Review, 58*, 54-84.

Freidenberg, J. (1995). Lower income urban enclaves: Introduction. In J. Freidenberg, (Ed.), *The anthropology of lower income urban enclaves: The case of East Harlem* (Annals of the New York Academy of Sciences, Vol. 749, pp. 1-40). New York: The New York Academy of Sciences.

Freire, P. (1970). *Pedagogy of the oppressed* (M.B. Ramos, Trans.). New York: Seabury. (Original work published 1968).

Gagné, R.M. (1966). The learning of principles. In J.M. Klausmeier & C.W. Harris (Ed.), *Analyses of concept learning.* New York: Academic Press.

García, S.B., & Dominguez, L. (1997). Cultural contexts that influence learning and academic performance. *Academic Difficulties, 6*, 621-655.

Garner, R., & Zhao, Y. (2000). Afterschool centers in four rural communities in Michigan. *Computers in Human Behavior, 16*, 301-311.

Gibson, M.A. (1985). Collaborative educational anthropology: Problems and profits. *Anthropology & Education Quarterly, 16*, 124-148.

Gibson, M.A. (1993). The school performance of immigrant minorities: A comparative view. In E. Jacob & C. Jordan (Eds.), *Minority education: Anthropological perspectives*, pp. 113-128. Norwood, NJ: Ablex.

Gibson, M.A. (2000). Situational and structural rationales for the school performance of immigrant youth. Three cases. In H. Vermeulen & J. Perlmann (Eds.), *Immigrants, schooling and social mobility. Does culture make a difference?* Basingstoke: Macmillian.

Gibson, M.A., & Ogbu, J.U. (Eds.). (1991). *Minority status and schooling: A comparative study of immigrant and involuntary minorities.* New York: Garland.

Goldenberg, C. (1990). Beginning literacy instruction for Spanish-speaking children. *Language Arts, 87*, 590-598.

González, N., Moll, L., & Amanti, C. (Eds.). (2004). *Funds of knowledge: Theorizing practices in households, communities, and classrooms.* Mahwah, NJ: Erlbaum.

González, N., & Moll, L. (2002). *Cruzando el puente:* Building bridges to funds of knowledge. *Educational Policy, 16,* 623-641.

González, R. (2002). *The No Child Left Behind Act: Implications for local educators and advocates for Latino students, families, and communities.* (Issue Brief No. 8). Washington, DC: National Council of La Raza. (ERIC Document Reproduction Service No. ED 471 049).

Hamilton, S.F. (1990). *Apprenticeship for adulthood.* New York: Free Press.

Hedegaard, M. (1988). *Skolebørns personlighedsudvikling set gennem orienteringsfagene* [The development of schoolchildren's personality viewed through the social science subjects]. Aarhus: Aarhus University Press.

Hedegaard, M. (1989). Motivational development in school children. *Multidisciplinary Newsletter for Activity Theory, 3/4,* 30-38.

Hedegaard, M. (1990). The zone of proximal development as basis for instruction. In L.C. Moll (Ed.), *Vygotsky and education: Instructional implications and applications of sociohistorical psychology,* pp. 349-371. Cambridge: Cambridge University Press.

Hedegaard, M. (1995). The qualitative analysis of the development of a child's theoretical knowledge and thinking. In L.M.W. Martin, & K. Nelson, & E. Tobach (Eds.), *Sociocultural psychology: Theory and practice of doing and knowing,* pp. 293-325. Cambridge: Cambridge University Press.

Hedegaard, M. (1996). How instruction influences children's concepts of evolution. *Mind, Culture, and Activity, 3,* 11-24.

Hedegaard, M. (1998) Activity theory and history teaching. In Y. Engestöm, R. Miettinen & R.L. Punamäki (Eds.), *Perspectives on activity theory.* Cambridge: Cambridge University Press.

Hedegaard, M. (2002). *Learning and child development: A cultural-historical study.* Aarhus: Aarhus University Press.

Hedegaard, M. (2004). *Krigsbørn i eksil.* Aarhus: Klim.

Hedegaard, M., Hakkarainen, P. & Engeström, Y. (Eds.) (1984). *Learning and teaching on a scientific basis: Methodological and epistemological aspects of the activity theory of learning and teaching.* Aarhus, Denmark: University of Aarhus, Department of Psychology.

Hedegaard, M., & Lompscher, J. (Eds.) (1999). *Learning Activity and Development.* Aarhus: Aarhus University Press.

Hedegaard, M., & Sigersted, G. (1992). *Undervisning i samfundshistorie.* Aarhus: Aarhus University Press.

Henriksen, D.L. (2003). *ProjectWeb as practice: On the relevance of radical localism for information systems development research.* Doctoral dissertation. Roskilde University, Computer Science.

Hernández, A.J. (1976). *Return migration to Puerto Rico.* Westport, CT: Greenwood.

Hill, K. (1992). The verbal folklore of Puerto Rican children: Implications for promoting school achievement. In A.N. Ambert & M.D. Alvarez (Eds.), *Puerto Rican children on the mainland: Interdisciplinary perspectives* (pp. 65-107). New York: Garland.

Hime, C. (1977). Ethnoscience: An educational concept. In V.L. Melnick & F.D. Hamilton (Eds.), *Minorities in science: The challenge for change in biomedicine* (pp. 259-266). New York: Plenum.

Historiedidaktik i Norden 2 (1985). Copenhagen: The Royal Institute for Educational Studies.

Historiediaktik i Norden 3 (1988). Malmö: The Royal Institute for Teachers Studies.

History Task Force (1979). *Labor migration under capitalism: The Puerto Rican experience.* New York: Monthly Review Press.

Hoffman, D.M. (1988). Cross-cultural adaptation and learning: Iranians and Americans at school. In H.T. Trueba & C. Delgado-Gaitan (Eds.), *School & society: Learning content through culture,* pp. 163-180. New York: Praeger.

Inclán, J.E., & Herron, D.G. (1989). Puerto Rican adolescents. In J.T. Gibbs & L.N. Huang (Eds.), *Children of color: Psychological interventions with minority youth,* pp. 251-277. San Fransisco: Jossey-Bass.

Irvine, J.J., & Armento, B.J. (with V.E. Causey, J.C. Jones, R.S. Frasher, & M.H. Weinburgh). (2001). *Culturally responsive teaching: Lesson planning for elementary and middle grades.* Boston: McGraw-Hill.

Jacob, E., & Jordan C. (1993). Understanding minority education: Framing the issues. In E. Jacob & C. Jordan (Eds.), *Minority education: Anthropological perspectives,* pp. 3-13. Norwood, NJ: Ablex.

Johansen, J., & Kreiner, S. *Tid til dansk 3B.* Copenhagen: The Danish Institute of Educational Research.

Jordan, C. (1985). Translating culture: From ethnographic information to educational program. *Anthropology & Education Quarterly, 16,* 105-123.

Kaufman, P., Kwon, J.Y., Klein, S., & Chapman, C.D. (2000). *Dropout rates in the United States: 1999.* Washington, DC: U.S. Department of Education, Office for Educational Research and Improvement.

Kerckhoff, A. (1990). *Getting started: The transition to adulthood in Great Britain.* Boulder, CO: Westview Press.

Kolata, G. (1989). Grim seeds of park rampage found in East Harlem streets. *The New York Times,* May 2, C1, C13.

Latino Commission on Educational Reform. (1992). *Toward a vision for the education of Latino students: Vol. 1. Community voices* (Interim report).

New York: New York City Board of Education. (ERIC Document Reproduction Service No. ED 359 287).

Latino Commission on Educational Reform. (1994). *Making the vision a reality: A Latino action agenda for educational reform*. New York: New York City Board of Education. (ERIC Document Reproduction Service No. ED 376 233).

Lave, J. (1988). *Cognition in practice: Mind, mathematics and culture in everyday life*. New York: Cambridge University Press.

Lave, J. (1992). Word problems: A microcosm of theories of learning. In P. Light & G. Butterworth (Eds.), *Context and cognition: Ways of learning and knowing*, pp. 74-92. New York: Harvester Wheatsheaf.

Lave, J. & Wenger (1991). *Situated learning. Legitimate peripheral participation*. Cambridge: Cambridge University Press.

Lektorsky, V.A. (1999). Historical change of the notion of activity: Philosophical presuppositions. In S. Chaiklin, M. Hedegaard, & U.J. Jensen (Eds.), *Activity theory and social practice*, pp. 100-113. Aarhus, Denmark: Aarhus University Press.

Leontiev, A.N. (1978). *Activity, consciousness, and personality* (M.J. Hall, Trans.). Englewood Cliffs, NJ: Prentice-Hall. (Original work published 1975).

Levin, H.M. (1995). Learning from accelerated schools. In J.H. Block, S.T. Everson, & T.R. Guskey (Eds.), *School improvement programs: A handbook for educational leaders*, pp. 267-288. New York: Scholastic.

Lockwood, A.T. (1995). A synthesis of four reforms. *New Leaders for Tomorrow's Schools, 1*(2), 3-13. (ERIC Document Reproduction Service No. ED 426 478).

Lockwood, A.T., & Secada, W.G. (1999). *Transforming education for Hispanic youth: Exemplary practices, programs, and schools* (NCBE Resource Collection Series No. 12). Washington, DC: The George Washington University, Center for the Study of Language and Education. (ERIC Document Reproduction Service No. ED 434 788).

Lompscher, J. (1984). Problems and results of experimental research on the formation of theoretical thinking through instruction. In M. Hedegaard, P. Hakkarainen, & Y. Engeström (Eds.), *Learning and teaching on a scientific basis: Methodological and epistemological aspects of the activity theory of learning and teaching*, pp. 293-357. Aarhus, Denmark: University of Aarhus, Department of Psychology.

Lompscher, J. (1985). *Persönlichkeitsentwicklung in der Lerntätigkeit* [The development of personality in learning activity]. Berlin: Volk und Wissen.

Lompscher, J., & Hedegaard, M. (Eds.) (1999). *Learning Activity and Development*. Aarhus: Aarhus University Press.

Lucas, T., Henze, R., & Donato, R. (1990). Promoting the success of Latino language-minority students: An exploratory study of six high schools. *Harvard Educational Review, 60*, 315-340.

Maldonado-Denis, M. (1972). *Puerto Rico: A socio-historic interpretation* (E. Vialo, Trans.). New York: Random House. (Original work published 1969).

Malik, K. (1996). *The meaning of race: Race, history and culture in Western society*. New York: New York University Press.

Margolis, R. (1968). *The losers: A report on Puerto Ricans and public schools*. New York: ASPIRA.

Markova, A.K. (1979). *The teaching and mastery of language* (M. Vale, Trans.). White Plains, NY: M.E. Sharpe. (Original work published 1974).

Matute-Bianchi, M.E. (1986). Ethnic identities and patterns of school success and failure among Mexican-descent and Japanese-American students in a California high school: An ethnographic analysis. *American Journal of Education, 95*, 233-255.

Mayor's Committee on City Planning of the City of New York. (1937). *East Harlem Community Study*. New York: Author.

Mayor's Committee on Puerto Rican Affairs in New York City. (1951). *Puerto Rican pupils in American schools*. New York: Author. (Reprinted in Cordasco & Bucchioni, 1982).

Mayor's Committee on Puerto Rican Affairs in New York City. (1953). *Interim report, 1949-1953*. New York: Author.

McDermott, R.P. (1993). The acquisition of a child by a learning disability. In S. Chaiklin & J. Lave (Eds.), *Understanding practice. perspectives on activity and context*, pp. 269-305. New York: Cambridge University Press.

McIntyre, A., Rosebery, A., & González, N. (Eds.) (2001). *Classroom diversity: Connecting curriculum to students' lives*. Portsmouth, NH: Heinemann.

Mehan, H., Villanueva, I., Hubbard, L. & Lintz, A. (1996). Constructing school success. New York: Cambridge University Press.

Meier, D. (1995a). How our schools could be. *Phi Delta Kappan, 76*, 369-373.

Meier, D. (1995b). *The power of their ideas: Lessons for America from a small school in Harlem*. Boston: Beacon Press.

Mencher, J. (1995). Growing up in Eastville, A barrio of New York: A retrospective view. In J. Freidenberg (Ed.), *The anthropology of lower income urban enclaves: The case of East Harlem* (Annals of the New York Academy of Sciences, Vol. 749, pp. 51-59). New York: The New York Academy of Sciences.

Mercado, C.I. (1992). Researching research: A student-teacher-researcher collaborative project. In A.N. Ambert & M.D. Alvarez (Eds.), *Puerto Rican children on the mainland: Interdisciplinary perspectives* (pp. 167-192). New York: Garland.

Mercado, C.I. & Moll, L.C. (2000). Student agency through collaborative research in Puerto Rican communities. In S. Nieto (Ed.), *Puerto Rican students
   in U.S. schools*, pp. 297-329. Mahwah, NJ: Erlbaum.

Mercer, N. (1992). Culture, context and the construction of knowledge in the
   classroom. In P. Light & G. Butterworth (Eds.), *Context and cognition: Ways
   of learning and knowing*, pp. 28-46. New York: Harvester Wheatsheaf.

Minick, N. (1993). Teacher's directives: The social construction of 'literal mean-
   ings' and 'real worlds' in classroom discourse. In S. Chaiklin & J. Lave (Eds.)
   Understanding practice: Perspectives on activity and context, pp. 343-374.
   New York: Cambridge University Press.

Moll, L.C., & Greenberg, J.B. (1990). Creating zones of possibilities: Combining
   social contexts for instruction. In L.C. Moll (Ed.), *Vygotsky and education:
   Instructional implications and applications of sociohistorical psychology*,
   pp. 319-348. Cambridge: Cambridge University Press.

Moll, L.C., Amanti, C., Neff, D., & Gonzalez, N. (1992). Funds of knowledge
   for teaching: Using a qualitative approach to connect homes and classrooms.
   Anthropology and Education Quarterly, 23, 132-141.

Morales, M., & Tarr, E.R. (2000). Social action projects: Apprenticeship for
   change in school and community. In S. Nieto (Ed.), *Puerto Rican students
   in U.S. schools*, pp. 249-266. Mahwah, NJ: Lawrence Erlbaum.

Morales Carrión, A. (1983). *Puerto Rico: A political and cultural history*. New
   York: Norton.

Morris, N. (1995). *Puerto Rico: Culture, politics, and identity*. Westport, CT:
   Praeger.

Morrison, J.C. (1958). *The Puerto Rican study, 1953-1957. A report on the
   education and adjustment of Puerto Rican pupils in the public schools in the
   City of New York*. New York: New York City Board of Education.

Narvaez, O. (1974). Clubs in city substitute for Puerto Rican plazas. *New York
   Times*, 23 March, p. 43.

National Commission on Secondary Education for Hispanics. (1984). *Make
   something happen: Hispanics and urban high school reform (Vol. 1)*. New
   York: Hispanic Policy Development Project. (ERIC Document Reproduction
   Service No. ED 253 598).

National Council of La Raza. (1992). *State of Hispanic America 1991: An overview*. Washington, DC: Author.

National Council of La Raza. (1996). *Curriculum: Academia del Pueblo*. Washington, DC: Author.

National Council of La Raza. (1998). *Curriculum: Project Success (PS)*. Washington, DC: Author.

National Council of La Raza. (1999). *ADP-MAS: A math and science curriculum*. Washington, DC: Author. (ERIC Document Reproduction Service No.
   ED 443 922).

National Council for the Social Studies. (1994). *Expectations of excellence: Curriculum standards for social studies.* Silver Spring, MD: Author.

Navarro, M. (2000). Puerto Rican presence wanes in New York. *New York Times,* February 28, pp. A1, B7.

Negrón de Montilla, A. (1975). *Americanization in Puerto Rico and the public school system 1900-1930.* Río Piedras: Editorial Universitaria.

Negt, O. (1971). *Soziologische Phantasie und exemplarisches Lernen: Zur Theorie und Praxis der Arbeiterbildung.* Frankfurt am Main: Europäische Verlagsanstalt.

Negt, O. (1978). Skolen som erfaringsproces – samfundsmæssige aspekter af Glocksee-projektet [The school as a process of experience – societal aspects of the Glocksee project]. *Kontext, 35.*

New York City Board of Education. (1947). *A program of education for Puerto Ricans in New York City: Report of the assistant superintendents.* New York: Author.

New York City Board of Education. (1953). *Teaching children of Puerto Rican background in New York City schools.* New York: Author.

New York City Department of City Planning. (1992). *A portrait of New York City's community districts from the 1980 & 1990 censuses of population and housing. A: Demographic profiles.* New York: Author.

New York City Department of City Planning. (1993). *Puerto Rican New Yorkers in 1990.* New York: Author.

New York City Department of City Planning. (2001a). *Demographic profile: New York City 2000. Community districts.* New York: Author. (Available at http://www.nyc.gov/html/dcp/pdf/census/59cdprof.pdf).

New York City Department of City Planning. (2001b). *Population growth and race/Hispanic composition* (NYC DPC #01-11). New York: Author. (Available at http://www.nyc.gov/html/dcp/pdf/census/nyc20001.pdf).

New York City Schools. (1982). Puerto Rican Study recommendations. In F. Cordasco & E. Bucchioni (Eds.), *The Puerto Rican community and its children on the mainland,* pp. 395-407. Metuchen, NJ: The Scarecrow Press.

Nicolau, S., & Ramos, C.L. (1990). *Together is better: Building strong relationships between schools and Hispanic parents.* New York: Hispanic Policy Development Project. New York: Hispanic Policy Development Project. (ERIC Document Reproduction Service No. ED 325 543).

Nieto, S. (1995). A history of the education of Puerto Rican students in the U.S. mainland schools: 'Losers,' 'outsiders,' or 'leaders'? In J.A. Banks & C.A.M. Banks (Eds.), *Handbook of research on multicultural education,* pp. 388-411. New York: Macmillan.

Nieto, S. (1998). Fact and fiction: Stories of Puerto Ricans in U.S. schools. *Harvard Educational Review, 68,* 133-163.

Nieto, S. (2000). Puerto Rican students in U.S. Schools: A brief history. In S. Nieto (Ed.), *Puerto Rican students in U.S. schools*, pp. 5-37). Mahwah, NJ: Erlbaum.

Ogbu, J.U. (1987). Variability in minority responses to schooling: Nonimmigrants vs. immigrants. In G. Spindler & L. Spindler (Eds.), *Interpretative ethnography of education: At home and abroad*, pp. 255-278. Hillsdale, NJ: Erlbaum.

Ogbu, J.U. (1993). Frameworks – Variability in minority school performance: A problem in search of an explanation. In E. Jacob & C. Jordan (Eds.), *Minority education: Anthropological perspectives*, pp. 83-111. Norwood, NJ: Ablex.

Ogbu, J.U., & Simons, H.D. (1998). Voluntary and involuntary minorities: A cultural theory of school performance with some implication for education. *Anthropology & Education Quarterly, 29*, 155-188.

Orum, L.S. (1988). *Making education work for Hispanic Americans: Some promising community-based practices.* Washington, DC: National Council of La Raza, Innovative Education Project.

Orum, L.S. (1991). *Project EXCEL: A mid-course report.* Los Angeles: Project Excellence in Community Educational Leadership, National Council of La Raza.

Pantoja, A. (1989). Puerto Ricans in New York: A historical and community development perspective. *Centro: Journal of the Center for Puerto Rican Studies, 2*(5), 21-31.

Paredes Scribner, A. (1999). High-performing Hispanic schools: An introduction. In P. Reyes, J.D. Scribner, & A. Paredes Scribner (Eds.), *Lessons from high-performing Hispanic schools: Creating learning communities*, pp. 1-18. New York: Teachers College Press.

Paradise, R. (1998). What's different about learning in schools as compared to family and community settings? [Commentary]. *Human Development, 41*, 270-278.

Pastor, R.A. (1985). Puerto Rico as an international issue: A motive for movement? In R.J. Bloomfield (Ed.), *Puerto Rico: The search for a national policy*, pp. 99-136. Boulder, CO: Westview Press.

Pedraza, P. (1989). The 'El Barrio' children's program. *Centro: Journal of the Center for Puerto Rican Studies, 2*(6), 62-65.

Pedraza, P. (1997). Puerto Ricans and the politics of school reform. *Centro: Journal of the Center for Puerto Rican Studies, 9*(1), 75-85.

Pedraza, P., & Ayala, J. (1996). Motivation as an emergent issue in an after-school program in El Barrio. In L. Schauble & R. Glaser (Eds.). *Innovations in learning: New environments for education* (pp. 75-91). Mahwah, NJ: Erlbaum.

Pérez, S.M. (1993). *Moving from the margins: Puerto Rican young men and family poverty.* Washington, DC: National Council of La Raza, Office of Research, Advocacy, and Legislation. (ERIC Document Reproduction Service No. ED 362 604).

Pérez, S.M. (2000). *U.S. Latino children: A status report.* Washington, DC: National Council of La Raza, Office of Research, Advocacy, and Legislation. (ERIC Document Reproduction Service No. ED 451 294).

Pérez, S.M., & Cruz, S. (1994). *Speaking out loud: Conversations with young Puerto Rican men.* Washington, DC: National Council of La Raza, Office of Research, Advocacy, and Legislation. (ERIC Document Reproduction Service No. ED 374 203).

Perloff, H. (1950). *Puerto Rico's economic future: A study in planned development.* Chicago: University of Chicago Press. (Reprinted in 1975 by Arno Press).

Phelan, P.; Davidson & Cao, H.T. (1991). Student's multiple worlds: Negotiating the boundaries of family, peer and school cultures. *Anthropology and Education Quarterly, 22,* 224-249.

Philips, S.U. (1983). *The invisible culture: Communication in classroom and community on the Warm Springs Indian Reservation.* New York: Longman.

Pietri, P. (1973). *Puerto Rican obituary.* New York: Monthly Review Press.

Pousada, A. (1987). *Puerto Rican community participation in East Harlem bilingual programs* (Language Policy Task Force No. 11). New York: Hunter College of the City University of New York, Centro de Estudios Puertorriqueños.

Puckett, J.L. (1989). *Foxfire reconsidered: A twenty-year experiment in progressive education.* Urbana: University of Illinois Press.

Puerto Rican Workshop. (1957). *Our children from Puerto Rico: A report on their island home by the visiting Puerto Rican Workshop of 1955.* New York: New York City Board of Education.

Purkey, S.C., & Smith, M.S. (1983). Effective schools: A review. *Elementary School Journal, 83,* 427-452.

Quintero, A.H. (1989). The University of Puerto Rico's partnership project with schools: A case study for the analysis of school improvement. *Harvard Educational Review, 59,* 347-361.

Ramos-Zayas, A.Y.(1998). Nationalist ideologies, neighborhood-based activism, and educational spaces in Puerto Rican Chicago. *Harvard Educational Review, 68,* 164-192.

Reyes, L.O. (2000). Educational leadership, educational change: A Puerto Rican perspective. In S. Nieto (Ed.), *Puerto Rican students in U.S. schools,* pp. 73-89. Mahwah, NJ: Erlbaum.

Reyes, L.O. (2003). Surviving the 'perfect storm': Bilingual education policy-making in New York City. *Journal of Latinos and Education, 2*, 23-30.

Rivera, E. (1982). *Family installments: Memories of growing up Hispanic.* New York: William Morrow.

Rivera, K.M. (1999). Popular research and social transformation: A community-based approach to critical pedagogy. *TESOL Quarterly, 33*, 485-500.

Rivera, M., & Pedraza, P. (2000). The spirit of transformation: An education reform movement in a New York City Latino/a community. In S. Nieto (Ed.), *Puerto Rican students in U.S. schools,* pp. 223-243. Mahwah, NJ: Erlbaum.

Rodríguez, A., Jr. (1992). On to college: Dropout prevention is possible. In A.N. Ambert & M.D. Alvarez (Eds.), *Puerto Rican children on the mainland: Interdisciplinary perspectives,* pp. 193-216. New York: Garland.

Rodriguez-Morazzani, R.P. (1997). Puerto Ricans and educational reform in the U.S.: A preliminary exploration. *Centro: Journal of the Center for Puerto Rican Studies, 9*(1), 59-73.

Rodriquez, C.E. (1992). *Toward a vision for the education of Latino students: Vol. 2. Student voices: High school students' perspectives on the Latino dropout problem* (Interim Report from Latino Commission on Educational Reform). New York: New York City Board of Education. (ERIC Document Reproduction Service No. ED 359 286).

Royal Commission on Aboriginal Peoples. (1996). *Report of the Royal Commission on Aboriginal Peoples: Vol. 3. Gathering strength.* Ottawa: Author.

Sánchez Korrol, V.E. (1994). *From colonia to community: The history of Puerto Ricans in New York City* (updated ed.). Berkeley: University of California Press.

Sánchez Korrol, V. (1996). Toward bilingual education: Puerto Rican women teachers in New York City schools, 1947-1967. In A. Ortiz (Ed.), *Puerto Rican women and work: Bridges in transnational labor,* pp. 82-104. Philadelphia: Temple University Press.

Santiago Santiago, I. (1978). *A community's struggle for equal educational opportunity* (OME Monograph Number Two). Princeton, NJ: Educational Testing Service, Office for Minority Education. (ERIC Document Reproduction Service No. ED 162 034).

Santiago Santiago, I. (1986). ASPIRA v. Board of Education revisited. *American Journal of Education, 95*, 149-199.

Schneider, S.G. (1976). *Revolution, reaction or reform: The 1974 bilingual education act.* New York: Las Americas.

Schorr, L.B. (with D. Schorr). (1988). *Within our reach: Breaking the cycle of disadvantage.* New York: Doubleday.

Scribner, J.D., & Reyes, P. (1999). Creating learning communities for high-performing Hispanic students: A conceptual framework. In P. Reyes, J.D. Scribner, & A. Paredes Scribner (Eds.), *Lessons from high-performing Hispanic schools: Creating learning communities*, pp. 188-210. New York: Teachers College Press.

Scribner, S. (1984). Studying working intelligence. In B. Rogoff, & J. Lave (Ed.), *Everyday cognition: Its development in social context*, pp. 9-40. Cambridge, MA: Harvard University Press.

Scribner, S. (1985). Vygotsky's uses of history. In J.V. Wertsch (Ed.), *Culture, communication, and cognition*, pp. 119-145. Cambridge: Cambridge University Press.

Scribner, S. (1992). Mind in action. *Quarterly Newsletter of the Laboratory of Comparative Human Cognition, 14*, 103-110.

Secada, W.G., Chavez-Chavez, R., Garcia, E., Muñoz, C., Oakes, J., Santiago-Santiago, Slavin, R. (1998). *No more excuses: The final report of the Hispanic Dropout Project*. Washington, DC: U.S. Department of Education, Office of the Under Secretary. (Available at http://www.ncela.gwu.edu/miscpubs/hdp/final.htm).

Sewell, W.H., & Hauser, R.M. (1975). *Education, occupation, and earnings: Achievement in the early career*. New York: Academic Press.

Sexton, P.C. (1965). *Spanish Harlem: An anatomy of poverty*. New York: Harper and Row.

Slavin, R.E., Madden, N.A., Dolan, L.J., & Wasik, B.A. (1996). *Every child, every school: Success for All*. Newbury Park, CA: Sage.

Smith, D., Gilmore, P., Goldman, S., & McDermott, R. (1993). Failure's failure. In E. Jacob & C. Jordan (Eds.), *Minority education: Anthropological perspectives*, pp. 209-231. Norwood, NJ: Ablex.

Sødring-Jensen, S. (1978). *Historieundervisningsteori* [The theory of history teaching]. Copenhagen: Chr. Ejlers' Forlag.

Sødring-Jensen, S. (1990). *Historieundervisning* [History teaching]. Copenhagen: Danmarks Lærerhøjskole.

Sorzano, J.S. (1985). Comment. In R.J. Bloomfield (Ed.), *Puerto Rico: The search for a national policy*, pp. 137-140. Boulder, CO: Westview Press.

Stedman, L.C. (1987). It's time we changed the effective schools formula. *Phi Delta Kappa, 69*, 215-224.

Stedman, L.C. (1988). The effective schools formula still needs changing: A reply to Brookover. *Phi Delta Kappa, 69*, 439-442.

Steel, D. (1980). *Discovering your family history*. London: British Broadcasting Company.

Steel, D.J., & Taylor, L. (1973). *Family history in schools*. London: Phillimore.

Steinberg, L., Dornbusch, S.M., & Brown, B.B. (1992). Ethnic differences in

adolescent achievement: An ecological perspective. *American Psychologist,*
47, 723-729.

Suarez-Orozco, M.M. (1993). "Becoming somebody": Central American im-
migrants in U.S. inner-city schools. I E. Jacob & C. Jordan (Eds.), *Minority*
Education: Anthropological Perspectives. Norwood N.J.: Ablex Publishing
Cooperation.

Sutter, B., & Grensjo, B. (1988). Explorative learning in school? Experiences of
local historical research by pupils. *The Quarterly Newsletter of the Labora-*
tory of Comparative Human Cognition, 10, 39-54.

Swanson, M.C., Mehan, H., & Hubbard, L. (1995). The AVID classroom: Academic and social support for low-achieving students. In J. Oakes & K.H.
Quartz (Eds.), *Creating new educational communities* (Ninety-fourth yearbook of the National Society for the Study of Education, pp. 53-69). Chicago:
National Society for the Study of Education.

Tapia, J. (1998). The schooling of Puerto Ricans: Philadelphia's most impoverished community. *Anthropology & Education Quarterly, 29,* 297-323.

Teddlie, C., & Reynolds, D. (2001). Countering the critics: Responses to recent
criticisms of school effectiveness research. *School effectiveness and school*
improvement. 12, 41-82.

Torres, L. (1997). *Puerto Rican discourse: A sociolinguistic study.* Mahwah,
NJ: Erlbaum.

Torres-Guzmán, M.E. (1992). Stories of hope in the midst of despair: Culturally responsive education for Latino students in an alternative high school
in New York City. In M. Saravia-Shore & S.F. Arvizu (Eds.), *Cross-cultural*
literacy: Ethnographies of communication in multiethnic classrooms, pp.
477-490. New York: Garland.

Torres-Guzmán, M.E., & Martínez Thorne, Y. (2000). Puerto Rican/Latino
student voices: Stand and deliver. In S. Nieto (Ed.), *Puerto Rican students*
in U.S. schools, pp. 269-291. Mahwah, NJ: Erlbaum.

Torruellas, R.M. (1989). Alfabetización de adultos en 'El Barrio' ¿Destrezas
básicas o educación popular? *Centro: Journal of the Center for Puerto Rican*
Studies, 2(6), 66-70.

Torruellas, R.M., Benmayor, R., Goris, A., & Juarbe, A. (1991). Affirming cul-
tural citizenship in the Puerto Rican community: Critical literacy and the El
Barrio Popular Education Program. In C.E. Walsh (Ed.), *Literacy as praxis:*
Culture, language, and pedagogy, pp. 183-219). Norwood, NJ: Ablex.

Trueba, H.T. (1988). Peer socialization among minority students: A high school
dropout prevention program. In H.T. Trueba & C. Delgado-Gaitan (Eds.),
School & society: Learning content through culture, pp. 201-217. New York:
Praeger.

Urciuoli, B. (1996). *Exposing prejudice: Puerto Rican experiences of language,*
race, and class. Boulder, CO: Westview Press.

U.S. Census Bureau. (2002). *The big payoff: Educational attainment and synthetic estimates of work-life earnings.* Washington, DC: U.S. Department of Commerce, Economics and Statistics Administration. (ERIC Document Reproduction Service No. ED 467 553).

U.S. Commission on Civil Rights. (1974). *Counting the forgotten: The 1970 census count of persons of Spanish speaking background in the United States.* Washington, DC: Author.

U.S. Commission on Civil Rights. (1976). *Puerto Ricans in the continental United States: An uncertain future.* Washington, DC: Author.

U.S. Department of Agriculture. (1941). *Census of agriculture 1940.* Washington, DC: Government Printing Office.

Valdes, G. (1996). *Con respecto: Bridging the distance between culturally diverse families and schools.* New York: Teachers College Press.

van Oers, B. (1999). Teaching Opportunities in Play. In M. Hedegaard & J. Lompscher (Eds.), *Learning Activity and Development.* Aarhus: Aarhus University Press.

Vasquez, O.A., Pease-Alvarez, L., & Shannon, S.M. (1994). *Pushing boundaries: Language and culture in a Mexicano community.* Cambridge: Cambridge University Press.

Vélez-Ibáñez, C.G., & Greenberg, J.B. (1992). Formation and transformation of funds of knowledge among U.S. Mexican households. *Anthropology and Education Quarterly, 23,* 313-335.

Vélez-Ibáñez, C.G., & Greenberg, J.B. (1994). Schooling processes among U.S. Mexicans, Puerto Ricans and Cubans: A comparative, distributive and case study approach. In T. Weaver (Ed.), *Handbook of Hispanic cultures in the United States: Anthropology,* pp. 270-281. Houston, TX: Arte Público Press.

Vibe-Hastrup, H., & Mørkøv Ullerup, B. (1988). *New approaches to adult education.* Copenhagen: Danish Research and Development Centre for Adult Education.

Villaronga, M. (1954). Program of education for Puerto Rican migrants. *Journal of Educational Sociology, 28,* 146-150.

Vogt, L.A., Jordan, C., & Tharp, R.G. (1993). Explaining school failure, producing school success: Two cases. In E. Jacob & C. Jordan (Eds.), *Minority education: Anthropological perspectives,* pp. 53-65. Norwood, NJ: Ablex.

Vygotskij, L.S. (1982). *Om barnets psykiske udvikling: En artikelsamling* (N. Måge, Trans.) [On the child's mental development]. Copenhagen: Nyt Nordisk Forlag.

Vygotsky, L.S. (1987). Thinking and speech (N. Minick, Trans.). In R.W. Rieber & A.S. Carton (Eds.), *The collected works of L. S. Vygotsky: Vol. 1. Problems of general psychology,* pp. 39-285. New York: Plenum Press. (Original work published 1934).

Vygotsky, L.S. (1997). *The collected works of L. S. Vygotsky: Vol. 4. The history of the development of higher mental functions* (M. Hall, Trans.; R.W. Rieber, Ed.). New York: Plenum Press. (Original work written 1931).

Vygotsky, L.S. (1998). *The collected works of L. S. Vygotsky: Vol. 5. Child psychology* (M. Hall, Trans.; R.W. Rieber, Ed.). New York: Plenum Press. (Original work written 1931).

Vygotsky, L.S. (1998a). Development of thinking and formation of concepts in the adolescent (M. Hall, Trans.). In R.W. Rieber (Ed.), *The collected works of L. S. Vygotsky: Vol. 5. Child psychology*, pp. 29-81. New York: Plenum Press. (Original work published 1930).

Vygotsky, L.S. (1998b). The problem of age (M. Hall, Trans.). In R. W. Rieber (Ed.), *The collected works of L. S. Vygotsky: Vol. 5. Child psychology* (pp. 187-205). New York: Plenum Press. (Original work written 1933-1934).

Walsh, C.E. (1991). *Pedagogy and the struggle for voice: Issues of language, power, and schooling for Puerto Ricans.* New York: Bergin & Garvey.

Walsh, C.E. (1998). 'Staging encounters': The educational decline of U.S. Puerto Ricans in [post]-colonial perspective. *Harvard Educational Review, 68,* 218-243.

Wehlage, G., & Rutter, R. (1986). Dropping out: How much do schools contribute to the problem? *Teachers College Record, 87*(3), 374-392.

White, J. (1990). *Education and the good life: Beyond the national curriculum.* London: Kogan Page.

Wigginton, E. (1989). Foxfire grows up. *Harvard Educational Review, 59,* 24-49.

Willis, P.E. (1977). *Learning to labour: How working class kids get working class jobs.* Farnborough, Hants: Saxon House.

Yzaguirre, R. (1992). Foreword. In *State of Hispanic America 1991: An overview.* Washington, DC: National Council of La Raza.

Zentella, A.C. (1997). *Growing up bilingual: Puerto Rican children in New York.* Oxford: Blackwell.

Ziehe, T. (1978). *Subjektiv betydning og erfaring. Om Glockseeskoleforsøgets didaktiske konception* [Subjective meaning and experience: On the Glocksee experimental school's didactical conception]. *Kontext, 35.*

Zinn, H. (1980). *A people's history of the United States.* New York: Harper & Row.

List of Figures

Index